THE BRITISH ISLES

KIM
DIXON
SARAH
DIXON
SIMON
BURTON
ROBERT
CROFT
DAVID
PENROSE
JENNY
LEINERT
BERLIN
BECKY
BURTON
MAXI
MY
A B C
BOOK
MARK
PENROSE
MINI

Learning English

Red Line new 1

Unterrichtswerk für Realschulen

von
Paul Aston, Claudia Finkbeiner,
Rosemary Hellyer-Jones, Marion Horner,
Harriette Lanzer, Alan Posener, Rolf W. Roth,
Margaret Winck, Harold S. Wonham
sowie
Werner Beile, Alice Beile-Bowes,
Peter Lampater, Peter Pasch,
Helmut Slogsnat, Klaus Stenzel
und Dorit Stribel

Ernst Klett Verlag
Stuttgart Düsseldorf Leipzig

Learning English – *RED LINE* NEW 1
für Klasse 5 an Realschulen

von
Paul Aston, Wells; Prof. Dr. Claudia Finkbeiner, Heilbronn; Rosemary Hellyer-Jones M.A., Ehingen (Donau); Marion Horner M.A., Cambridge; Harriette Lanzer B.A., London; Alan Posener, Berlin; Rolf W. Roth M.A., Idar-Oberstein; Margaret Winck B.A., Tübingen; Harold S. Wonham M.Litt., Stone, sowie Prof. Dr. Werner Beile, Alice Beile-Bowes M.A., Wuppertal und Iserlohn; Peter Lampater, Ehingen (Donau); Prof. Dr. Peter Pasch, Tübingen; Dr. Helmut Slogsnat, Neckargemünd; Klaus Stenzel, Bopfingen, und Dorit Stribel, Nürtingen

Beratende Mitarbeit
Falko Alig, Hitzacker (Elbe); Walter Düringer, Ketsch; Siegfried Kemmler, Calw; Brigitte Leber, Löffingen; Brunhilde Müller, Stuttgart; Manfred Nigmann, Donzdorf; Dr. Gudrun Steinbach, Halle; Wolfgang Weber, Lebrade; Gerhard Wildermuth, Esslingen

Visuelle Gestaltung
Elsie Lennox, London;
Kirsten Walther, Bochum (z. T. Grammatik, Vokabular)

Kassetten und CDs zu diesem Band

SB *Begleitkassette zum Schülerbuch* für zu Hause und für den Unterricht mit Unittexten,Liedern, Ausspracheübungen (Klettnummer 546402).
Die *Begleit-CD zum Schülerbuch* mit demselben Inhalt hat die Klettnummer 546499.
Lieferung durch jede Buchhandlung oder, wo dies auf Schwierigkeiten stößt, zuzüglich Portokosten per Nachnahme vom Verlag.

HV *Kassette zum Hörverstehen* für den Unterricht mit den Hörverstehenstexten aller Werkteile (Klettnummer 546419).
Die *CD zum Hörverstehen* für den Unterricht hat die Klettnummer 546482.
Lieferung direkt an Lehrerinnen und Lehrer. Schulstempel erforderlich.

Lernsoftware

Passend zu diesem Band gibt es ein Vokabel- und ein Grammatiktrainingsprogramm. Die Programme bieten abwechslungsreiche Übungsformen, zahlreiche Abfragevarianten, Leistungs- und Lernzielkontrolle und ein Lexikon mit dem Wortschatz der gesamten Lehrbuchreihe.

1. Auflage A 1 6 5 4 3 2 | 2003 2002 2001 2000 99

Alle Drucke dieser Auflage können im Unterricht nebeneinander benutzt werden, sie sind untereinander unverändert.
Die letzte Zahl bezeichnet das Jahr dieses Druckes.

Internetadresse: http://www.klett-verlag.de

Redaktion: Christa Weck, Christa Meier, Jennifer Wood

Layout: Dieter Gebhardt, Graphic- und Foto-Design BFF, Asperg
Umschlaggestaltung: Christian Dekelver, Weinstadt
Satz: DTP-Verlag und Lihs GmbH, Medienhaus, Ludwigsburg
Reproduktion: Repro Maurer GmbH + Co, Tübingen
Druck: Druckerei Auer, Donauwörth
ISBN: 3-12-546470-6

Gedruckt auf Papier aus chlorfrei gebleichtem Zellstoff, säurefrei.

Inhaltsverzeichnis

Hallo!
Ich heiße Monny. Englischlernen macht Spaß – vor allem, wenn man es gemeinsam macht. Deshalb begleite ich dich durch dieses Buch und gebe dir ab und zu ein paar Tipps. Damit du dich in deinem Englischbuch leicht zurechtfindest, erkläre ich dir kurz, wie das Buch aufgebaut ist. Auf Seite 7 heißt es **Let's start**. Das bedeutet soviel wie: Jetzt geht's los. Dann kommen zehn **Units** (Kapitel) zu verschiedenen Themen. Am Ende jeder *Unit* kannst du auf einer **Let's check**-Seite überprüfen, was du in dieser *Unit* dazugelernt hast. Ab Seite 116 beginnt die **Extra line** mit weiteren interessanten Geschichten und einem Theaterstück. Ab der Seite 122 findest du den **Grammatikanhang**. Das **Vokabular** beginnt auf Seite 145. Hier findest du alle neuen Wörter aus den *Units*. Wenn du einmal ein Wort aus einer früheren *Unit* nicht mehr weißt, kannst du in der **alphabetischen Wortliste** am Ende des Buches nachschlagen.
Alles klar? Na dann – **Let's start!** Viel Spaß!

Erläuterungen:

- SB: Begleitkassette/CD zum Schülerbuch
- HV: Kassette/CD zum Hörverstehen
- Your turn: Hier kannst du über dich, deine Familie oder Freunde sprechen.
- Partnerarbeit
- Gruppenarbeit
- WORD POWER: Wortschatzübungen
- Wiederholungsübungen
- ⟨ ⟩ fakultativ (wahlfrei)
- schwierigere (wahlfreie) Aufgaben
- besonders für den fächerverbindenden Unterricht geeignet

1 In Nottingham

2 Hello

ⓐ *Becky:* Hello.
Robert: Hello.
Becky: My name is Becky Burton.
Robert: I'm Robert. Robert Croft.
Sarah: Robert is new, Becky.
Robert: Yes. I'm from London.

ⓑ Woof! Woof!

Robert: Oh hello, dog.
What's your name?
Becky: Maxi. – And that's Mini.
Robert: Hello, Mini.

Woof! Woof!

what's = what is
that's = that is

1 My name

1. "Hello. I'm … ."
   – "Hello. I'm … ."
2. "Hello. My name is … ."
   – "Hello. My name is … ."
3. "Hello. What's your name?"
   – "… ."
4. "Hello. My name is … . What's … ?"
   – "… ."

2 I'm from Nottingham

1. *Sarah:* I'm Sarah. I'm from Nottingham.
2. *Robert:* … Robert. … from London.
3. *Becky:* … . … Nottingham.

"I'm … . I'm from … ."

⟨3 A song: Sarah Dixon⟩

©Text: M. Horner, Melodie: trad.; Gitarrenakkorde: M.Hauschild

ⓒ *Sarah:* I'm at Haywood School.
Robert: Oh, that's my new school! And Becky? Is she at Haywood School?
Sarah: Yes. She's in my tutor group.

ⓓ *Sarah:* Look. That's David Penrose. He's in my tutor group, too.
Robert: Is he nice?
Sarah: Yes. He's a friend. Hello, David!

I'm = I am
she's = she is
he's = he is

4 That's Sarah

She's He's	from Nottingham. from London. at Haywood School.

1. That's Sarah. **She's** from Nottingham. She's at Haywood School.
2. That's … . **He's** from … . He's at … .
3. That's … 4. That's …

Your turn "That's … . She's in my class."
"That's … . He's in my class."

5 My friend

1. *Robert:* Becky is my friend.
Mrs Croft: **Is she** at your school?
Robert: Yes. She's in my tutor group.

2. *Robert:* David is my friend.
Mrs Croft: **Is he** at your school?
Robert: Yes. … in my tutor group.

3. *Robert:* Sarah … .
Mrs Croft: …
Robert: …

6 A poster

Your turn *Make a poster.*

3 School!

(a) *Sarah:* School, Becky!
Becky: I'm here. Am I late?
Sarah: Yes!
Robert: Look! Maxi is here, too.
Becky: Goodbye, Maxi.
Oh no! You crazy dog!
David: Your bag, Becky!

here's = here is

1 Here's your pen

1. Here's your pen, Becky. – Thank you.
2. Here's your book. – … .
3. Here's your … . – … .

Please go on.

2 In your bag

Your teacher: What's in your bag?
You: My folder

3 My English folder

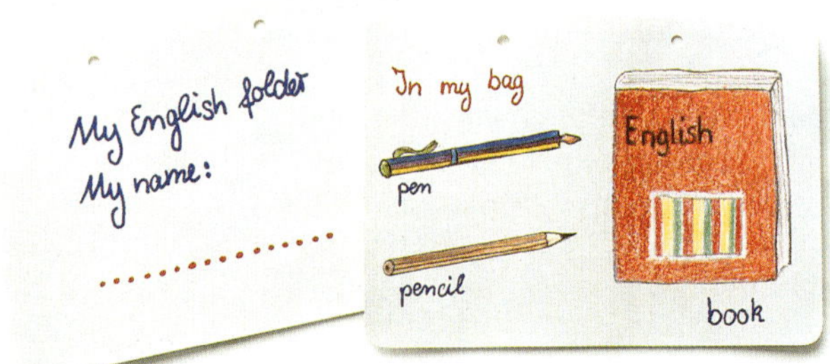

4 Sound practice

Look, listen and say.

[aɪ]	[æ]	[əʊ]
My dog is nice.	Maxi is a dog.	Hello.
Am I late?	That's your bag.	A folder. A poster.
Goodbye.	Thank you.	Oh no!

SB (b) *Robert:* I'm twelve.
Are you twelve, too, David?
David: No. I'm eleven.
Robert: How old are you, Sarah?
Sarah: I'm eleven. And Becky, too.
Becky: I'm not eleven!
Sarah: Oh. Sorry, Becky. You're ten.
Becky: Ten? Sarah Dixon, you crazy girl.
I'm *twelve*.

you're = you are

5 How old?

Sarah	
Robert	11?
David	
Becky	12?

a) How old is Sarah? – She's ... eleven
How old is Robert? – He's ... twelve
How old is ... ? – ... *Please go on.*

Your turn b) "How old are you?" – "I'm ... ."
"How old is ...?" – "She's ... ."
"How old is ...?" – "He is ... ."

10 – ten
11 – eleven
12 – twelve

6 Are you new in Nottingham?

1. Are you new in Nottingham? → – Yes. I'm new here.
2. Am I late?
3. You're crazy!
4. Are you at Haywood School?
5. Hello, Becky.
6. You're a nice dog, Mini.

– Yes. That's my school.
– I'm not Becky. I'm Sarah.
– Yes. You're late.
– Woof! Woof!
– Yes. I'm new here.
– I'm not crazy!

7 Becky and Robert

a) Becky

1. Sarah? – Becky
   – Are you Sarah?
   – No, I'm not Sarah. I'm Becky.
2. eleven? – twelve
   – Are you eleven, Becky?
   – No, I'm not ... . I'm ... .

b) Robert

1. David? – Robert
   – ... you ...?
   – No, ... I'm ... .
2. from Nottingham? – from London
   – ...?
   – No, ...

8 I – you

Robert:
1. ...'m Robert. What's your name?
2. Are ... at Haywood School?
3. Oh, ...'m at Haywood School, too!
4. How old are ..., Sarah?
5. ...'re a crazy girl, Sarah!

9 he – she

Sarah:
1. Robert is new. ...'s from London.
2. That's Becky. ...'s in my tutor group.
3. David is my friend. Is ... your friend, too?
4. Is Robert late? Oh no. ...'s here.
5. How old is Becky? Is ... ten?

4 Tutor group 7MD

ⓐ *Robert:* Is that your teacher, David?
David: Yes. She's my English teacher. And she's my tutor, too. Her name is Mrs Dane. – Good morning, Mrs Dane.
Mrs Dane: Good morning, David. – Oh, are you the new boy?
Robert: Yes. I'm new here.
David: His name is Robert Croft.
Mrs Dane: Good morning, Robert. You're in my tutor group, too. That's tutor group 7MD.

she – **her**
he – **his**

1 Her name and his name

Is that
- your tutor
- girl in your tutor group
- boy in your tutor group

?

– Yes. Her name is
– Yes. His name is

Robert | Becky | David | Mrs Dane | Sarah .

ⓑ *Robert:* Becky! Sarah! You're in tutor group 7MD, right?
Becky: Yes. We're in 7MD.
Robert: That's my tutor group, too! Are the teachers OK?
Sarah: The teachers? They're …
Mr Cooper: *Guten Morgen*, girls and boys!
David: *Guten Morgen*. – That's Mr Cooper.
Robert: He's the German teacher, right?

we're = we are
you're = you are
they're = they are

2 What's the answer?

Teacher:
1. Good morning, girls and boys. – Good morning.
2. Becky Burton! David Penrose! – We're … .
3. You're late, boys! – …
4. Are you eleven? – …
5. Are you in tutor group 7MD? – … .

Sorry we're late.
We're here.
Good morning. ✓
Yes. We're eleven.
Yes. We're in 7MD.

3 Questions

1. Are Becky and Robert eleven? – No. **They're** twelve.
2. Are Sarah and David twelve, too? – No. … .
3. Are David, Sarah and Becky from London? – No. … from … .
4. Are they German? – No. … .
5. Are they at Greenwood School? – No. … at … .

c) *Sarah:* Hey, David! What's that?
David: What? Where? On my desk?
Sarah: No. Under your chair.
David: Aaah! It's a snake!
Sarah: It's Sneaky Snake! Here. Look.
David: Oh, Sarah!

it's = it is

4 What and where?

a) 1. Look! What's on the desk? – A pen and a book.
2. What's in the bag? – A … . *Please go on.*
3. What's under the chair?
4. What's on the chair?
5. What's under the desk?
6. And under the bag? What's that?

b) Where's the biro? – It's on the … .
Where's the comic? – It's … .
Where's the …? *Please go on.*

5 A game

Play the game.

6 Sound practice

[eɪ]	[ð]	[w]
Please **say** your **name**.	**The** boys are late.	**W**e're here, Mrs Dane.
That's a cr**a**zy g**a**me.	**The**y're in my tutor group.	**Wh**at? **Wh**ere?
It's a sn**a**ke.	**Th**at's **th**e teacher.	**W**oof! **W**oof!

5 Haywood School

ⓐ Here is Haywood School.
It is in Nottingham.

The girls and boys in the picture are in year 7.
They are eleven or twelve.
They are at school in the morning and in the afternoon.

1 Please *say* the sentences

1. I am ten. ⟶ **I'm** ten.
2. She is a teacher. ⟶ **She's** a …
3. They are in year 7. ⟶
4. You are my friend. ⟶ …
5. He is a new boy. ⟶ …
6. I am from London. ⟶ …
7. We are from Nottingham. ⟶ …
8. You are late, boys. ⟶ …
9. It is a nice picture. ⟶ …
10. They are here. ⟶ …

I am	– I'm
you are	– you're
he is	– he's
she is	– she's
it is	– it's
we are	– we're
you are	– you're
they are	– they're

2 Make questions

is am are

1. **Is** Mr Cooper the German teacher?
2. … I late?
3. … they from Nottingham?
4. … it a good comic?
5. … you the new boy?
6. … the girls and boys nice?
7. … Sarah eleven?
8. … we in your tutor group, Mrs Dane?

3 Let's learn words

Girl and boy, you and I,
Yes and no, hello and goodbye,
Her and his, desk and chair,
Words are easy in a pair!

Write the pairs in your folder.

question – answer she – he
Mrs – Mr my – your morning – afternoon

(b) *David:* Where's Sarah, Becky?
Becky: I'm not sure. She isn't here.
David: And Robert isn't here.
Becky: No. They aren't in the playground.
David: Hmm. – Chocolate, Becky?
Becky: Oh yes, please!

Robert: Chocolate?!
Sarah: Hello! We're here!

isn't = is not
aren't = are not

4 Where's Sarah?

1. Sarah? Where's Sarah? – I'm not sure. **She isn't** here.
2. Mr Cooper? Where's …? – I'm not sure. **He isn't** here.
3. David?
4. Mrs Dane?
5. Becky?
6. Robert?

5 Crazy sentences

Maxi and Mini	are teachers.
David and Robert	are girls.
Mrs Dane and Mr Cooper	are eleven.
Sarah and David	are dogs.
Sarah and Becky	are boys.

a) 1. That's crazy! Maxi and Mini aren't teachers.
2. That's crazy! David and Robert aren't … .
3. That's … ! Mrs Dane and Mr Cooper … .
Please go on.

b) *Find the right words.*
1. Maxi and Mini are … .
2. David and Robert are … . *Please go on.*

6 Listening practice: Thank you!

Listen and find the answer.

Becky: Where's my … ?

David: It's under your … .

7 Sound practice

[s]
Sorry, **S**arah.
Say ye**s**.
A ni**c**e
pen**c**il ca**s**e.

[z]
Cra**z**y dog**s**.
Where'**s** hi**s** pen?
Look here, plea**s**e,
girl**s** and boy**s**.

[s] – [z]
Ni**c**e dog**s**!
Sarah i**s** cra**z**y.
Say hello, plea**s**e.

6 The lesson

The girls and boys are in the classroom.
Mrs Dane is late.

Sarah: Let's play a game!
I'm your teacher.
Becky: What's your name?
Sarah: Oh, I'm – Mrs Dixon.
David: You're funny, Mrs Dixon!
Sarah: Sit down, please.
Now, here's your homework.
Becky: Homework?
Robert: No, thank you!
David: Now you're the teacher, Robert.

Robert: OK. I'm the new teacher.
David, what's that on your desk?
David: It's a comic, Mr Croft.
Robert: A comic? In my lesson?
Bring the comic here, please.
David: It's my comic!
Sarah: Yes. It's his comic!
Robert: Quiet, please!
David, bring the comic here. –
Thank you. –
Oh good. It's a new comic.
David: You aren't the teacher now,
Robert.
I'm –
Mrs Dane: I'm the teacher now!
David: Oh! Mrs Dane!
Mrs Dane: Good afternoon. Sorry I'm late.

1 Right or wrong?

Are the sentences right or wrong?
Please correct the wrong sentences.

That's right.

That's wrong. …

1. The girls and boys are in the playground.
   – That's wrong. The girls and boys are in … .
2. Mrs Dane is late.
   – That's … . *Please go on.*
3. Mrs Dixon is a funny teacher.
4. David is the new teacher.
5. It's a book on the desk.
6. Mr Cooper is the teacher now.
7. It's the afternoon.

7 Let's check

1 In your classroom

Example: 1. *You:* Good morning. – *Your teacher:* Good morning. *Please go on.*

What's *Kugelschreiber* in English, please?
Here's my folder.
Good morning. ✓
Where's my book?
Sorry I'm late.

You:
1.
2.
3.
4.
5.

Your teacher:
– Good morning.
– Thank you.
– A biro.
– On your desk. Look.
– That's OK.

2 My, your, his or her?

1. *Robert:* Are Maxi and Mini your dogs?
   Becky: Yes. They're ... dogs.
2. *Sarah:* The new boy is from London.
   David: What's ... name?
3. *Becky:* Is Robert at Haywood School?
   Sarah: Yes. That's ... new school.
4. *Robert:* Is Mrs Dane your tutor?
   David: Yes. I'm in ... tutor group.
5. *Sarah:* What's that under your chair?
   David: Oh Sarah! You and ... snake!
6. *David:* Where's my comic?
   Robert: ... comic? It's on the desk.

3 Maxi and Mini

in on under

1. Mini is ... the folder. 2. Maxi is ... . 3. Mini ... . *Please go on.*

4 Find the right words

a) I'm / you're / we're

1. – Hello. ... David.
   – Hello, David.
2. – Becky! Sarah! Where are you?
   – ... here!
3. – Are we late, Mr Cooper?
   – Yes. ... late!
4. – Maxi, ... a crazy dog!
   – Woof! Woof!

b) he's / it's / she's / they're

1. Robert is new. ... from London.
2. David and Becky are from Nottingham. ... at Haywood School.
3. Haywood School is in Nottingham. ... a good school.
4. Sarah is eleven. ... in tutor group 7MD.
5. Mr Cooper is nice. ... the German teacher.

5 What's your answer?

1. Hello.
2. What's your name?
3. How old are you?
4. Is your school nice?
5. Goodbye.

Unit 1

At home with the Burtons

Step A

Superdogs

SB ⓐ Becky is at home. She is with her brother Simon.

Becky: Look, Simon. Mini is a superdog. What's one and one, Mini?
Mini: Woof! Woo-
Becky: Clever dog! That's right. One and one is two.
Simon: Wow! Now you, Maxi! What's two and two?
Maxi: Woof! Woof! Woof! Woof! Woof! Woof!
Simon: No. That's wrong, Maxi. It's: Woof! Woof! Woof! Woof!

1 Let's play school

Find the answer.
Example: 5 + 3 = ?

What's five and three?
Eight.
That's right.

1. 9 + 2 = ? 2. 1 + 6 = ? 3. 5 + 5 = ? 4. 7 + 5 = ? 5. 4 + 2 = ? *Please go on.*

2 Find the number

1. | 4 | 3 | ? | 1 | 2. | 2 | ? | 6 | 8 | 3. | 3 | 6 | 9 | ? | 4. | 12 | 10 | ? | 6 | 5. | 1 | 2 | 4 | 7 | ? |

SB

ⓑ *Simon:* Hm, where are my comics? – Oh yes, in my bag. Clever dog, Maxi. Thank you. – Now, let's look. Books, pens, my lunch box, a biscuit, a car. – Oh, here are my comics. But where's my new comic? – Clever dog, Mini. It's under my bed!

3 What's under the bed?

One comic, four books, ... *Please go on.*

SB **4 Sound practice**

[s]	[z]	[ɪz]
two book**s**	two girl**s**	two sentenc**es**
three desk**s**	three boy**s**	three pencil cas**es**
four comic**s**	four dog**s**	one box – two box**es**
	five friend**s**	

Step B

The Burtons

Becky and Simon are in the kitchen.
Their mother and father aren't at home.
Their friend Robert is in the kitchen, too.

Robert: I'm hungry.
Becky: Where are our biscuits?
Simon: Here's a nice biscuit, Robert.
Robert: Thanks, Simon. – Hey, it's a dog biscuit!
Here! – Oh, sorry.
Becky: Oh, hello Dad. Here's our new friend Robert.
Mr Burton: Your friend? Hm. Hello, Robert.

we – **our**
you – **your**
they – **their**

1 Becky and Simon

1. Becky and Simon	their new friend.
2. Their mother and father	is hungry.
3. Robert is	aren't at home.
4. He's in	Mr Burton.
5. Their friend	are in the kitchen.
6. Here's their father,	the kitchen, too.

⟨2 Say it to the beat⟩

- Clap your hands.
- (clap, clap, clap)
- Stamp your feet.
- (stamp, stamp, stamp)

Say it to the beat.
Say it to the beat.
Clap your hands
And stamp your feet.

We're OK.
Our friends are OK.
Let's go together
All the way.

Now all together.
Say it to the beat!

We're OK.
Our friends are OK.
Let's go together
All the way.

Your turn 3 Our school

Our	German teacher / class / school / English book / English teacher	is	crazy. / easy. / new. / old. / good. / OK. / funny. / nice.

Two rooms

ⓐ Simon has got a football in his room.
And he has got a skateboard.
His radio is new.
Is that a CD player, too?

ⓑ Becky has got a computer in her room.
She has got a nice poster.
She hasn't got a radio.
But that's her new CD and – oh no!
Has Simon got her CD player? Brothers!

4 What has Simon got?

Look at the picture.

1. He's got a football.
2. He's got three cars.
3. He's got … .

Please go on.

he has got = **he's got**
she has got = **she's got**

5 She's got a computer

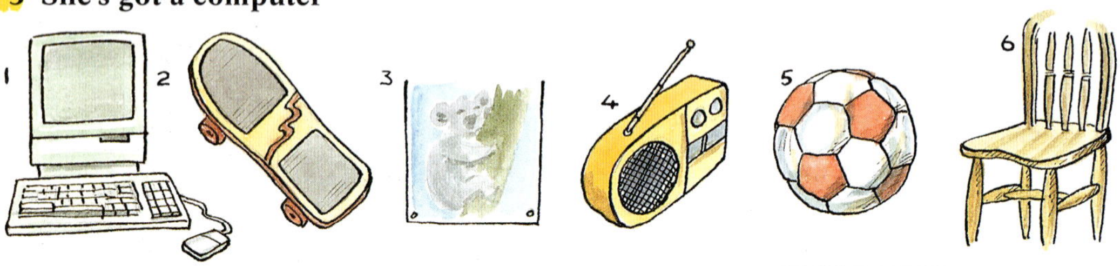

a) Becky
1. She's got a computer.
2. She hasn't got a skateboard.

Please go on.

b) Simon
1. He hasn't got a computer.
2. He's got a skateboard.

Please go on.

6 Becky or Simon?

Becky
Simon

a poster a computer a football a skateboard a CD player a new CD a box a radio ?

1. Has Becky got a poster? – Yes. That's right.
2. Has Simon got a computer? – No. Becky has got a computer.
3. Has Becky got a football? – No. Simon … . *Please go on.*

Good idea!

ⓐ *Robert:* Let's play football.
Becky: OK. – Oh sorry,
I haven't got a ball.
Robert: Simon, have you got a ball?
Simon: Yes, I've got a *new* football.
Look! Oops!
Becky: Oh no! Simon! My CD player!
Simon: Sorry, Becky. Let's play football
in the garden.
Robert: Good idea.

I've got = I have got

7 Your room

What have you got in your room at home?
– "I've got … ."

? ? a game
a desk ? …

8 Brothers and sisters

Example:

Work with a partner.

Have you got … ?
I've got … .
I haven't got … .

ⓑ *Robert:* Hey, you've got a big tree.
We haven't got a tree in our garden.
Simon: Oh yes, we've got a big tree and …
Oh, bad dogs, Maxi and Mini!
Now we've got a hole in our garden.
Becky: Bad dogs? No, they're clever dogs.
It's a nice big hole. Let's make
a pond.
Simon: Good idea! Clever dogs! –
Let's ask Mum.

9 Your classroom

What have you got in your classroom? What haven't you got?

We've got
We haven't got

a computer. a nice poster. a football.
a radio. …

LOOKING AT THE UK:
Nottingham

This is Nottingham.

1 Nottingham

Look at the pictures.

1. This is … .
2. Nottingham is in … .
3. … is in Sherwood.
4. This is … .
5. This is … Road.
   The Burtons have got a house here.

2 My English folder

Step C

Look!

ⓐ Becky, Simon and Robert are in the garden. Now David is there, too.

David: What's this, Simon?
Simon: Hmmm – it's an apple.
Becky: Right. And what's this?
Simon: It's a ball. No. It's an egg – oops!
Robert: Yes. Look! It's an egg – a broken egg.

1 Sound practice

a pen	an apple	a nice apple	an English book
a biro	an egg	a broken egg	an easy question
a house	an idea	a big bag	an old football

2 WORD POWER

Play the game.

– What's this?
– Is it a / an … ?
– Yes. Right.
No. Sorry.

ⓑ

3 This isn't your chocolate!

1. Hey! This isn't your chocolate!
   That's your chocolate. *Please go on.*

4 Role play: Let's make a pond

Work with your partner.

Let's
- play football together.
- play a game.
- play with cars.
- play with the computer.
- make a poster.
- make a pond.

– Yes. Good idea.
Oh no.
Look. That isn't a good idea. Let's ....

5 In your classroom

Your teacher: Where's your pen / homework / folder / book / biro ?

You: Sorry, I haven't got my ... .
Here it is.

6 Listening practice: A crazy morning

Listen and find the right words.
Becky: I haven't got a biro pen ball.
Robert: It's a book picture comic.
Sarah: I haven't got my homework folder pen.

7 What's your telephone number?

690472
673351

Robert: What's your telephone number, Becky?
Becky: Six nine o four seven two. What's your number?
Robert: My number is six seven double three five one.

0 = **o** [əʊ]
33 = **double three**

Your turn *What's your telephone number?*

8 Listening practice: Telephone numbers

Listen, and write their telephone numbers:
David Penrose, Sarah Dixon, Robert Croft,
Becky and Simon Burton, Margaret Dane, Tim Cooper.

Step D

The frog

1. Sarah and Robert are on their bikes in Arnot Hill Park.

Sarah: Look, Robert. Is that a frog?
Robert: Where?
Sarah: There, look! Yes. It *is* a frog.
Robert: I've got an idea.
It's a nice frog – a frog for Becky.
Becky hasn't got a frog.

2. Becky and her mother are at home. Robert and Sarah are there, too.

Sarah: Hello, Mrs Burton! Hi, Becky!
Mrs Burton: Hello, you two!
What have you got there, Robert?
Robert: Hello, Mrs Burton.
This is for Becky. It's a frog.
Look, Becky – oops!
Your frog! Where's your frog?

3. Where is the frog?
It's under the table.
It's on a chair.
Where is it now?
Is it in the bag?

4. Now Becky has got the frog.

Robert: It's for your new pond, Becky.
Becky: Oh, Robert! We haven't got a pond.
Our pond isn't ready yet.
Poor frog!

5. Becky, Robert and Sarah are in the park.

Becky: Look frog. Now you're at home.
Sarah: Hey, look! More frogs! Two, three …
Robert: And there: four, five …
Becky: That's nice.
Our frog has got friends here.
Goodbye, frog.
Robert: Goodbye, frog. Sorry.

Unit 1

1 The frog

1. Sarah and Robert are
2. Is that
3. Robert and Sarah
4. But the pond
5. Now the frog is
6. The frog has got

have got a frog for Becky.
at home in the park.
on their bikes in Arnot Hill Park.
friends here.
a frog?
isn't ready yet.

⟨2 A song: At the door⟩

© Text: Alan Posener, Melodie: Petra Scheil

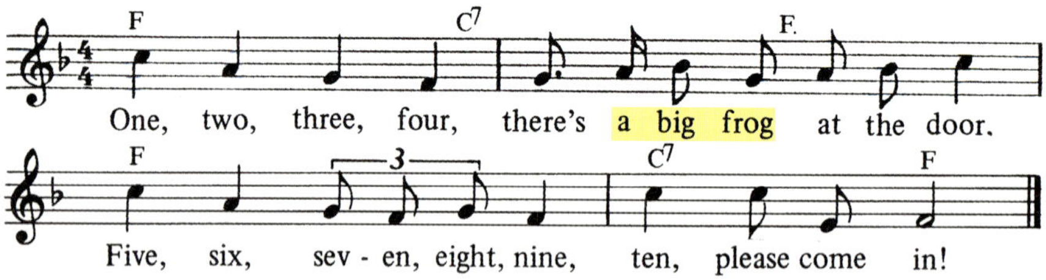

an old dog
a new girl
a nice boy
a teacher
…

3 Sound practice

[ə]
That's a computer.
Mrs Dane is a clever teacher.
Simon and Becky are at home.

[r]
That's **r**ight, Sarah.
That's w**r**ong, **R**obert.
This is my f**r**iend Superf**r**og.

4 Have you got a pen?

Have you got a pen? / …? – No. Sorry.
– No. Ask … . She's got a pen. / He's … .
– Yes. Here your are.

Please go on.

5 What have you got?

Write the answers.
Example:

Ilona: radio, bed, frog
Kemal: computer, pond, dog

a) You've got a house and a garden with three nice things. What are your things?
Write the words in a picture.

b) *Ask five friends. Example:*

What have you got in your house and garden?

I've got a radio, and a bed, and a frog.

c) What have your friends got?

Ilona has got … .
Kemal … . …

Step E

Let's Check

1 Has got or have got?

a) *Put in 'has got' or 'have got'.*

1. The Burtons *have got* a house in Arndale Road.
2. Simon *has got* a radio.
3. The frog … friends in the park.
4. Becky … a computer.
5. Maxi and Mini … beds in the kitchen.
6. David … a brother.
7. Sarah and Robert … bikes.
8. The frogs … a nice pond in the park.

b) *Write the sentences in a) with 'he's got', 'she's got', 'it's got' or 'they've got'.*

1. They've got a house in Arndale Road.
2. He's got … . *Please go on.*

2 WORD POWER

a) *Find the right words.*

b) *Write the words in groups.*

3 Our, your or their?

1. *Sarah:* Where are Becky and Simon?
   Mrs Burton: In … rooms.
2. *David:* Hi, Becky! Hi, Simon! Where are … dogs?
   Simon: In the garden.
3. *Simon:* Let's play football in the park.
   Becky: No. Let's play in … garden.
4. *David:* Let's learn … German words together.
   Robert: Yes. Good idea.
5. *Sarah:* Let's play with Becky and Simon.
   Robert: OK. What's … telephone number?
6. *Robert:* Are … mother and father at home?
   David: No. They aren't here yet.

4 In your classroom

1. I haven't got my book. - - - - - - - - →
2. My biro is broken.
3. Let's work together.
4. Is this my book?
5. Where's my folder?

– Yes. Good idea.
– That's your folder over there.
– Here's a biro. I've got two.
– Here. Look at my book.
– No. It's my book. Here's my name.

The Dixons

Step A

Sarah and her family

ⓐ This is Sarah Dixon on her new bike. The poor man in the picture is her father. His name is Eddy and he is a bank clerk.

The woman in this picture is her mother. Her name is Janet and she is a vet's assistant. Here she is in the kitchen with their cat Tabby.

This is Sarah with her sister Kim. The children are in the garden. Sarah is in the tree. Tabby is in the picture, too – but where?

1 What's in the pictures?

1. One child, ... *Go on.*

ⓑ Sarah and Kim are at home.

Sarah: Kim, have you got a red crayon for my German homework? My pencil case is at school.
Kim: No, but I've got a blue crayon.
Sarah: OK, that's a good colour, too. And have you got a green crayon?
Kim: No, but I've got a green biro. Here you are.

2 What colour are the school bags?

a) Sarah has got a brown bag, and Kim has got a black bag. *Go on.*
b) What colour are the school bags?
– The school bags are brown and black. *Go on.*

3 My English folder

Draw your school things and write sentences.

Step B

What a crazy family!

ⓐ In the morning.
Mr Dixon and the girls are in the kitchen.

Sarah: Where's my knife? Hey, the knives and spoons aren't on the table, Kim. It's your turn, today.
Kim: No, it's your turn, Sarah.
Mr Dixon: Girls, please! I've got the knives here.
Sarah: Thank you, Dad. – Kim, where's my lunch box?
Mr Dixon: It's on that shelf over there.
Kim: And where's my apple?
Mr Dixon: Oh no! What a crazy family!

family – famil**ies**
shel**f** – shel**ves**
kni**fe** – kni**ves**

Unit 2

1 Sound practice

[f]
Where's my knife?
The funny frog is on the shelf.

[v]
I've got five knives.
I've got twelve shelves.

[æ]
That man has got a bag.
You're a bad cat, Tabby.
What's that, Dad?

[e]
This pen is for my friend.
The men are in the garden.
Are you ready? Let's check.

2 Sarah and her teachers

Find the words.
Sarah: I've got ten teachers at Haywood School, four  and six . Two have got big . For example, Mr Wood has got six , three boys and three girls. Mr Miller is nice. He's got chocolate and biscuits on the  in his classroom. That's great!

ⓑ In the afternoon. Sarah and Kim are at home. Their parents aren't there yet.

Kim: Look, Dad is very untidy. His folders are on the chair.
Sarah: And Mum is very untidy, too. Her books are under the chair. And her new CD isn't in its box.
Kim: What a crazy family!

he – **his**
she – **her**
it – **its**

3 The Dixons

Put in 'his', 'her' or 'its'.

1. Sarah and … sister are at home.
2. Kim has got an apple in … lunch box.
3. Mr Dixon is untidy. … folders are on the chair.
4. And Mrs Dixon? … books are under the chair.
5. That cat is crazy. … ball is under the bed.
6. And that CD? It isn't in … box.

In the garage

Sarah and Robert are in the garage.

Robert: Let's go, Sarah. Are you ready?
Sarah: No, I'm not.
My bike has got a flat tyre.
Robert: Where's your pump?
Sarah: Is it on that shelf over there, Robert?
Robert: No, it isn't.
Sarah: Oh – er – is it in that black box?
Robert: Yes, it is. Here you are.
Sarah: Thank you, Robert. ...
Robert: Are you ready now?
Sarah: Yes, I am. Let's go and find Becky.

Yes, he is. – No, he isn't.
Yes, she is. – No, she isn't.
Yes, it is. – No, it isn't.
Yes, they are. – No, they aren't.

4 Questions and answers

1. Are Sarah and Robert in the garage?
2. Is the pump on the chair?
3. Are Mr and Mrs Dixon in the garage, too?
4. Is the cat there?
5. Is Robert there?
6. Is Sarah his sister?

No, they aren't.
Yes, she is.
No, it isn't.
Yes, they are.
No, she isn't.
Yes, he is.

5 What's your answer?

Yes, I am. – No, I'm not.
Yes, we are. – No, we aren't.

1. Are you at Haywood School?
2. Are you eleven?
3. Are you English?
4. Are you and your friends in class 5?
5. Are you at home now?
6. Are you from Berlin?

6 A question game

Throw the dice and look at the numbers.
Find the words and make questions.

Have you got two dice? That's 'Würfel' in German.

Examples: (3) + (4) Are Sarah and Becky at Haywood School? – Yes, they are.
(2) + (6) Are Mr and Mrs Dixon teachers? – No, they aren't.

(1)	Sarah and Robert	(4)	Robert and Becky	+	(1)	sisters	(4)	at Haywood School
(2)	Mr and Mrs Dixon	(5)	Kim and Sarah		(2)	ten	(5)	English
(3)	Sarah and Becky	(6)	the girls and boys in your class		(3)	German	(6)	teachers

In Larwood Grove

Sarah, Becky and Robert are in Larwood Grove.

Robert: Hey, Becky, have you got a new bag for your bike?
Becky: Yes, I have. It's from our shop.
Robert: Oh, have your parents got a bike shop?
Becky: Yes, they have.
Sarah: The bag is very nice. – Er, have your parents got yellow bags, too?
Becky: Yellow– er – no, they haven't. But they've got other colours. They've got red and blue and …
Robert: And have they got pumps, too?
Becky: Yes, they have.
Sarah: Let's go to the shop now.
Robert: Good idea.

Yes, they have. – No, they haven't.
Yes, he has. – No, he hasn't.
Yes, she has. – No, she hasn't.

7 What have they got?

a) Have the Dixons got a house in Larwood Grove? – Yes, they have.
Have the Burtons got a book shop?
Have Sarah and Becky got bikes?
Have the Burtons got blue bags?

b) Has Becky got a new bag?
Has Sarah got an old bike?
Has Robert got a bike, too?
Has Sarah got a blue bag for her bike?

8 What have you got?

Work with your partner.

Have you got
a bike
a bag for your bike
a red biro
a poster in your room
…
? –
Yes, I have.
No, I haven't.
Yes, we have.
No, we haven't.

9 Sarah and Mr Nosy

Sarah is in Larwood Grove with Mr Nosy, a neighbour. *What are her answers?*

Mr Nosy:	*Sarah:*
1. Hello, Sarah. Is that boy your friend?	Yes, he is.
2. Is he from Nottingham?	…
3. Is he at your school?	
4. Has he got a bike, too?	
5. Have you got two dogs now, Sarah?	
6. Oh, and the Burtons? Have they got two dogs?	

Step C

Unit 2

Is that my new CD, Sarah?

Sarah is in her room with Becky.
Kim is there, too.

Kim: Have you got my new CD, little sister?
Sarah: No, I haven't. This is my CD.
Becky: Hi, Kim.
Kim: No, it isn't. Look, Sarah. That's my CD. – And those comics over there are my comics, too.
Sarah: No, they aren't. They're …
Becky: Er – Kim, these are my comics.
Kim: Oh – sorry!

1 In the classroom

Work with a partner. Act the dialogues. Examples:

books ✓ crayons pens folders pencils biros

a) "Are these your books here?"
– "Yes, they are. Thank you."

b) "Are these my books here?"
– "No, those are your books over there."
– "Oh, yes. Thanks."

2 Are you ten?

a) *Find a partner and ask questions.*

Questions	Jens yes	Jens no
Are you ten?	x	
Have you got a brother?		x
Have you got a cat?		
Have you got a bike?		

Yes, I am. – No, I'm not.
Yes, I have. – No, I haven't.

b) *Now talk about your partner:*
Jens is ten. He hasn't got… .

Your turn 3 Is that right?

1. Yellow is a nice colour.
2. Cats are funny.
3. English is OK.
4. Football is a good game.
5. Comics are funny.
6. Snakes are nice.

You:

Yes, it is./No, it isn't.
Yes, they are./No, they aren't.
Go on, please.

4 Sound practice

[ʊ]
That's a g**oo**d b**oo**k.
L**oo**k at my f**oo**tball!
Kim is from Sherw**oo**d.

[u:]
She is in my t**u**tor gr**ou**p.
She's at sch**oo**l this aftern**oo**n.
This is for y**ou**, t**oo**.

[ʊ] – [u:]
G**oo**d aftern**oo**n.
Let's play f**oo**tball at sch**oo**l.
That w**o**man has got tw**o** dogs.

Step D

The ring

1. Sarah is at home with Robert, Becky and David. They are in the living-room.

Sarah: Look! My sister Kim has got a new ring. Isn't it nice?
Becky: Yes, it is.
David: Let's see the ring.
Sarah: Here you are. Be careful! – Oh no! Where is it?
David: Is it under the table?
Becky: No, it isn't.
Sarah: Are you sure? Let's look again. It isn't *my* ring!
Robert: Has Tabby got the ring?
Becky: Tabby? – No, that's silly. She hasn't got the ring.
Robert: Yes, I'm sure. Look, she's in the garden now.
David: Come on. Let's get Tabby.

2. The children are outside now.

Becky: Look, she's in that tree. Oh no, Kim is over there.
Robert: Come on. Let's get Tabby.
David: She's at the top of the tree now.
Robert: The silly cat!
Sarah: I've got an idea! Let's get those red boxes over there. Here, Tabby, Tabby! Come here. Good, I've got Tabby.
Robert: Has she got the ring?
Sarah: No, she hasn't. Where *is* it?
Robert: It's in Tabby, I'm sure.
Becky: What? Where?
Sarah: *In* Tabby?
David: Poor Tabby!

3. Sarah, David, Robert and Becky are in the living-room again. Sarah has got Tabby. Kim is not there yet. She is in the kitchen.

Robert: Tabby, where's the ring?
Becky: I'm sure she hasn't got the ring.
David: Hey, Sarah, look! What's that under those shelves over there?
Becky: What? Where? Is it the ring?
Sarah: Yes, it is. Oh, great! Let's put the ring in its box again.
Kim: Hello! – Hey, what's all this noise?
Sarah: Ha, ha. It's nothing, Kim. Everything is OK.

1 Find the right answer

1. Where are the friends?
   Has Sarah got a new ring?
   Is the ring under the table?
2. Where is Tabby?
   Have the friends got blue boxes?
3. Where is the ring?
   Where is it now?
   Is Kim there now, too?

No, it isn't.
She is at the top of the tree.
The friends are in the living-room.
It is in its box again.
It is under the shelves.
No, Kim has got a new ring.
Yes, she is.
No, they have got red boxes.

2 WORD POWER

1. The Dixons are a … .
2. Eddy Dixon is the … .
3. Janet Dixon is the … .
4. Kim and Sarah are their … .
5. Mr and Mrs Dixon are the … .
6. Kim and Sarah are … .
7. Sarah hasn't got a …, but she's got a sister.

3 My English folder

Draw your family in your folder and write about your family.

4 Where are my books?

a) *Put in 'this' or 'these'.*

Mr Dixon: Please put … comics here in your room, Sarah.
Sarah: OK, Dad. Oh, and please put … bank folder here on your desk.
Mr Dixon: Thank you, Sarah. And are … your pictures here on the chair? And is … your pencil under the table?

b) *Put in 'that' or 'those'.*

Mrs Dixon: Where are my books?
Mr Dixon: The green book is under … chocolate biscuits on … chair over there. And the new books are on … shelves over there.

⟨5 A song: Little boxes⟩

6 Four families

Put in 'he's' or 'his'.

1. Simon — … ten and Becky is … sister. … parents have got a bike shop.
2. Mr Burton — Becky and Simon are … children.
3. Mr Dixon — … a bank clerk. … girls are at Haywood School.
4. Robert — He and … mother are from London. Sarah is … friend.
5. David — … in tutor group 7 MD. Becky and Sarah are … friends.

7 Listening practice: At the bike shop

Listen and find the colours.

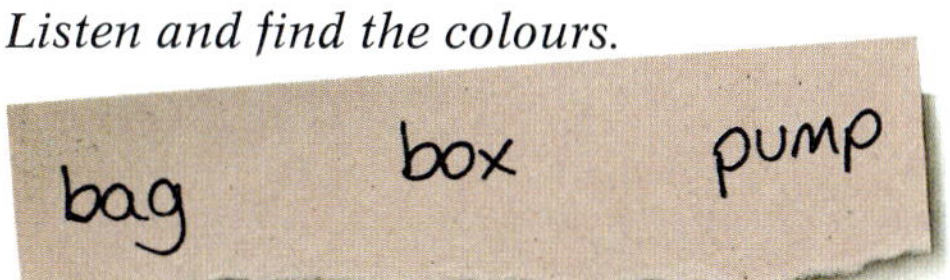

1. The bag is … .
2. The box … . *Go on.*

Step E

Let's check

1 Colours

1. These apples are ..., ... and ... .

2. Chocolate is ... . 

3. This car is ... and ... . 

2 These or those?

1. *Sarah:* Hello, Mrs Burton. ... comics here are for Becky.
2. *Robert:* ... pictures here and ... posters over there are for our classroom.
3. *Mrs Dane:* Sarah, please put ... books here on my desk.
4. *Kim:* ... boys over there are in my tutor group.
5. *Mr Dixon:* Are my folders on ... shelves over there, Sarah?

3 WORD POWER

Four shelves, ...

4 Becky and Mr Nosy

Find the answers for Becky.

a) Is Robert your little brother? – No, he isn't.
Are you new here in Nottingham?
Are your friends at Haywood School?
Are they eight?

b) Have your parents got a shop?
Has your brother got a CD player?
Has Robert got a dog?
Have you got a black cat?

5 His, her or its?

1. *Becky:* Simon isn't here. He's in ... room.
2. *Mrs Dixon:* Please put the CD in ... box, Sarah.
3. *Simon:* Becky is outside with ... friends.
4. *Sarah:* Please put the ring in ... box, Becky.

The new girl from Germany

Step A

At the airport

ⓐ These people are at Heathrow Airport in London. There are men, women and children. There is a girl with a big red bag. She is from Germany.

1 The people at the airport

There's ... . | There are ... .

Examples: There's a family with four children. There's a man with ... .

There are two women with black bags. There are three girls with ... .

ⓑ Jenny Leinert is from Berlin. Her father is German, but her mother is British. She has got an aunt, an uncle and two cousins in England.

David: Hi, Jenny! We're here!
Mark: Jenny! Jenny!
Mrs Penrose: Hello, Jenny.
Mr Penrose: Welcome to England.
Jenny: Oh thank you. This is great!
David: Come on, Mark. Let's help Jenny with her bag.

2 I'm German

"Hi. I'm Christian. I'm German."
"My name is Laura. I'm Italian."
"I'm Maria and I'm Spanish."
"Melina is my name. I'm Greek."
"My name is Kemal. I'm Turkish."

a) *Talk about these people.*
Start: Christian is German. Laura is ... .

Your turn

b) "I'm ... ." Ask your teacher for new words.

c) *Ask your friends questions.*
Example: "Are you German?"
– "No, I'm not. I'm Italian."
– "My parents are from Poland."

3 Sound practice

[tʃ]
Where's my lun**ch** box?
What's in the pic**t**ure?
There are four **ch**ildren.

[dʒ]
Look at this pa**g**e.
My name is **J**anet.
Are you **G**erman?

[tʃ] – [dʒ]
The **ch**ild is from **G**ermany.
There's a big pic**t**ure on this pa**g**e.
Thank you for the **ch**ocolate, **J**anet!

Step B

In the car

The Penroses and Jenny are in the car.

David: You're lucky, Jenny. You can speak German and English.
Mrs P.: You can speak German, too, David.
Jenny: Oh, can you speak German now?
Mark: Yes, he can.
David: No, I can't. I can say one or two things, but –
Jenny: Hey, I can do your German homework!
David: Oh yes, that's a good idea.

Mrs P.: A good idea? I'm not sure. – What about Mr Cooper?
Jenny: Who's Mr Cooper?
David: He's my German teacher. He's OK.

Unit 3

1 Your English lessons

What can you and your friends do in English?
Example: We can ask questions in English.

We can | ask✓ write play talk about make | sentences questions✓ pictures posters dialogues answers games people … | in English.

2 Mark

1. write 2. draw 3. make 4. play 5. speak

a) *Make sentences with 'can' or 'can't'.*
1. Mark can't write his name. 2. He … draw a … . *Please go on.*

b) *Now make questions and answers.*
1. Can he write his name? – No, he can't.
2. Can he …? – Yes, he can. *Go on.*

Can he …? – Yes, he can.
– No, he can't.

3 A name quiz

Who?

Who's from Berlin? – That's Jenny.
Who's a bank clerk? – That's Mr Dixon.
Who's …? – …

Make a name quiz with people from this book.

4 Who can do what?

a) *Write questions with 'Can you …?'*

b) *Go to your friends. Ask the questions.*
"Can you speak Turkish, Nadine?"
– "No, I can't."

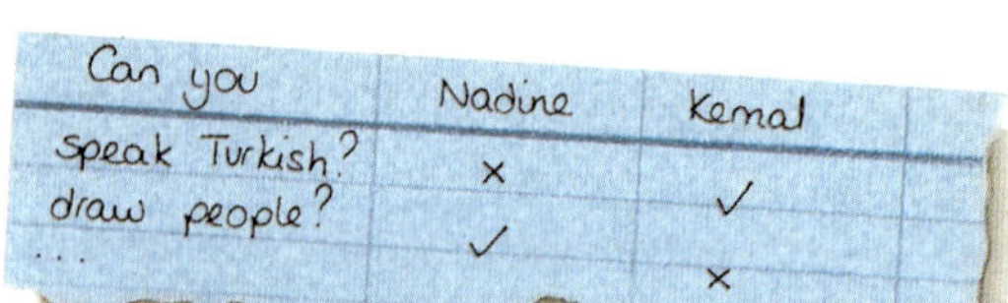

Can you	Nadine	Kemal
speak Turkish?	×	✓
draw people?	✓	×
…		

c) *Who can or can't do what? Tell the class.*
"Nadine can't speak Turkish, but she can … ."

At home in Sherwood

SB

ⓐ The Penroses are at home now.
Mark is in Jenny's room.

Mark: Is my mum your aunty, Jenny?
Jenny: Yes, she is.
Mark: Are we cousins?
Jenny: Yes, we are.
Your mother is my mother's sister.
So we're cousins.
Mark: Hey, what have you got in your bag?
Presents?!

5 Jenny and the Penroses

Please make sentences. You can start:
1. Jenny is David**'s** cousin.
2. She is … cousin, too.
3. Mrs Penrose is … . *Go on.*

Jenny Mrs Penrose Mr Penrose David Mark	is	Jenny's David's Mark's	aunt. uncle. cousin. brother. mother. father.

HV

6 Listening practice: Presents

Please listen. What are their presents?
"Mrs Penrose's present is … ."

ⓑ

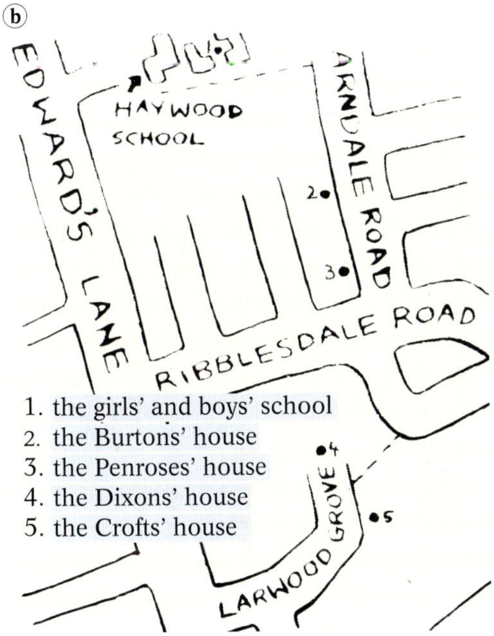

1. the girls' and boys' school
2. the Burtons' house
3. the Penroses' house
4. the Dixons' house
5. the Crofts' house

7 Where?

1. The girl**s'** and boy**s'** school is in Edward's Lane.
2. The Burtons'house is in … *Go on.*

my friend**'s** house
my friend**s'** house

8 Friends and neighbours

friends ✓ Burtons parents girls dogs Dixons

What can David tell Jenny?
Write the right forms.
1. My friends' houses are in Sherwood.
2. There's Becky. Her … bike shop is in Mansfield Road. 3. But the … house is in Arndale Road. 4. Their … names are Maxi and Mini. 5. The Dixons are a crazy family! Their … names are Sarah and Kim. 6. There's Robert Croft, too. He and his mother are the … neighbours in Larwood Grove.

Let's say hello

Ⓐ Becky is in Arndale Road. Sarah is with her.

Sarah: Can you give me your ball, please? I've got an idea for a game, and – Hey, look. David is in his garden.
Becky: Yes, I can see him. And he's got a girl with him.
Sarah: It's his German cousin. Let's go and say hello to her.

Becky: Hi. I'm Becky. My German isn't very good.
Sarah: And I'm Sarah. My German is terrible!
Jenny: Oh! My name is Jenny. And it's OK – you can speak to me in English.
Sarah: Good! – Where's Robert, David?
David: I'm not sure. Maybe he's at home. Let's phone him.

I	–	**me**
she	–	**her**
he	–	**him**

9 Can you give me my ball, please?

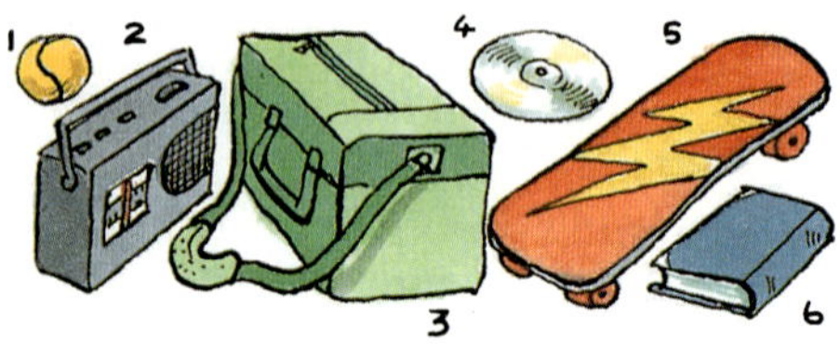

Your friend has got your things. What can you say?

1. Can you give me my ball, please?
2. Can you give me my …, please? *Go on.*

10 On the telephone

1. Robert? – not at home 2. Sarah? – at Becky's house 3. David? – at the Crofts' house
4. Jenny? – not here 5. Becky? – in the park with the dogs 6. Mark? – in bed

1. "Hello. Is Robert there? Can I speak to **him**, please?" – "Sorry. He isn't at home."
2. "Hello. Is Sarah there? Can I speak to **her,** please?" – "Sorry, she's at … ." *Go on.*

Ⓑ Now the friends are at the Burtons' house.

Becky: Can you help me with the pond this afternoon?
David: Sorry, we can't. We must go to the shops.
Jenny: I must get my school uniform.
David: Jenny is at our school now.
Sarah: Oh, good. That's great.

11 Sorry, I can't

Can you | go to the park / play football / go to the shops / … | with me? – Sorry, I can't. I must | do my homework. / help my parents. / phone my friend. / help in the garden. / …

LOOKING AT THE UK:

How can you get there?

by plane

1 Look at the pictures

You can get there by plane.
You can get there by … . *Go on.*

2 Look at the map

There are ferries from Belgium to England.
There are ferries from … to … .
There is a tunnel from … . *Go on.*

by train through the Channel Tunnel

by car and hovercraft

by ferry

3 Work with a partner

Make a poster for planes or trains or ferries – or for the Channel Tunnel. Find photos or draw pictures. What can you write on your poster?

Go by … . You can get there by … .
It's great by … . You can see more by … .

Step C

Tea

It is late in the afternoon. Mr Penrose and Jenny are in the kitchen.

Jenny: Can I help, Uncle Colin?
Mr Penrose: Oh, thank you, Jenny. Yes, you can help me with the tea. Can you put the ham and the cheese on the table, please?
Jenny: Yes. – Er – is this the cheese?
Mr Penrose: Yes, that's right.
Jenny: English cheese is a funny colour. Mmm – but it's nice.

Unit 3

1 Role play: Can I help?

How can you help at home?
"Can I help?"
– "Oh, thank you.
Can you help me in the kitchen, please?"

help me with the tea | go to the shops | put the bikes in the garage | make the beds | help me in the garden ...

2 WORD POWER

What's for tea?

– There's salad.
– And there's ... .
– There are ... .
– You can have ... .

Can you go on?

3 What you can say at the table

Work in groups of four or five. Draw pictures of things for tea. Put your pictures on the table. Now sit at the table and act little dialogues.

4 Sound practice

[l]
Hello, Uncle Colin.
Can I help?
Can I have more milk, please?

[r]
It's brown bread.
Where are our CDs?
They're in my room.

Step D

The photo

1. Sarah, Becky and Robert are with David. They are in the Penroses' garden. Robert has got his mother's camera with him.

Robert: It's a good camera.
You can see the photos right away.
Sarah: Ha, ha. This is a great idea!
David: Yes, we can take a nice photo of her.
Becky: But where *is* Jenny?
Sarah: In the house. Let's go and find her.

2. Now Jenny is in the garden, too. She is in her new school uniform.

Jenny: Oh no, this isn't a good idea.
This silly uniform –
Sarah: It isn't silly. It's – er –
Becky: It's very English.
David: And the photo is for your family in Berlin. Please, Jenny!
Jenny: Oh, OK. But you must all be in the photo with me.
Robert: Who can take the photo?
Your father, David?

3. But they cannot find Mr Penrose. Here is little Mark. He can help. He is only four. This is great for him!
Mark: Are you all ready? Say 'cheese'!

4. Now they have got the photo.

Robert: Oh no!
David: You can only see our legs!
Becky: Oh Mark, it isn't a very good photo.
Jenny: Yes, it is. It's a great photo. You can't see me in my uniform! Thanks, Mark!

Unit 3

1 Tell the story

Find the right sentences.

a) 1. The friends are in David's garden.
2. … But Jenny is in the house.
3. … Robert has got a camera.
4. … It is for a photo of Jenny.

b) 1. Now Jenny is in the garden.
2. … But Mark can help.
3. … Robert cannot take the photo.
4. … She is in her new school uniform.

What can you say about Mark's photo?

2 Questions for Jenny

Jenny is new at Haywood School. *What can she tell the boys and girls there?*

1. Are you eleven, Jenny? – No, I'm not. I'm twelve.
2. Is your father German? – Yes, he … .
3. Are David and Mark Penrose your cousins?
4. Is your mother German?
5. Are you from Hamburg?
6. Is Berlin big?
7. Are your parents in England, too?

3 Who and where?

a) 1. Who's that? – It's Jenny.
Where is she? – She's in her room.
2. Who's that? – It's … .
Where is he? – He's in the … .
Go on. Make more questions and answers.

Your turn b) *Draw a picture of a girl or boy in your class. Can the others say who it is?*

4 Let's play *me her him*

1. *Jenny:* Here's David. Let's play a game with … .
2. *Mark:* Where am I? Can you find …?
3. *David:* Jenny is under the table. Look at … !
4. *Mark:* I can play football. Look at … .
5. *David:* Jenny can draw good pictures. Have you got a crayon for …, Mark?
6. *Jenny:* Mark can't write his name. But I can help … .

5 Pictures from this unit

Can you find the pictures? Make sentences like this:
1. That's the Burtons' garden. 2. That's Mrs …'s camera. 3. That's …s' … . *Go on.*

6 What's right?

you're – your	**You're** late. Is that **your** book?	it's – its	Look. **It's** Sarah's snake. What's **its** name?

Sarah:
1. Oh good, Jenny. … in our tutor group.
2. … new uniform is OK. 3. … lucky, David.
4. … cousin is German. 5. She can do …
German homework!

Becky:
1. What's that? Oh, … a frog. 2. Look at … little green legs! 3. Where's … home?
4. … from the pond in Arnot Hill Park.
5. … a funny frog!

Step E

Let's Check

1 Find the right word

What? Who? Where?

1. ...'s that? – It's David's cousin.
2. ...'s your name? – Jenny.
3. ...'s Uncle Colin? – In the kitchen.
4. ...'s that? – It's a dog biscuit.
5. ...'s Jenny's home? – In Berlin.
6. ...'s the little boy? – Mark Penrose.

2 Pairs

Make sentences with these pairs.
You can start:
1. Becky is David's friend.
2. Tabby is the Dixons' ... . *Go on.*

1. Becky/David 2. Tabby/the Dixons 3. Jenny/Mark
4. Mrs Penrose/Jenny 5. Maxi/the Burtons
6. Kim/Sarah 7. Mr Cooper/the girls and boys

3 What can Maxi and Mini do? What can't they do?

play football | take a photo | speak German | make a hole | get a comic | draw a picture

1. Maxi **can** play football. 2. Mini **can't** ... . 3. Maxi ... . *Please go on.*

4 Me, her or him?

Jenny is on the telephone to her mother. *Can you find the right words?*

1. I'm at Haywood School now. The German lessons are easy for ... .
2. David is lucky. I can help ... with his German homework.
3. David's friend Becky has got two dogs. I can play with ... and with the dogs, too.
4. I've got a funny photo of ... and my friends. You can only see our legs!
5. Aunty Pat? No, sorry – you can't speak to ... . She isn't at home.
6. But here's Uncle Colin. You can speak to ... now.

5 WORD POWER

What's different?
Look at the two pictures. Make sentences. Start:
– In picture 1 there's one ball. In picture 2 there are two balls.

⟨Revision 1⟩

1 Jenny at Haywood School

Put in 'am', 'is' or 'are'.

David: Here we ..., Jenny! This ... our classroom. – Mrs Dane! This ... my cousin, Jenny Leinert.
Jenny: Hello, Mrs Dane.
Mrs Dane: Hello, Jenny. ... you the girl from Germany?
Jenny: Yes, I ...
Mrs Dane: Where ... you from in Germany?
Jenny: Berlin.
Mrs Dane: ... your parents German?
Jenny: Well, my father ... German. But my mother ... English. I can speak English, and German, too.
Mrs Dane: Ah! Good! You can help David with his German.
Jenny: Oh – ... I in David's group for German?
Mrs Dane: Yes, you ... So David ... lucky!
David: Yes, I ...!

2 Who am I?

Now you are Becky Sarah Kim Simon Robert David Mark *or* Jenny .

Play the game with a partner. Example:
You: Who am I?
Partner: Are you a girl?
You: No, I'm not.
Partner: Are you David's brother?
You: Yes, I am.
Partner: Oh, are you Mark?
You: Yes, I am!

Are you
a girl/a boy ten/eleven/twelve
from England/from Germany
David's cousin/brother
Becky's brother/friend
Simon's sister ...'s ...
? – Yes, I am. / No, I'm not.

3 At the Penroses' house ***the boy's football the boys' football***

Example:
1. The boys have got a new football.
   – The boys' football is new.
2. David has got a big blue bag.
3. Mark has got a little red bag.
4. The Penroses have got a new CD player.
5. David has got an old radio.
6. Mrs Penrose has got a big computer.

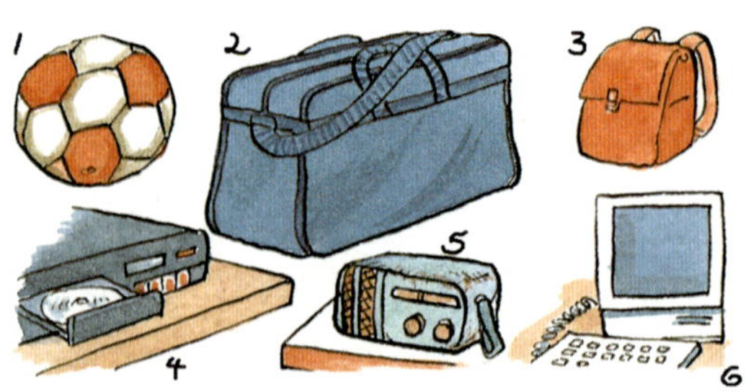

Free time

Step A

The alphabet

David and Jenny are at the Crofts' house. They are in Robert's room. Mark is there, too. He has got a new book.

Mark: Robert! Look at my new ABC book.
Robert: That's nice. – Can you say all the letters in the alphabet, Mark?
Mark: A – B – C – D. Er ... E – F ... er ...
David: It's G! Let's make a rhyme. Then it's easy.
A – B – C – D – E – F – *G* –
Say the alphabet with *me*!
Jenny: Hey, that's good! Let's go on. Er ...
H – I – J – K – L – M – *N* –
Mark can count from one to *ten*! – Can you, Mark?
Mark: Of course I can! One, two, three ...
David: OK. – Now listen. *This* is clever ...
O – P – Q – R – S – T - *U* –
Mark's new shoes are brown and *blue*.
Mark: No, they aren't. They're red and blue!
Jenny: OK. Mark's new shoes are *red* and blue. Now the last letters. Oh yes ...
V and W – X – Y – Z –
Now it's late and time for *bed*!
Mark: No, it isn't. That's silly!
Robert: It's time for 'Camera box' now. Let's watch TV.
David: Oh, no. That's boring. Let's read our comics.
Jenny: Oh, you've got a kite, Robert.
Robert: Yes, but it's broken.
Jenny: Well, let's repair the kite and go to the park.

1 A is for APPLE

Find words for the letters in the alphabet. Work with a partner.
Example: Bettina: A is for APPLE.
Claudia: B is for BALL.
Bettina: C is for COMPUTER.
Go on.

2 Spell the words

Markus: Think of a word, Stefan.
Stefan: Apple.
Markus: Can you spell 'apple'?
Stefan: A – P – P – L – E.
Markus: Right. Now it's your turn.

'APPLE' has got two 'p's. So you can say: 'A – double P – L – E.'

Your turn: *Can you spell your name?*

3 Let's read our comics

Work with a partner.

Let's
watch
play
read
listen to
repair
make

a salad for tea.
our comics.
your old camera.
football on TV.
your new CD.
computer games.
....

–

Yes, OK. / great! / that's a good idea.

No, we haven't got time. / that's a silly idea. / not again!

Step B

In the living-room

Now the friends are in the Crofts' living-room.
Jenny is repairing Robert's kite.Robert is helping her.
David and Mark are looking at the ABC book.
David is reading the rhymes to Mark, and Mark is learning the letters.
The TV is on, but nobody is watching!

Unit 4

1 What are they doing?

He is read**ing**.
She is read**ing**.
They are read**ing**.

Look at the picture. Example: Robert is helping Jenny.

Robert		watching TV.
David		looking at the book together.
Jenny	is	reading the rhymes to Mark.
Mark	are	repairing the kite.
David and Mark		helping Jenny.
Jenny and Robert		learning the ABC.
Nobody		working together.

Is he read**ing**?
Is she read**ing**?
Are they read**ing**?

2 In the evening

At the Burtons' house

1

2

3

4 At the Dixons' house

5

6

a) *Ask your friends questions.*
– What is Simon doing? – He's … .
– What are Mr Burton and Becky doing?
– They're … .

b) *Now ask different questions.*
– Is Simon working in the garden?
– No, he's … .
– Are Mr Burton and Becky …?
– No, they're … .

read a book
play a game
work in the garden
draw a picture
listen to the radio
watch TV

Mrs Croft

Becky: Hi, Robert! We're just going to our house. We've got an idea for the pond. Can you come, too?
Robert: In a minute. I'm just washing up.
Simon: Ugh, terrible.
Robert: Yes, but Mum is working late today. So it's my turn in the kitchen.
Simon: Ah! You're listening to Radio 1.
Robert: No, I'm not listening to Radio 1. It's Radio Nottingham. I'm listening to my mum.
Becky: Your mum? But she isn't at home. Robert, are you crazy or what?
Robert: Of course I'm not. Listen … .

Simon: Hmm??
Robert: There! That's my mum. She's on Radio Nottingham. That's her job.
Becky: Hey, that's an exciting job!

I am work**ing**.
You are work**ing**.
We are work**ing**.

3 What are you doing?

1. *Mrs Penrose:* Colin! What are you doing?
   Mr Penrose: I'm working in the kitchen.
2. *Mrs Burton:* Becky, Simon! What …?
   Becky: We're … . *Go on.*

4 Let's play a game: What am I doing?

Think of an activity. Then act – and say, 'What am I doing?' Your friends must find out.

"Are you doing your homework?"
"No, I'm not."
"Are you reading a book?"
"No – but your question isn't bad!"
"Er … Are you reading a comic?"
"Right! Yes, I am."

The idea

Becky and Simon are in their garden. They are looking at the hole. Robert is with them.

Robert: Oh, it's big now. – And what's your idea for the pond?
Simon: Big stones round it.

I	–	**me**
you	–	**you**
he	–	**him**
she	–	**her**
it	–	**it**
we	–	**us**
you	–	**you**
they	–	**them**

Robert: Stones? But where can you get them?
Becky: From the hole! – Look, we've got these stones here. And there are more stones in the hole. But we must get them out. And that isn't easy. Can you help us?
Robert: Of course I can help you. Give me the spade!

5 Please help

it *you* *us* *them*

Please put in the right words.

1. *Mrs Croft:* I've got this ham for tea. Please put … on the table, Robert.
2. *Simon:* These stones are terrible! We can't get … out. Can you help …, Robert?
3. *Mrs Burton:* Becky! Maxi and Mini are hungry. Please give … their biscuits. *Becky:* OK, Mum. Maxi! Mini! I've got biscuits for …!
4. *Mr Penrose:* David! Mum and I are just going out. Can you and Jenny wash up for …, please?
5. *Mark:* 'Playtime' is on TV. Please watch … with me, Jenny!
6. *Becky:* Simon and Robert and I are working in the garden, Dad. Can you give … your big spade?

6 Where are they?

Where is Where are	my lunch box Dad the chocolate biscuits Mum Maxi and Mini my new shoes	?	I can't find	them him it her .

7 Sound practice

[ʌ]
Your brother is funny.
One is my lucky number.
What colour is your pump?

[æ]
There's a black cat in the flat!
Dad! The apples are in that bag.
Pat hasn't got Tabby.

[ʌ] – [æ]
Can I come in?
I'm hungry.
– There's bread and butter with ham and salad.

LOOKING AT THE UK:
Free time

1

2

3

4

5

1 What are they doing?

In picture 1 they're playing tennis.
In picture 2 … . *Go on.*

tennis ✓ | football | computer games | cricket | pop music

2 It's great!

Your turn

Work with your partner. *Example:* "Football is boring." – "Yes, it is."

Tennis
Cricket
Football
TV
Pop music
Computer games
…

is
are

great.
OK.
exciting.
boring.
terrible.
nice.
silly.

Yes, it is.
No, it isn't. It's … .
Yes, they are.
No, they aren't. They're … .
No idea.

3 WORD POWER

These are English words – but they are the same in German.
Think of more words like these.
Draw pictures – maybe you can find photos, too – and make a poster.

badminton | tennis | sweatshirt | pop | T-shirt | computer

Step C

What's the weather like?

In the morning

It's warm and sunny today, and Becky is playing cricket with David.

In the afternoon

But now it's windy. Becky and Robert are out with their kites. Jenny is with them.

In the evening

Becky is going for a walk with the dogs, but the weather isn't nice now. It's raining, and it's cold, too. The dogs are very wet.

Unit 4

1 What can you do today?

Example: It's sunny today. We can play football in the garden, **or** we can go to the park.
It's raining. We can't play outside, **but** we can … .

It's sunny today. It's raining. It's warm. It's wet now. It's very windy today. It's cold here today.	We can We can't	go for a walk. play outside. listen to CDs. watch TV. play football in the garden. sit in the garden. play in the house. go to the park. …

⟨2 A song: Sailing⟩

© Polygram Songs Musikverlag GmbH, Hamburg

2. We are sailing, we are sailing
Home again, 'cross the sea.
We are sailing stormy waters
To be near you, to be free.

3 Listening practice: At home

Listen. Then answer the questions.

a) Where is Becky? And Simon? What's the weather like?

b) What is Robert doing? Is tea ready? Is Mrs Croft watching TV?

Step D

The flowerpot

1. It is Saturday morning, so there is no school today. The children are at Robert's house. The weather is cold, but it is not raining.

Robert: Let's go in and watch TV.
David: Oh no!
Sarah: Not again! TV is boring. Let's go out on our bikes.
David: But Jenny can't come with us – she hasn't got a bike here. Let's play football. We can play here.
Jenny: Oh yes! Sarah and I can be one team. And you boys can be the other team.
Robert: OK. We're Team A, and you're Team B. I've got a ball in the garage.

2. The game is exciting. The garage door is the boys' goal. Sarah has got the ball. She is good at football, and now she is kicking the ball.
Jenny: Great, Sarah! Goal!

Unit 4

3. Crash! There is a terrible noise. The ball is in the garage and Mrs Croft's big flowerpot is on the floor. It is broken.
Jenny: Oh, Sarah, look – the flowerpot!
Sarah: It's broken! Oh, sorry, Robert.
Robert: Oh no! Mum's pot! A present from Aunty Audrey.
David: Well, we must tell your mum.

4. Now Mrs Croft is there.
Mrs Croft: Hello!
Robert: Oh, Mum – your flowerpot from Aunty Audrey. It's broken.
David: We're very sorry, Mrs Croft. But we can get you a new pot.
Sarah: Or maybe we can repair it. I –
But Mrs Croft is laughing.
Mrs Croft: That big flowerpot from Aunty Audrey? It's a terrible old thing. I'm not angry about that – of course not.

1 The story

Put the sentences together.

1. It is Saturday today, and … ------→ there is no school.
2. It is cold, but …
3. David and Robert are Team A, and …
4. Sarah has got the ball, and …
5. The ball is in the goal, but …
6. Maybe the children can repair it, or …
7. They are sorry, but …

- she is kicking it now.
- they can get a new pot.
- there is no school.
- Mrs Croft's flowerpot is broken.
- Mrs Croft is not angry.
- the girls are Team B.
- the weather is OK for football.

2 Tell the story

Can you tell the story?

Start: The children are at Robert's house. They are outside. *Go on.*

children – at Robert's house / outside / cold – but – not raining / football – good idea / boys – Team A – girls – Team B / garage door – goal / now – Sarah – kicking – ball / Crash! / ball – in the garage – but – flowerpot – on the floor / broken / children – very sorry / must – tell Mrs Croft / but – Mrs Croft – laughing / flowerpot – Aunty Audrey – terrible old thing.

3 Can you help?

Put in 'me', 'you', 'him', 'her', 'it', 'us' or *'them'*.

1. *Mr Penrose:* Mark can't find his shoes. Can you see … , David?
2. *Jenny:* I haven't got the telephone number for Germany. Can you tell … the number, please, Aunty Pat?
3. *Robert:* David and I can't do this German exercise. Jenny, can you help … with …?
4. *Jenny:* Can I play cricket with …, Robert?
5. *Mark:* Mum, where are my crayons? *Mrs Penrose:* Oh, David. They're on that shelf. Can you get … for …?
6. *Mrs Burton:* Becky is going to the shops, Simon. Can you go with …?

4 They're there – in their beds!

Please write this exercise.
Put in 'there', 'their' or 'they're'.

1. Where are Maxi and Mini? … here! … are two beds for them on the kitchen floor. They have got … dog biscuits in … beds.
2. Now … playing with Simon. Where is … new ball? – Look, … it is.
3. Now Maxi is in the living-room. Mini is …, too. … watching TV together.

5 A new ball – an old bag

'A' or 'an'? Example: This ball is new. – It's **a new** ball. *But:* This bag is old. – It's **an old** bag.

1. This ball is new. 2. This bag is old. 3. This stone is big. 4. This room is untidy. 5. This game is silly. 6. This book is exciting. 7. This kite is good. 8. This exercise is easy!

6 WORD POWER

Find the pairs.
Example: watch – TV.

kick read throw
watch ✓ draw listen to

Let's check

1 Robert's photos

Robert is talking about his photos. *Put in 'me', 'her', 'him', 'us' or 'them'.*

1. In this photo, you can see … with Mum.
2. This is Becky. In this picture, you can see … with Maxi and Mini.
3. This is David. Here you can see … with Mark.
4. Here are Sarah and Kim. In this photo you can see … with Tabby.
5. Here I am again! In this photo, you can see … with Jenny.
6. Jenny and I are in this photo, too. Here you can see … with Becky and Simon.

2 WORD POWER

Put the opposites together in pairs. Example: 'Silly' is the opposite of 'clever'.

bad   boring   cold   wrong   good   everything   clever ✓   silly ✓   exciting   nothing   right   warm

3 A wet Saturday

…and…   …but…   …or…

Put two sentences together – and make one!

1. The weather is cold. It's raining.
2. It isn't nice outside. It's warm in the house.
3. We can play computer games in my room. We can watch TV in the living-room.
4. I haven't got a CD player. We can listen to the radio.
5. We can read comics. We can draw.
6. I've got two new pencils. My crayons are new, too.

4 What are they doing?

1. What's the weather like?
2. What are they doing?
   – Mrs Penrose is … . *Go on.*

Jenny's birthday

Step A

A surprise party

David, Becky and Sarah are outside the Penroses' house.

David: Jenny's birthday is in ten days. Let's have a surprise party for her.
Becky: Good idea! I can make the invitations.
David: Yes – we can invite six people from school.
Becky: That's six invitations.
David: Then there are you, Simon, Robert, Sarah, Mum and Dad, Mark, Jenny and me. That's nine people.
Sarah: Six and nine. That's fifteen. We must have a big cake then.
David: I can make it. That's no problem. And I can play the guitar, too.
Becky: Oh great! We can sing.
Sarah: And we can dance, too.

1 Numbers

1	one	11	eleven	21	twenty-one	10	ten
2	two	12	twelve	22	twenty-two	20	twenty
3	three	13	thirteen	23	twenty-three	30	thirty
4	four	14	fourteen	24	twenty-four	40	forty
5	five	15	fifteen	25	twenty-five	50	fifty
6	six	16	sixteen	26	twenty-six	60	sixty
7	seven	17	seventeen	27	twenty-seven	70	seventy
8	eight	18	eighteen	28	twenty-eight	80	eighty
9	nine	19	nineteen	29	twenty-nine	90	ninety
10	ten	20	twenty	30	thirty	100	a/one hundred

2 Let's play a game with numbers

Think of a number from 1 to 100. Your partner must ask questions and find your number.

You: What's my number?
Your partner: Is it over twenty?
You: No, it isn't.
Your partner: Is it under ten?
You: No, it isn't.
Your partner: Has it got a five in it?
You: No, it hasn't.
Your partner: Has it got an eight in it?
You: Yes, it has.
Your partner: Then your number must be eighteen.
You: Yes, that's right.

Jenny's letter

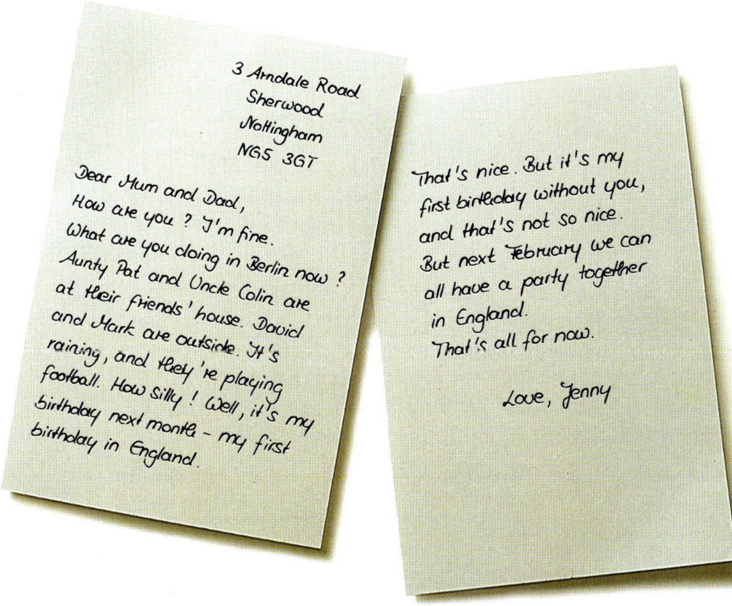
3 Arndale Road
Sherwood
Nottingham
NG5 3GT

Dear Mum and Dad,
How are you? I'm fine.
What are you doing in Berlin now?
Aunty Pat and Uncle Colin are at their friends' house. David and Mark are outside. It's raining, and they're playing football. How silly! Well, it's my birthday next month – my first birthday in England.

That's nice. But it's my first birthday without you, and that's not so nice.
But next February we can all have a party together in England.
That's all for now.

Love, Jenny

3 The months

January, February, March, April, May
Let's learn all the months today

June, July and August, too
all these names are new to you

September, October, November, December
but they are easy to remember.

4 Find the months

Can you find the months?
Example: 1. They have got 31 days.
– January, March … have got 31 days.
2. They have got 30 days.
– … *Please go on.*
3. It has got 28 or 29 days.
4. These months are warm.
5. And these months are cold.
6. It has only got 3 letters.
7. They have got a 'y' in them.

5 Sound practice

[ən]
I've got an invitation for you.
I've got an idea.

[ə]
It's a nice invitation.
It's a good idea.

[ði:]
Here's the invitation.
The idea is very good.

[ðə]
The new invitation is on the table.
That's the new idea.

Everyone is very busy

The children are getting everything ready for Jenny's surprise party. They are all sitting in the Burtons' kitchen. David is making a shopping list. Becky is writing invitations. And Sarah is helping her. Maxi is there, too. She is lying under a chair. She is playing with a balloon.

get – **getting**
sit – **sitting**
write – **writing**
make – **making**
lie – **lying**

1 Party invitations

Say what Becky is doing. Example: 1. Becky is getting a pen. *Go on.*

get a pen

sit at the table

make the invitation

draw a picture

write a name

2 In the afternoon

Example: 1. *Mrs Burton:* Is Becky playing with Maxi?
Simon: No, she isn't. She's working with her computer. *Go on.*

Mrs Burton: – play with Maxi?
Simon:

Mark: – make a cake?
Mrs Penrose:

Mr Burton: – do his homework?
Becky:

Mr Dixon: – write a letter?
Kim:

Jenny: – listen to the radio?
David:

David: – work in the kitchen?
Mr Penrose:

What is the date?

3 David's birthday list

Birthdays:
Mum - - - - - 18th January
Jenny - - - - - 7th February
My birthday! - - - 11th May
Becky - - - - - 24th June
Simon - - - - - 25th July
Mark - - - - - 31st August
Dad - - - - - 20th September
Sarah - - - - - 3rd October
Robert - - - - - 2nd December

first	1st
second	2nd
third	3rd
fourth	4th
fifth	5th
sixth	6th
seventh	7th
eighth	8th
ninth	9th
tenth	10th

a) *Ask questions and give the answers.*
1. When is Mark's birthday?
   – His birthday is on the thirty-first of August.
2. When is Mrs Penrose's …? *Go on.*

Your turn

b) *Now talk about all the birthdays in your family.*
– My mum's birthday is on the … .
  When is your mum's …?
– It's on … . *Go on.*

eleventh	11th
twelfth	12th
thirteenth	13th
fourteenth	14th
fifteenth	15th
sixteenth	16th
seventeenth	17th
eighteenth	18th
nineteenth	19th
twentieth	20th

4 My English folder

Make a list with all the birthdays in your family.
You can put your friends on the list, too.

twenty-first	21st
twenty-second	22nd
twenty-third	23rd
twenty-fourth	24th
twenty-fifth	25th
twenty-sixth	26th
twenty-seventh	27th
twenty-eighth	28th
twenty-ninth	29th
thirtieth	30th
…	…
hundredth	100th

Unit 5

What time is it?

Mark: What's this, Mum?
Mrs Penrose: It's Jenny's present from her parents. It's a surprise! David, can you put the present in my room, please? I must phone Jenny's mother now.
Mark: Can I say 'Guten Tag', Mum?
Mrs Penrose: OK, Mark. Let's see. What time is it?
David: It's quarter past six, Mum.
Mrs Penrose: Oh, then it's quarter past seven in Germany. Jenny's parents must be at home. Let's phone them now.

1 The time

It's four o'clock. It's quarter past four. It's half past four. It's quarter to five.

What time is it?

6.15	8.00	9.30	11.45
4.15	1.00	2.45	7.15
12.30	10.45	5.15	10.00

2 What time is it now?

It's ten to six. It's four **minutes** to six. It's twenty past six.

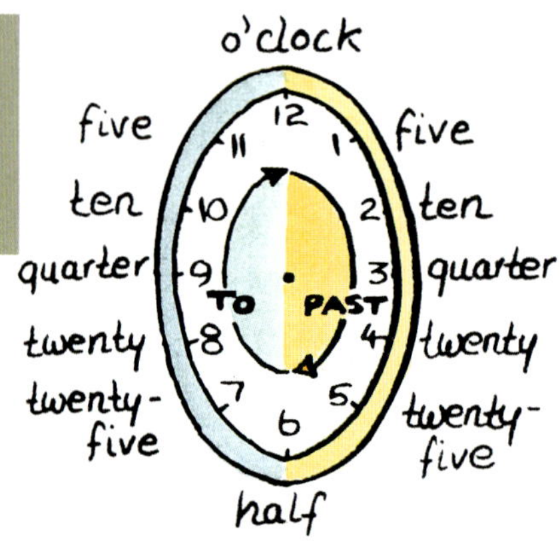

Can you tell the time?

2.15	2.22	3.20	11.10	8.05	10.25
11.30	4.57	9.35	1.30	7.18	10.40

3 Role play: Can you come?

Can you come to | my house / my party | on the 14th / at 3 o'clock / on Saturday / today / this afternoon | ?

On the 14th? Yes, I can.
Thank you.
Sorry, I can't. It's my friend's birthday.
No, sorry. I haven't got time then.

4 In the classroom

Find the answer to these questions.

1. Sorry, what page are we on? ----► We're at the top of page 61.
2. What exercise are we doing?
3. Can you help me with this?
4. Can I write in pencil?
5. What's our homework for tomorrow?
6. Must we do number 4, too?

Yes, number 3 and number 4.
Of course I can.
No, we must write in biro or pen.
We're doing exercise 6.
We're at the top of page 61.
Please do exercise 5 for tomorrow.

5 Listening practice: A present for Jenny

That's right. | That's wrong.

a) *Right or wrong? Say what is right.*

1. It is 5th February.
2. Jenny is at Sarah's house.
3. Sarah and Robert have got crayons for Jenny.
4. David and Becky have got an idea: a T-shirt with 'Germany' on it.
5. It is quarter to five.
6. Becky must go to the shops.

b) *Can you go on?*

1. It's Jenny's birthday in … .
2. David, Becky and Mark are talking about … .
3. Sarah and Robert have got … .
4. Now David and Becky have got a good idea: … .
5. They can get the present … .
6. Becky must go home. It's … .

Look. 'U' is the first letter in these words. The sound can be [ʌ] or [ju:].

6 Sound practice

[ən] [ʌ]
Simon has got an untidy room.
Jenny has got an uncle in England.

[ə] [ju:]
This is a **u**nit with numbers.
There is a **u**niform at Haywood School.

[ði:] [ʌ]
Mini is in the untidy room.
Colin Penrose is the uncle in England.

[ðə] [ju:]
The **u**nit is about Jenny's birthday.
The **u**niform is blue.

Unit 5

LOOKING AT THE UK:
A British house

These rooms are upstairs:

1 the children's bedroom

2 the bathroom and toilet

3 the parents' bedroom

These rooms are downstairs:

4 the living-room

5 the hall

6 the kitchen

1 What are these rooms?

1. You can have a bath in this room. It is the … .
2. In this room you can have breakfast or tea. It is … . *Go on.*
3. You can sit and talk or play games in this room.
4. This room has got a big bed in it.
5. The children have got their things in this room.
6. This is the first 'room' downstairs in a house.

2 My English folder

Draw a plan for a house or a flat. Put in the rooms.

Step D

A great birthday

1. It is 7th February. Robert is in the park with Jenny.
Robert: Are you having a good birthday, Jenny?
Jenny: Well, yes, it's nice, but very quiet.

2. At the Penroses' house. The friends are getting everything ready for the surprise party.
David: Is everyone from school here now?
Sarah: Yes. – Wow! Your cake is great, David.
David: Thanks, Sarah. – What time is it?
Becky: It's five past three. Oh, look, there are eleven candles on the cake – and it's Jenny's twelfth birthday. David, have you got another candle?
David: Oh, yes, there's a candle over there.
Sarah: Where's that present from Jenny's parents?
Becky: Look, Robert and Jenny are coming now. Ssh! Be quiet.

3. *David:* Hey, Jenny, I'm in the living-room.Can you come here?
Jenny: Yes, OK. Come on, Robert.
"Surprise, surprise!" "Happy birthday, Jenny."
Everyone is there: her aunt, her uncle, her cousins, her friends.
What a nice surprise!

4. *Mark:* Look, Jenny. More presents for you!
Jenny: Oh, thank you, everyone! What's this? Is it a game? No, it's a book.
David: Well, there's another present for you.
Jenny: Thanks, David. Let's see. Oh, a video. What is it?
David: I'm not sure, Jenny. Let's have a look.
Robert: Oh, yes, come on, Jenny.

5. The TV is on and the video is playing.
Everyone is watching.
Jenny: Oh look, it's Mum and Dad! And that's our flat!
Mark: That's Aunty Helen!
Jenny: Oh, what a great idea! It's a great birthday.

1 The birthday

Can you make sentences for the pictures?
Look at the pictures and at the words.
Example: 1. Robert and Jenny are in the park.

singing friends are 'Happy Birthday' the

living-room Jenny are Robert in and the now

watching friends Jenny are and the her video

are park Robert in Jenny and the ✓

looking Jenny at her is presents

getting David cake is the ready

2 Where's Mum's CD?

my your his her its our their

1. *Mark:* Let's play a game. Mum's new CD is in the house. Where is it?
2. *Mr Penrose:* Is it in Jenny's room?
   Mark: No, it isn't in … room.
3. *David:* Is it in Mum and Dad's room?
   Mark: No, it isn't in … room.
4. *Jenny:* Is it in David's and … room, Mark?
   Mark: Yes, it's in … room.
5. *Mrs Penrose:* Is it under David's bed?
   Mark: No, it isn't under … bed.
6. *David:* Is it under … bed, Mark?
   Mark: Yes, it's under … bed.
7. *Mrs Penrose:* Is it in … box?
   Mark: Of course it is, Mum.
   Mrs Penrose: Good. Then please put it on the shelf in … living-room.

3 Where are their things?

's s'

Example: 1. David**'s** cake is on the table. *Go on!*

Step E

Let's check

1 Making a video

Mr Penrose is making a video. It is for Jenny's parents.
Write down what time it is and what Jenny is doing.

1. It's quarter past eight. Jenny is getting … . *Go on.*

get her things for school — go to school — make tea — write a letter — lie in bed

lying

2 House numbers

Write these numbers in words, please.

3 Jenny's birthday list

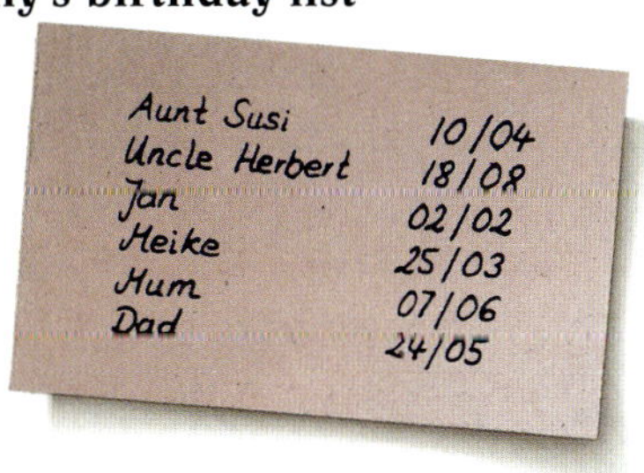

Aunt Susi	10/04
Uncle Herbert	18/08
Jan	02/02
Heike	25/03
Mum	07/06
Dad	24/05

When are their birthdays?
Example: Aunt Susi's birthday is on the tenth of April.
Go on, please.

4 Months and numbers

Find the months.

What is the eleventh / first / seventh / fifth / tenth / ninth / sixth month ?

The eleventh month is November. *Go on.*

5 WORD POWER

Can you put these words in three groups?
1. Months:
2. Time:
3. Party things:

cake, two minutes, candle, March, half past three, December, 4 o'clock, game, present, quarter past five, quarter to eight, August, balloon, July

Unit 5

⟨Revision 2⟩

1 The Sherwood video

Put in 'me', 'you', 'her', 'him', 'it', 'us' or 'them'.

a) *David:* The video from my aunt and uncle in Germany is very good. Now let's make a video for … !
Jenny: Great idea! 'The Sherwood video'! My parents can watch … on their TV.
Sarah: But we haven't got a camcorder.
Becky: Mrs Croft has! Maybe she can give … her camcorder for a day or two. Let's phone Robert and ask … .

b) It is OK. They can have Mrs Croft's camcorder. But everyone has got different ideas for the video!

Becky: Maxi and Mini are our superdogs. So we must have … in the video! Maxi! Mini! We're making a video – with … .
Sarah: Oh, Becky! OK, but the first scene must have Jenny in … . Then her parents can see … here in England right away.
Jenny: No, they must see … with all my new friends. Let's have everyone in the first scene.
Sarah: Everyone? But who can take the scene for …? Mark? So your parents can only see our legs again?
David: Oh, Sarah! My father can take … . He's in the kitchen now. Let's ask … .

2 All about Sherwood

Can you answer these questions about Sherwood – and the people there?

Examples: "Is there a school in Sherwood?" – "Yes, there is."
"Are there three dogs at the Burtons' house?" – "No, there aren't. There are two dogs at the Burtons' house."

1. Is there a pond in the Crofts' garden?
2. Is there a cat at the Penroses' house?
3. Are there frogs in Arnot Hill Park?
4. Are there four children in the Penrose family?
5. Is there a big tree in the Burtons' garden?
6. Is there a German cousin in the Dixon family?

3 All about Germany

Sarah has got a lot of questions for Jenny. *Can you give Jenny's answers?*

Are there
Have you got

good comics
tutor groups
British bikes
nice houses
school uniforms
chocolate biscuits
video shops
good pop groups

at German schools
in Germany
in German shops

? –

Yes, there are.
Yes, we have.
No, there aren't.
No, we haven't.
No idea.
I'm not sure.

4 A house puzzle

a) *Look at all the things.*
Make three lists.

1. upstairs: bed, … .
2. downstairs: telephone, … .
3. outside: car, … .

b) *Where can you put all the things?*
Make dialogues with your partner.
Example:
"Now, let's see. Oh yes!
We can put the telephone in the bathroom."
– "No, that's silly. Let's put the telephone in the hall."
"OK. – We can put … ." *Go on.*

Unit 6

In town

Step A

In Nottingham

This is the Robin Hood statue. It is in front of Nottingham Castle.

Old Market Square is in the city centre.

The Victoria shopping centre has got a lot of shops and restaurants.

Nottingham is a busy city. There are a lot of people in the streets. You can see St Peter's Church in this picture. It is near Old Market Square.

1 The city centre

What can you say about Nottingham?

Example: There's a Robin Hood statue in front of Nottingham Castle.
There are a lot of people in the streets.

There's There are	a castle a church shops and restaurants a Robin Hood statue a big square a lot of people	in the city centre. in front of Nottingham Castle. in the Victoria shopping centre. near Old Market Square. in Nottingham. in the streets.

Your turn

2 In your town

a) *Talk about your town.*

Examples: "We've got a nice market square."
"… is a little town, but it's got nice shops."
"We haven't got a castle, but we've got three churches."

b) *Now make a poster about your town. Find pictures for it and write about them.*

Step B

Days of the week

SB ⓐ It is half past four on Friday, the last day of the school week.

Jenny: It's Saturday tomorrow, Becky. Let's go into town together. We can look at the shops, and then maybe we can go to the cinema.
Becky: OK. What time?
Jenny: Let's go at eleven o'clock.
Becky: Eleven is too late.
Jenny: Why?
Becky: Because it's so busy on Saturdays. What about ten o'clock?
Jenny: OK then.
Becky: We can get the 88 bus near the end of Larwood Grove.
Jenny: Oh, is it a double decker?
Becky: Yes, it is.
Jenny: That's great. You can see everything from the top of a double decker.
Becky: OK. Ten o'clock at the bottom of Arndale Road. Then we can walk to the bus stop together.

1 Can you go on?

pond ✓ road week book town tree alphabet

Example: The little frog is at the bottom **of the pond.**

1. Saturday is the sixth day … .
2. The cat is at the top … .
3. The church is in the centre … .
4. Our house is at the end … .
5. B is the second letter … .
6. David is reading. Now he is on the last page … .

SB ⓑ

Monday  "Oh no, school again!"

Tuesday  "An easy day for me. We've got two German lessons."

Wednesday  "We've got football practice on Wednesday. That's great!"

Thursday  "My turn in the kitchen on Thursday!"

Friday  "It's my guitar lesson on Friday. That's nice."

Saturday  "The best day of the week – there's no school!"

Sunday  "My favourite day of the week. Mum and Dad and David and Jenny are all at home."

Unit 6

2 Why?

Example: Why is Monday a bad day for Sarah?
– Because there's school again.

1. Why is Tuesday easy for Jenny?
2. Why is Wednesday a great day for Simon?
3. Why is Thursday a busy day for Robert?
4. Why is Friday a nice day for David?
– Because he's got … .
5. Why is Saturday the best day for Becky?
6. Why is Sunday Mark's favourite day?

3 What day of the week?

Look at a calendar for this year. Then ask your partner questions.

Examples: "What day of the week is 1st April?"
– "It's a Monday this year."
"What day of the week is your birthday/your mum's birthday?"
– "It's a …." *Go on, please.*

Step C

At the Victoria shopping centre

Becky and Jenny are at the Victoria shopping centre.
They are trying on clothes in a shop.

Here is Jenny in jeans and in a pullover. The jeans are OK, but the pullover is very big! Becky is wearing black trousers and a yellow shirt. She is trying on a yellow anorak. Yellow is her favourite colour!

1 Clothes

a) What are Jenny and Becky wearing now?
Jenny is wearing a red and blue … .
Go on.

b) *What are you wearing?*
What is your teacher wearing?

2 My English folder

Draw your favourite clothes.
Then write about them.

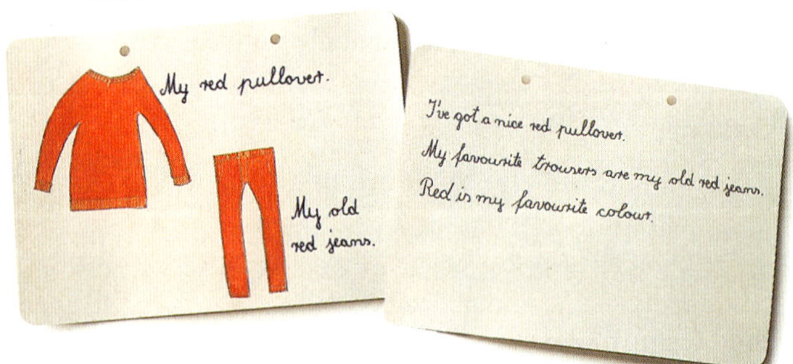

3 A game: Who is it?

Think of a boy or girl in your class. Look at his or her clothes.
Then the others must ask questions about him or her. You can only answer with 'Yes' or 'No'. Example:

Julia: I'm thinking of a girl in the class.
Patrick: Is she wearing blue jeans?
Julia: No, she isn't.
Melanie: Is she wearing black jeans?
Julia: Yes, she is.
Sascha: Then it must be Annette or Kathrin! Is she wearing a red pullover?
Julia: Yes, she is.
Nina: Then it must be Annette.
Julia: Yes, it is.

4 Sound practice

[ət]
I'm **at** Haywood School.
Is Jenny **at** home?
Let's look **at** your photos.

[əv]
That's the end **of** the story.
Today is the first **of** May.
We've got a lot **of** apples.

[ət] – [əv]
Our house is **at** the bottom **of** Old Street.
We're **at** the top **of** page ten.
There are a lot **of** people **at** the bus stop.

Unit 6

Excuse me, please

David is in Old Market Square.
There are a lot of people there today.

Woman: Excuse me, please. Can you tell me the way to the castle?
David: Yes, I can. Go down Friar Lane. Go straight on to the end. Then turn left into Maid Marian Way. Then turn right into Castle Gate. Then you can see the castle on the left.

5 Can you tell me the way?

Make dialogues. Here is an example:

1. *Girl:* Cinema in Mount Street?
David: – down Beastmarket Hill and Angel Row. – turn left – Mount Street. – cinema – on right

Girl: Excuse me, please. Can you tell me the way to the cinema in Mount Street?
David: Go down Beastmarket Hill and Angel Row. Then turn left into Mount Street.
The cinema is on the right then.
Girl: Oh, thanks!

2. *Man:* Victoria shopping centre?
David: – down Market Street. – turn right – Parliament Street. – straight on– end of Parliament Street.– Victoria shopping centre – on left.

3. *Woman:* St Peter's Church?
David: – down South Parade. – straight on – end. – turn left – Exchange Walk. – turn left – St Peter's Gate. – church – on right.

6 A game: Draw a castle

Example: Blackstone Castle is very old. It is at the top of a hill. It is behind the trees. There is a road on the right. There is a statue at the bottom of the hill. It is near a tree. There is a pond on the right.

Now draw your picture of a castle. Put a hill, trees, a pond, a statue and a road in the picture. Then your partner must ask questions about it – and maybe draw it, too!

Example: "Is your castle at the top of the hill?" – "Yes, it is."
"Are the trees in front of the castle?"
– "No, they're at the bottom of the hill." ...

Unit 6

David's grandma

It is five o'clock on a Tuesday afternoon. David and Robert are at the Twinning Office in Nottingham. David's grandma has got a job there.

David: Hello, Grandma!
Grandma: Oh, there you are, David! Hello, Robert.
David: Can we go and eat at the 'Hot Potato'?
Grandma: Oh yes, that's a good idea. Their 'Hot Potato Special' is very good.
Robert: What's that?
Grandma: It's a big potato with ham and tomatoes and two eggs.

David: Great! – Can we go now?
Grandma: In a minute. I must phone Karlsruhe first.
Robert: Carl Srour? Who's that?
David: Oh, Robert! Karlsruhe isn't a person, it's a town. It's our twin town in Germany.
Robert: Oh!

potato – potatoes
tomato – tomatoes

7 At the Twinning Office

Example: Woman: Hello. Can I speak to Mrs Penrose, please?
Clerk: Sorry. Mrs Penrose … (talk – on telephone)
Mrs Penrose is talking on the telephone.

1. *Man:* Good morning. Is that Mrs Penrose?
   Clerk: No, sorry. She … (just have lunch). Can you phone again at 2 o'clock?
2. *Woman:* Hello! My name is Bauer. I'm phoning from Karlsruhe.
   Clerk: Oh, Frau Bauer! Mrs Penrose … (talk to – group of Germans). Please phone again this afternoon.
3. *David:* This is David Penrose. Is my grandma there, please?
   Clerk: Yes, she's here today. But she … (work – in another room). Phone again in ten minutes, David!
4. *Mr Penrose:* Colin Penrose here. Can I speak to my mother, please?
   Clerk: Oh, sorry, Mr Penrose. Your mother is busy. She … (phone – office in Karlsruhe). – Oh, she … (just say – goodbye)! – Here she is now!

8 In town

Look at the people in the picture. What are they all doing?
Example: A man and a woman are looking at a map. *Go on, please.*

Step D

Robert and Jenny in town

1. It is half past five on Saturday afternoon. Robert and Jenny are in Nottingham together.

Jenny: Let's get the bus back to Sherwood now. Our bus stop is near the Victoria shopping centre.
Robert: Look, Jenny. A bus is coming. Number 37. It's going to Beeston. That's near Sherwood.
Jenny: Are you sure, Robert? The 88 and 89 are the Sherwood buses.
Robert: The 37 bus is OK, too. Beeston Park is near Sherwood. Come on, Jenny. Let's get on.
Jenny: OK then.

2. Six o'clock
Mr Penrose: It's six o'clock. Tea is ready. – Where's Jenny, David? Isn't she home yet?
David: No, she isn't. Maybe she's at the Crofts' house.
But Jenny isn't there. She and Robert are on the way to Beeston – on the 37 bus.

3. Robert and Jenny are sitting upstairs. They can see a big park on the right now.
Jenny: Robert, where are we? This isn't the way to Sherwood.
Robert: It's OK, Jenny. The bus is going a different way, that's all.
Jenny: Well, I'm not sure. Maybe we're on the wrong bus. Let's ask the driver at the next stop.

4. *Driver:* Yes, you're on the right bus for Beeston.
Jenny: And Beeston Park is near Sherwood?
Driver: Near Sherwood? Oh, no. Maybe you're thinking of Bestwood. Bestwood Park is near Sherwood.
Jenny: Oh, Robert, you are silly! It's Bestwood, not Beeston!
Robert: Oh, sorry, Jenny!
Jenny: Well, I must phone Aunty Pat. It's six o'clock now, and we're a long way from home.
Robert: No, let's get back to the city centre right away.

5. Mr and Mrs Penrose are worried now.
Mrs Penrose: It's half past six. Where can Jenny be?
David: Telephone! Maybe that's Jenny now.
But it is Mrs Croft on the telephone. She is worried, too.

6. Jenny and Robert are back in the city centre.
They are standing at the 88 bus stop.
Jenny: The next bus is in twenty minutes! That's terrible. I *must* phone Aunty Pat now!
Robert: Look. That red car over there is stopping.
Jenny: Oh, who is it?
Robert: Hey, it's David's grandma! Hello, Mrs Penrose!
Grandma: Hello, you two! Can I give you a lift?

1 Is that right?

Example: It is half past five. Robert and Jenny are at home.
– No, that's wrong. They're in Nottingham.

1. The bus to Beeston is number 37.
2. At six o'clock Robert and Jenny are at the Crofts' house.
3. The children can see a big park from the top of the bus.
4. They are on the right bus.
5. Beeston Park is near Sherwood.
6. The Penroses are worried because they aren't sure where Jenny is.
7. Robert and Jenny are on the 88 bus at half past six.
8. Now a red bus is stopping at the bus stop.
9. David's grandma is in the bus.
10. She can give the children a lift.

2 WORD POWER

What can you see in the kitchen?
Work in pairs, and make two lists:
1. a list of the things to eat
2. a list of the other things.

Then check your partner's list.

3 A lot of questions

What Where Who Why When

Put in the right words.

1. ... is the castle? – It's at the top of the hill.
2. ... has got a map of London? – I have!
3. ... is the name of this road? – Park Lane.
4. ... can't we go by car? – Because it's so busy in town on Saturdays.
5. ... is the next bus? – At quarter past four.
6. ... time is it now? – It's five past four.
7. ... is the bus late? – No idea!
8. ... is the bus stop? – At the end of this road.
9. ...is market day? – On Wednesdays and Saturdays.
10. ... can give us a lift into town? – My mum can!

4 Listening practice: People in town

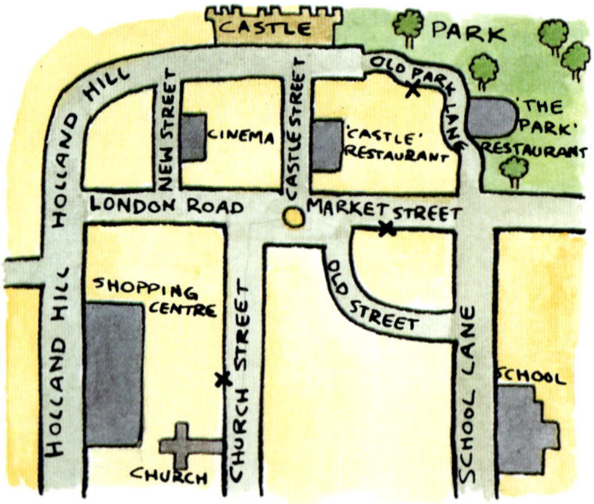

a) *Look at the map. Find the castle, the cinema, the restaurants, the shopping centre and the church.*

b) *Now listen to the first two dialogues. Can you find the way on the map?*

c) *Listen to the third dialogue now. Where is the woman going?*

d) *Now work with the map – with a partner. Ask the way and your partner must tell you.*
1. From School Lane – to the cinema.
2. From the castle – to the church.
3. From the shopping centre – to the castle.

Step E

Let's Check

1 Sarah's clothes

Sarah's room isn't very tidy.
Look at all her clothes!
Her jeans are on the floor.
Her ... .
Go on, please.

2 What is different?

in on under behind in front of near round

Example: In picture 1, the apples are on the tree.
But in picture 2, they're under the tree.

3 WORD POWER

This is a letter from Jenny to her friend Sandra in Berlin. *Can you read it?*

Unit 6

School days

Step A

Lunch time

ⓐ *David:* I'm hungry. Let's go to lunch.
Sarah: Hey, look at this. There's a competition.
Becky: A healthy living competition – you must make a poster. Oh, great.
Robert: Ugh, competitions are boring.
Becky: No, they aren't. Look, there are good prizes – a T-shirt, a sweatshirt, … .
Sarah: But I've got a lot of T-shirts and sweatshirts.
David: I'm very hungry. Can you lend me 50p for sausage and chips?
Sarah: How much? Er … No, sorry, I can't.
Becky: Here you are. I can lend you £1.
David: Great! Then I can buy a packet of crisps, too.
Becky: Sausage and chips and crisps for lunch again, David? That isn't very healthy!

ⓑ British money

There are 100 pence (p) in a pound (£).

1 Listening practice: School lunch

Listen to the three dialogues.
How much money must Sarah, Becky and Robert give Mrs White?

(Reduced in size)

Step B

Jenny's day

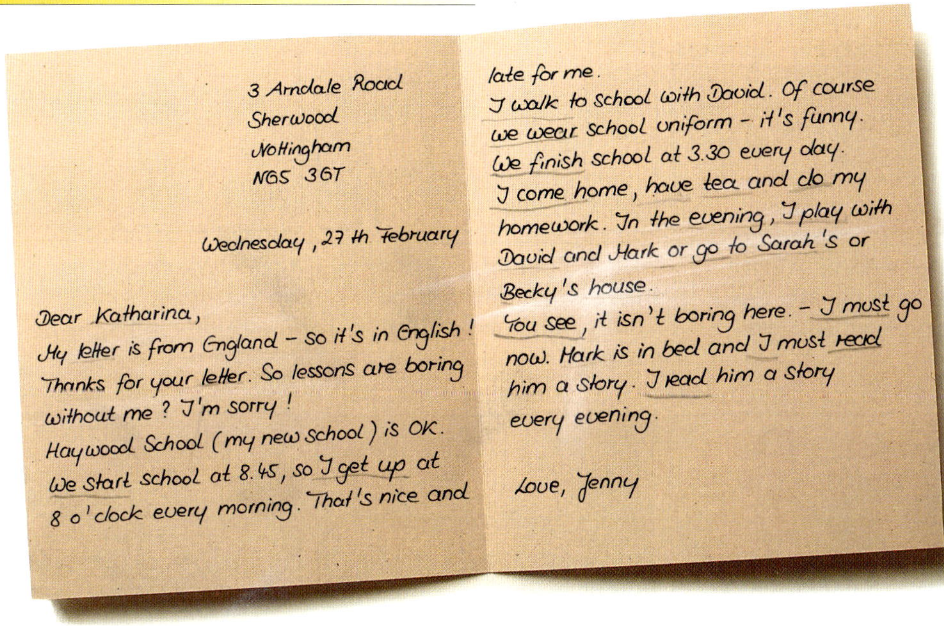

3 Arndale Road
Sherwood
Nottingham
NG5 3GT

Wednesday, 27th February

Dear Katharina,
My letter is from England – so it's in English! Thanks for your letter. So lessons are boring without me? I'm sorry!
Haywood School (my new school) is OK. We start school at 8.45, so I get up at 8 o'clock every morning. That's nice and late for me.
I walk to school with David. Of course we wear school uniform – it's funny. We finish school at 3.30 every day. I come home, have tea and do my homework. In the evening, I play with David and Mark or go to Sarah's or Becky's house.
You see, it isn't boring here. – I must go now. Mark is in bed and I must read him a story. I read him a story every evening.

Love, Jenny

1 My school day

Talk about your school day.
Say when you get up every morning,
how you go to school every day,
when your lessons start,
what you do after school,
when you go to bed.

I go to bed at … .
Our lessons start at … .
After school I go to my friend's house and we … or I … or I … .
I get up at … every morning.
I go to school by bus (by train) every day.
I walk to school with … .

Unit 7

2 Free time

go | play ✓ | play | go | make | work

Say what they do in their free time.
Example: 1. Every Tuesday David and Jenny play tennis. 2. Every … . *Go on.*

Mark's day

Mark gets up very early every morning. He goes into his parents' room.

At 8 o'clock Mr Penrose makes breakfast for the family. Mark helps him. He puts the cornflakes on the table.

At 8.30 Mark gets ready for nursery school.

At 8.40 Mark walks to nursery school with his father.

School finishes at 12.30. Mr Penrose collects Mark.

When Mark comes home, he has lunch. And then he does his 'homework'.

I walk you walk we walk you walk they walk	he walk**s** she walk**s** it walk**s**

I go – he, she, it go**es**
I do – he, she, it do**es**

3 Jenny and Mark

Talk about their day.
Example: Jenny gets up at 8 o'clock every morning, but Mark gets up at 7 o'clock.

1. She walks to school with David every morning, but Mark … with his father.
2. Jenny has lunch at school every day, but Mark … lunch at home.
3. Jenny helps Mr Penrose with tea, but Mark … with breakfast.
4. Jenny listens to music in the evening, but Mark … in the morning.
5. Jenny goes to bed at 9.30, but Mark … at 7.30.

4 Every week

play go write play make go go

Say what they do every week.
Example: Every week, Mr and Mrs Dixon go to the shops.

1. Jenny – a letter to her parents
2. David – to his guitar lesson
3. Becky – tennis at school
4. Mr and Mrs Penrose – a cake for Grandma
5. Sarah and Kim – to the shops
6. Mr and Mrs Burton – badminton

A busy day

ⓐ What is it?
It sometimes goes to school,
 but it never goes to a lesson.
It often makes a noise,
 but it never says a word.
It sometimes has an upstairs,
 but it never has a hall.
It always takes people home and to town,
 because that is its job!
What is it? That's easy. It's a … .

5 You and your family

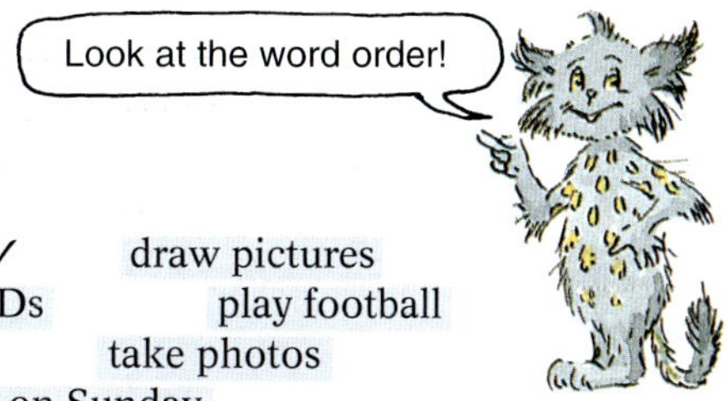

Make sentences.
Example: My sister sometimes goes to the cinema.

I My sister My brother My parents	always often sometimes never	go to the cinema ✓ draw pictures listen to CDs play football write stories take photos go for a walk on Sunday read a book write letters

ⓑ Robert cannot finish his poster for the competition today. He must help in the house. After breakfast Mrs Croft goes to the shops. First Robert does the washing-up. Then he goes upstairs to his bedroom … oh dear, it is in a mess! First he makes his bed. After that he tidies up his desk. That is boring, but he finds an old comic there. He reads the first story. It is very good, so he sits down and reads the next story.

There is a noise downstairs. Mrs Croft is home again! Robert kicks his clothes under his bed and puts his skateboard behind the door. Then Mrs Croft walks in.
"Wow, Robert. Your room looks very tidy now. Well done!"
"Thanks, Mum," Robert says. "Housework isn't bad!"
"Good," says Mrs Croft. "Now we can tidy up the living-room!"

I tidy up – he/she tidies up

6 Robert at home

Say what Robert does.

First Robert does the … . | Then … . | After that … . | After that … . | And then … .

LOOKING AT THE UK:
Haywood School

School starts at 8.45. There is an assembly every Monday morning.

Pupils play hockey at school.

Pupils usually have lunch in the school canteen.

Pupils wear school uniform. at Haywood School.

Unit 7

1 My English folder

Here are some words about school.
Can you find more words?
Write them in your English folder.

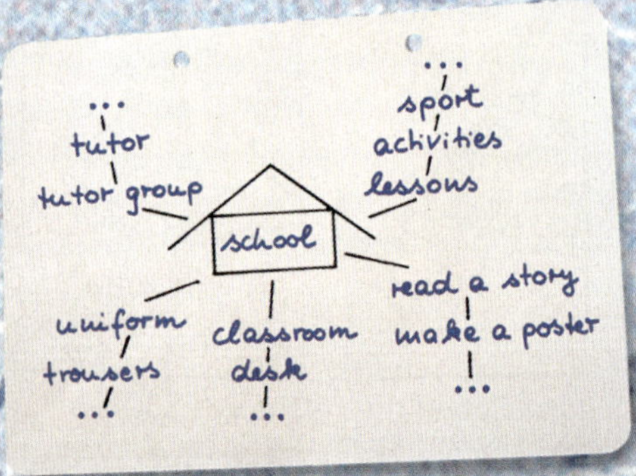

There are a lot of activities for pupils at lunch time and after school. For example, they can go to a drama group.

Step C

The poster

On Sunday the friends are in Becky's garage. They finish their healthy living posters. They go home for lunch. When they come back, they find Maxi and Mini in the garage.

Sarah: Oh, look! Maxi and Mini are on our posters!
Becky: Maxi! Mini! Get out! You're all wet!
David: Ugh! Our posters are all wet and dirty.
Sarah: Well – no prize for us now.
David: Look. Robert's poster is OK here. You can see his legs.
Sarah: Oh, yes. And there's your head, David. It's very big!
Robert: Ha, ha.
Becky: Hey, let's make *one* big poster together.
Sarah: Good idea.

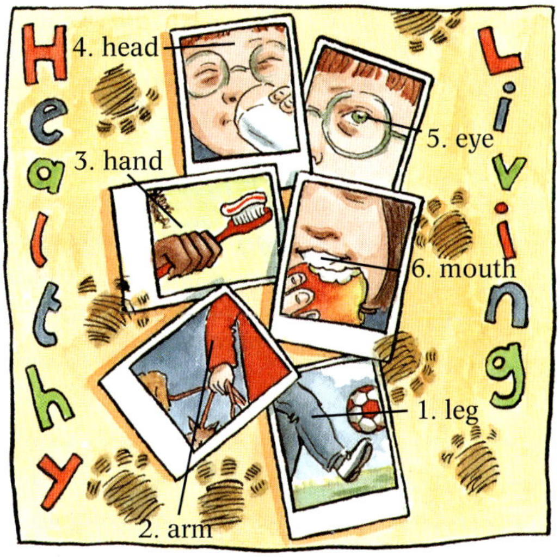

1 WORD POWER

Look at the poster. Say what the numbers are.
Number 1 is Robert's leg. Number 2 is … . *Go on.*

2 Beetle – a dice game

Take the dice and start the game. You must throw a six first and draw the body in your exercise book. Then it's your friend's turn. When your beetle has everything, you are the winner.

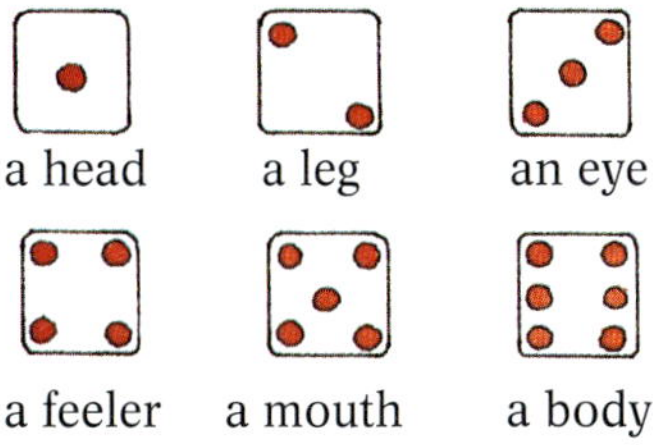

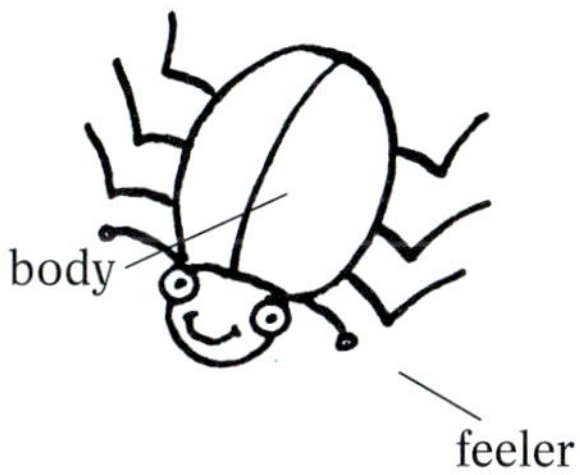

I've got a one (a six, a five …).
Oh, no. I can't draw an eye.
I haven't got a head!
I can draw a leg now.
Can I have the dice, please?

⟨3 A Song: Head and shoulders⟩

(trad.; Gitarrenakkorde: M. Hauschild)

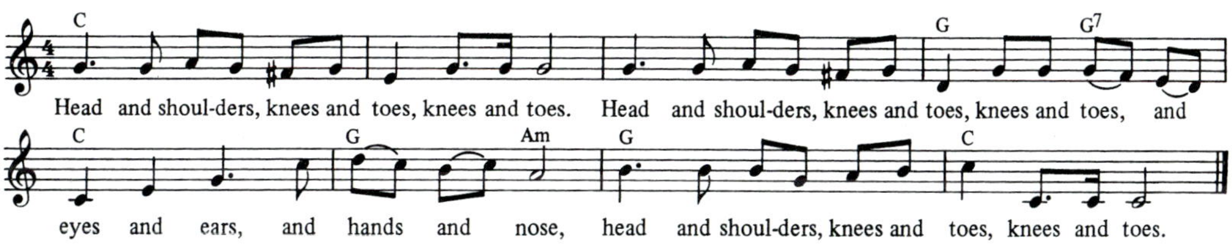

Unit 7

At the shops

ⓐ *Assistant:* Hello. Can I help you?
Sarah: Hello. Can I have a pound of bananas, please?
Assistant: Yes, of course. Here you are. Anything else?
Sarah: Yes, this pint of milk, please.
Assistant: OK. That's £1.40, please.
Sarah: Thank you. Here you are. Goodbye.

ⓑ *David:* Excuse me. How much is this bottle of lemonade?
Assistant: That's 68p.
David: And how much is this bar of chocolate?
Assistant: 25p.
David: Oh, good. I've got £1. I can buy the chocolate, too.

4 What goes together?

	bottle	
	packet	
a	pound	of
	bar	
	pint	

Make pairs. Example:
A bottle of lemonade, a … of … .

5 Role play: At the shops

Work with your partner. Make dialogues and then act them.

Hello. Can I have a …, please? → Yes, of course. Here you are.
How much …? ← → It's … .
Here you are. Here's £… . ← → Thank you. Goodbye.

6 Listening practice: At the supermarket

Listen. What must Mr Penrose, Mark and David get? *Find the right pictures.*

Step D

The healthy living prize

1. It is Monday morning and the end of assembly. Mrs Benson, the headteacher, gets up and puts a big box on the table. "Oh, look," David says. "Prizes for the healthy living competition!" Mrs Benson takes the prizes – a T-shirt, a sweatshirt and a football – and gives them to the three lucky winners – Peter Wall, Annabel Barker and Suvina Adib.
"Oh no!" David says. "There's no prize for us!"
"Oh, well," Sarah says. "Maybe next time!"
"Ssh," Jenny says. "Listen!"

2. Mrs Benson starts to talk again.
"I've got an extra prize today," she says. "It's for a very funny poster. The prize goes to a group in 7MD. Come on, Becky, Robert, Jenny, Sarah and David. Come and get your prize!"
What a surprise for the friends!
They all stand up and walk to Mrs Benson and the box of prizes.

3. "Here you are," Mrs Benson says. "A funny prize for a funny poster. Well done!"
"Thank you," Becky says, and she takes the prize from Mrs Benson.
"What is it?" Sarah asks.
"Oh, no," Becky laughs. "Look! Five bars of soap and five bottles of bubble bath!"
"Hey, I can't see," David says.
"Be careful, David!" Mrs Benson says. But it is too late. David trips and falls over.

4. "Are you OK?" Jenny asks.
"I'm not sure," David says. "Oh no, my money is all over the floor."
"Here's 50p," Becky says.
"And here's 20p," Sarah says.
"And there's your packet of crisps," Mrs Benson says.
"Oh, no. I'm very sorry." David says.
"And that's your chocolate," Robert laughs.
"Well, David Penrose!" Sarah says, "You aren't very healthy!"
"And you've got a healthy living prize! That's crazy!" Becky laughs.

1 Assembly

Put in the right names. Example: 1. Mrs Benson puts a big box on the table.

1. … puts a big box on the table.
2. … gives the prize to the winners.
3. … says: "There's no prize for us!"
4. … walk to Mrs Benson for the extra prize.
5. … takes the prize from Mrs Benson.
6. … get five bars of soap and five bottles of bubble bath.
7. … trips.
8. … sees David's packet of crisps.
9. … finds David's bar of chocolate.

2 Your Sunday

sometimes **never** **often** **always**

Write down what you do on Sunday.
Example:
On Sunday I often get up late.
Go on.

tidy up my room	watch TV
read a book	help Mum and Dad
go and see Grandma	play with my friends
write letters or birthday cards	

3 Poor Simon!

Put in the verbs. **go buy put look see fall go take**

Tennis is on TV. But Simon can't watch it today. He must go to the shops. He … the list from the kitchen table and … at it. He … to the supermarket and … a packet of dog biscuits, a pint of milk and other things. After that he … Becky. They … back home together. Simon is happy now – he can watch TV. He … the bag on the kitchen table. But, oh no! The bag … to the floor. The dog biscuits are all over the floor. Poor Simon – he must tidy up the kitchen now.

Unit 7

4 Sound practice

[v]
David is eleven.
The **v**et is se**v**enty-fi**v**e.
Your pullo**v**er is **v**ery big.

[w]
He al**w**ays **w**alks to school.
March is al**w**ays **w**et and **w**indy.
Wo**w**, you're the **w**inner.

[v] – [w]
It's **v**ery **w**arm in here.
Where is Lar**w**ood Gro**v**e?
We **w**atch TV in the e**v**enings.

5 What time is it?

Fill in the times. Example: 1. Let's play football at half past two.

Step E

Let's check

1 What is that?

That is a … of …

2 Their day

Correct the wrong sentences.

1. Mr and Mrs Dixon go to the park every Tuesday.
   – No, that's wrong. Mr and Mrs Dixon go to the shops every Thursday.
2. Robert helps his mum with the housework.
3. Becky goes to assembly every Friday.
4. Mark gets up at 9 o'clock every morning.
5. Mrs Penrose makes breakfast every morning.
6. David walks to school with his dad every morning.

3 Kim's activities

Write down what Kim sometimes/often/never/always does.
Example: Kim never makes her bed.

	sometimes	often	never	always
make her bed ✓			x	
go to the shops		x		
do the washing-up	x			
tidy up her bedroom				x
make tea		x		
repair Sarah's bike			x	
help in the garden	x			

Your turn *Say what you do in the house.*
Example: I often tidy up my bedroom. *Go on.*

4 WORD POWER

Can you repair the broken words? Make a list.
Example: supermarket, …

super break home skate some corn flakes times fast board work market

5 My mascot

Draw a funny mascot.
Give it a name. Then tell your friends about it.
Example: My mascot's name is Lucky. It has got two yellow legs, a big mouth and six black feelers. It hasn't got … .

Unit 7

Unit 8

The accident

Step A

Money and jobs

SB ⓐ Sarah always gets her pocket money on Fridays.
She often buys sweets or magazines with it.
She never saves her pocket money!

Your turn 1 You and your money

Talk about your money.

I often buy crisps.

I sometimes save my pocket money.

I always get comics with my pocket money.

I sometimes buy a CD.

SB ⓑ Kim has got a Saturday job.
She sells clothes in a jeans shop.

Sarah: Hey, I like your new shirt, Kim.
Kim: Thanks, Sarah. It's from the jeans shop.
Sarah: You're lucky. You've got a Saturday job.
Kim: Yes. I can buy nice things with the money.
Sarah: I want a job, too. I need money for a new CD.
Kim: Well, you can't be a shop assistant. You're only eleven.
Sarah: I know. Hm. Maybe I can do jobs for the neighbours. I can repair bikes.
Kim: Oh, right! Sarah the bike mechanic!

2 I like it

Has your friend got nice things? What can you say?

I like your T-shirt. / new pen. / pullover. / bag. / ring. / …
– Oh, thank you. It's a present from … . / …

3 People and their jobs

repair help work in work with sell

1

2

3

4

5

What can you say about these people?

1. This woman is a mechanic. She repairs cars.
2. This woman is a … . She … cats and dogs.
3. This … . *Go on.*

Step B

Saturday morning

Kim: Oh no – not 'Two'n'Two'!
Sarah: I like 'Two'n'Two'. They're my favourite group.
Kim: Well, I don't like them. They're terrible.
Sarah: They aren't! They sing great songs.
Kim: Sing? They don't sing – they make a noise!
Mr Dixon: Girls, please! – Look at the time, Kim.
Kim: Oh yes. I must go. – Bye, Dad. Bye, Sarah. Have a nice day with 'Two'n'Two'!

1 Sisters

Sarah is eleven, and Kim is sixteen. So the two girls don't like the same things.
Make sentences about them.
Example: They don't listen to the same music.

They don't	listen to ✓ like — read — wear watch — do	the same	magazines — music ✓ things on TV — pop groups activities — clothes

2 Everyone likes different things

Say what you like and don't like.
Examples: "I like red, but I don't like black."
"I like football, but I don't like tennis."

colours	*activities & games*	*pop groups*
red yellow brown …	tennis TV computer games …	…

3 Your school

What can you tell an English friend about your school in Germany?
Say what you do and what you don't do.
Examples: We don't wear school uniform. We get homework.

wear school uniform — get homework — finish school at lunch time — have lunch at school — go to school on Saturdays — learn English — work with computers — have assembly — play … .

In Edward's Lane

David is on his bike, and Jenny has got Mrs Penrose's bike. They see Sarah with a packet of sweets and a new magazine.

Jenny: Hello, Sarah!
Sarah: Hello, you two. Here. Do you want a sweet?
David: Oh yes, please.
Jenny: No, thank you, Sarah. Oh, you've got a music magazine. Do you buy it every week?
Sarah: No, I don't. But this week there's a good poster in it.
David: Do people in Germany listen to English pop music, Jenny?
Jenny: Yes, they do. A lot of English groups are very popular.
David: Hey, Jenny. Look at the time. We must go home for lunch. Come on.
Jenny: OK. Bye, Sarah. – Careful, David. Be careful with your bike! – Oh!
David: Aaah!
Sarah: Are you OK?
Jenny: Yes, I'm OK, thanks.
David: Oh, my leg … .
Sarah: Oh, David!

Do you …? – Yes, I do.
– No, I don't.

4 Do you want a sweet?

Make dialogues. Your answer can be 'Yes, please' or 'No, thank you'.
Example: "Do you want a cake?" – "No, thank you."

5 What about you?

1. Do you listen to English pop music?
2. Do you and your friends like football?
3. Do you and your family watch TV every day?
4. Do your parents like pop music?
5. Do you save all your pocket money?
6. Do a lot of people in Germany play cricket?
7. Do you speak Turkish (Spanish, …)?

Yes, No,	I we they	do. don't.

6 What's popular?

a) *Write 4 questions about different activities.*

Questions	Yes	No
1. Do you read a lot of comics?	III	I
2. Do you play badminton?	I	III
3. Do you like computers?	II	II

listen to pop music	watch a lot of TV
play football	like computers
read a lot of books	…

b) *Ask 4 friends the questions.*
Example: "Do you read a lot of books?"
– "Yes, I do."
"Do you play badminton?"
–"No, I don't."

c) *What can you tell the class?*
"Comics are popular. But badminton isn't so popular. And computers aren't very popular."

Step C

In hospital

David is in hospital now, with a broken leg. Here are all his friends.

Jenny: Hello, David!
Sarah: How are you, David?
David: Oh, OK, thanks.
Robert: How's your leg?
David: Well, it hurts a bit. So please don't sit on it!
Becky: Poor David! I hope you're better soon.
David: Thanks, Becky. – It's good to see you all. The nurses are very nice, but it's a bit boring in hospital.
Robert: Hm. Have you got chocolate biscuits there on your cupboard?
David: Yes, Robert! Here you are. Don't eat them all.
Sarah: Can I write on your leg, David? Please!
David: Hm. OK. But only your name. No funny pictures, please.

1 What you can say to a friend in hospital

Make dialogues with a partner.

How are you? → – Oh, OK thanks. / not so bad. / terrible!

How's your leg? / arm? / head? → – It hurts a bit. / It hurts a lot / It's not too bad.

I hope you're better soon. / Get well → – Thank you.

2 A word game: What's my job?

Look at exercise 3 on page 86 for more ideas and words.

You can't do a lot of things when you've got a broken leg – but you can play word games! *Write down the name of a job. Your partner must ask questions and find the job.*
Example: nurse

You: What's my job?
Partner: Do you sell things?
You: No, I don't.
Partner: Do you work in a school?
You: No, I don't.
Partner: Do you help people in hospital?
You: Yes, I do.
Partner: Oh, are you a nurse?
You: Yes, that's right.

3 Sound practice

[uː]
"Do you repair shoes?"
– "Yes, I do. Yes, I do."
"Can I have them back soon?"
– "Yes, at half past two."

[əʊ]
"Phone your mum and say hello."
– "Is she at home now?"
"I don't know."

4 A get well card

Make a card for a friend in hospital.
Put or draw a picture on the card:
a present, a girl/boy in hospital, a funny picture, … .
What can you write in your card?

Get well soon.
This card is for you.
It isn't the same without you!
…

5 Please don't!

Can you finish the sentences?

1. *Becky:* This card is a surprise for David, Simon, so please **don't tell** him.
2. *David:* You can have one or two of my biscuits, Robert, but please don't … .
3. *Robert:* The bus goes at 10 o'clock, Jenny, so please … .
4. *Mr Dixon:* You can have £5, Sarah, but … .
5. *Kim:* I like pop music, Sarah, but … .
6. *Mrs Penrose:* Mark is in bed, Jenny, so … .

be late.
make a noise.
play your 'Two'n'Two' CD.
eat them all.
ask for more money.
tell him. ✓

6 Listening practice: Radio requests

Right or wrong? Please correct the wrong sentences.

a) 1. Anna Hunt's birthday is on April 9th.
   2. She is twelve years old today.
   3. The request comes from her sister.

b) 1. Michael Hilton goes to school by bike. 2. The request is from a girl on the number 19 bus.
   3. The girl has got brown eyes.

c) 1. The third request is for a boy in hospital. 2. David can go home today. 3. The request is from his parents.

7 Robert's photo

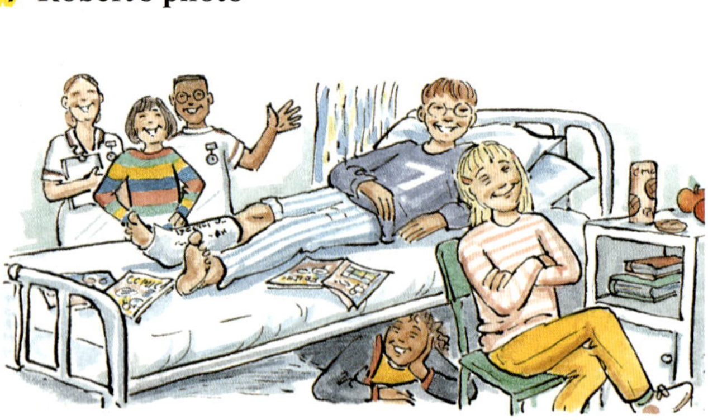

Make sentences about Robert's photo. Can you use all these words?

in   on   under   behind   in front of

Example: David is lying **on** the bed.
or: There are books **in** the cupboard.

LOOKING AT THE UK:

Help!

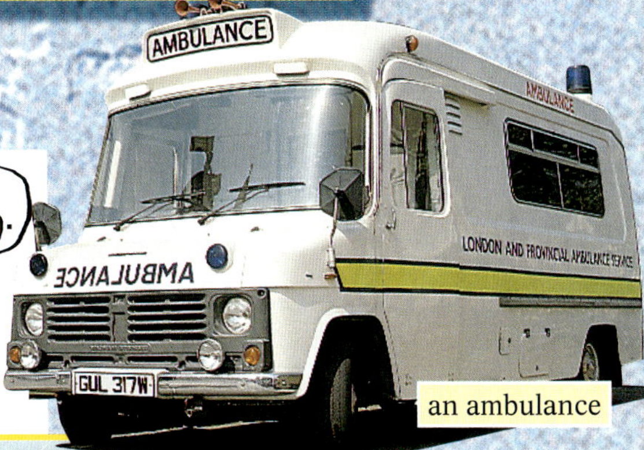

an ambulance

the fire brigade

the police

A fireman

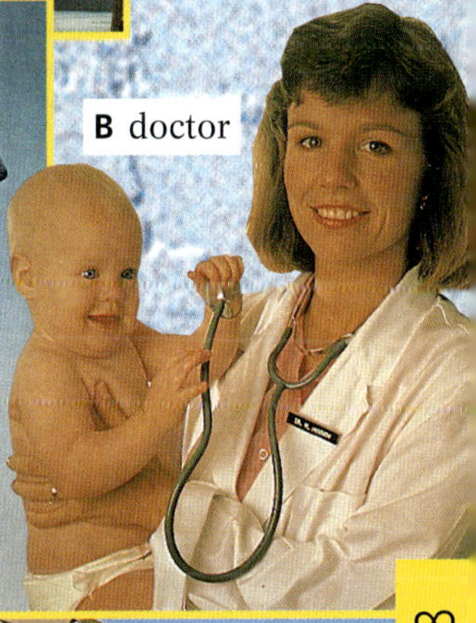

B doctor

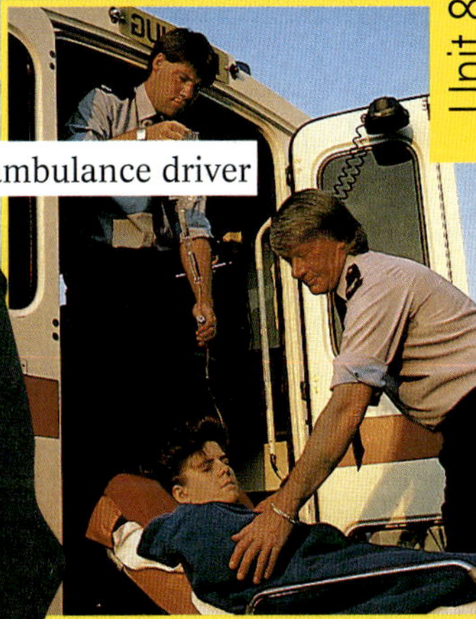

C ambulance driver

D police officer

1 Look at the pictures

You can call the fire brigade.
You can call an ... . *Go on.*

2 What's their job?

1. He takes people to hospital. He's an ... .
2. She helps people in hospital. She's a ... .
3. She wears a blue uniform. She's ... .
4. He's in the fire brigade... .

3 The UK and Germany

What is the same? What is different?

1. What number must you call in the UK? What about Germany?
2. What colour are police cars in the UK? Are German police cars the same colour?
3. What can you say about the colour of the uniforms? Are they the same in the UK and Germany?

Fish fingers and ice cream

1. "Goodbye, Jenny. Grandma is on her way here. She can make tea for you and Mark today. OK?"
"Yes, OK, Uncle Colin. Goodbye. And please give my love to David."
It is five past five on Tuesday afternoon.
Mr Penrose is usually at home with the children, but today he is going to the hospital.
Mrs Penrose works for a computer firm.
She is working late today.

2. Grandma gets to the Penroses' house at quarter past five. Jenny and Mark open the front door for her.
"Hello, you two," Grandma says.
"Do you like fish fingers and ice cream?"
"Oh no, we don't," Jenny laughs.
"We do, we do!" Mark answers. "Don't listen to Jenny, Grandma!"
Grandma laughs, too. "Come on. Let's get the things from the car."

3. They go to the car. Grandma gives Jenny the ice cream. Then she gives Mark the fish fingers. But it is a windy day, and the front door closes behind them.
"Oh, come on. Let's go round to the back door," Jenny says.
But at the back door they get a surprise.
They can't open the door. It is locked.

4. They can't get into the house.
Mark is hungry. "What can we do?" he asks.
"Must we wait for Mum or Dad?"
"Hm. The fish fingers and the ice cream don't like that idea," Grandma says.
But Jenny is looking at the house. "Aha!" she says. "The bathroom window is open. And there's a ladder in the garage ... ."

1 Tell the story

Can you find the right words? (Don't look at the text!)
1. Mr Penrose is going to the … . 2. And … is working late today. 3. But Grandma can make … for Jenny and Mark. 4. Grandma has got … and … in her car. 5. It is a … day, and the … closes. 6. And they can't … the back door – because it's … . 7. Now they can't get into the … . 8. But the … is open. 9. And there's a … in the garage.

2 Let's go on with the story

a) *Read the endings.*

A Grandma climbs up the ladder. She gets into the house through the bathroom window. Then she opens the front door. Now she can make tea for the children.

B A neighbour sees Grandma at the top of the ladder. "Who's that?" he thinks. "Maybe it's a burglar!" So he calls the police, and a police car comes.

C Jenny climbs up the ladder. But she gets stuck in the bathroom window. Grandma goes to the neighbours' house, and they call the fire brigade.

b) *Talk about the endings.*
Example: I like ending B. It's an exciting ending.

I	like don't like	ending … . It's a (an)	exciting good silly boring funny …	ending.

c) *Have you got an idea for another ending?*

d) *Now listen to this ending. Do you like it?*

3 Kim's Saturday job

a) Jenny asks Kim a lot of questions about her Saturday job.
What are her questions?
Example: 1. Do you work in a jeans shop?

1. you/work in a jeans shop?
2. the other assistants/work there every day?
3. your friends/buy their jeans from you?
4. you/sell sweatshirts in the shop, too?
5. shop assistants/get a lot of money?
6. you/save your money?
7. your parents/give you pocket money, too?

b) *Give answers for Kim (your ideas!), and make a dialogue. Start like this:*

Jenny: Do you work in a jeans shop, Kim?
Kim: Yes, I do. I work in 'Just Jeans' in the Victoria shopping centre.
Jenny: Do the …? *Go on.*

Step E

Let's check

1 Problems

Can you find all the jobs?

The problem:

1. You and your friend see a burglar.
2. There's a problem with a car.
3. You're in a shop. Your friend wants a red pullover.
4. A cat gets stuck at the top of a tree.
5. Your friend's arm hurts.

You say:

– We must tell that p… o… over there.
– Sorry, but I'm not a …!
– Can't you find a red pullover? Let's ask the s… a… .
– Maybe a f… can bring the cat down.
– You must go and see the d… .

2 Questions and answers

Make questions and answers with **do** **don't**

Example:

1. **Do** Mr and Mrs Burton sell clothes? – No, they **don't**.

1. Mr and Mrs Burton/sell clothes
2. the Crofts/come from London
3. Maxi and Mini/eat dog biscuits
4. Kim and Sarah/like the same music
5. David and Jenny/go to school by bus
6. the friends/wear jeans at school

3 Don't do that!

How can you say 'no' to your friends?

Example: 1. Hey, … look in my bag! *Go on.*

4 What can you do with these things?

Look at the words in the box.

(Have you got more ideas?)

Example: 1. You can eat fish fingers. (You can buy fish fingers, too.)

1. fish fingers 2. door 3. money 4. ladder 5. song 6. magazine

to open	to climb up	to eat
to read	to save	to sing …

5 Just for fun

A day at the seaside

Step A

On the train

Grandma Penrose, David, Mark, Simon, Becky and Maxi are getting on the train to Skegness.

Grandma: Come on, everyone! Get in, please!
Becky: Oh, look! There are five seats together there. Sorry, Maxi. You must sit on the floor.
Grandma: Oh, no! Who has got the tickets?
David: It's OK, Grandma. I've got them.
Simon: Why isn't Jenny here?
David: She's at home. Her parents are coming to Nottingham today.
Becky: Oh, that's nice. Now they're all together again.
Mark: What can we do at Skegness? Can we eat ice creams?
Becky: Yes, of course. We can go to the beach and go swimming, too. Have you all got your swimming things?
David: No, I haven't. I can't go swimming with a broken leg.
Grandma: Never mind, David. We can go to the boating lake.
Mark: Oh, can I come, too, Grandma? I like boats *and* ice creams, too.
Grandma: It's OK, Mark. We can all have an ice cream at Skegness.

1 What can you do at Skegness?

a) *Look at the pictures. What can you say?*
Example: 1. You can eat … . *Go on, please.*

b) *Now you are at the seaside with your friends. What can you do there? Please make dialogues.*
Example: "Let's go to the beach."
– "Oh no. Let's buy ice creams first. I'm hungry."
"OK. But then we can … ." *Go on.*

⟨2 A song: The sun has got his hat on⟩

Step B

At Skegness

Now they are at Skegness station.
They are looking at the map.

Simon: Where's the beach?
Becky: Look at the map.
You go down the High Street.
Simon: Does that road go to the sea?
Becky: Yes, it does. Look – it says 'High Street'.
Grandma: Oh, but the beach is a dog-free zone.
We can't go there with Maxi.
Mark: Oh great, Maxi. You can come with David and me to the boating lake.
Becky: Does your leg hurt, David?
David: No, it doesn't, but I can't go swimming.
Grandma: OK, come on, then. Let's all meet at 3 o'clock on the beach. Then we can go to a snack bar.

Does he/she/it …?
– Yes, he/she/it does.
– No, he/she/it doesn't.

1 Activities

Say what Becky, Simon and the others do and don't do. Example:

1. Becky: go to the drama group ✗
go to a music group ✓

Becky doesn't go to the drama group, but she goes to a music group.

2. Simon: play tennis ✗
play football ✓
3. Sarah: take photos ✗
draw pictures ✓
4. David: play cricket ✗
play the guitar ✓
5. Mark: go to school ✗
go to nursery school ✓
6. Robert: play the guitar ✗
take photos ✓

2 Does Simon like ice cream?

	Simon	Becky	David	Mark
ice cream	✓	✓	✓	✓
fish fingers	✓	✗	✗	✓
sausage and chips	✓	✗	✓	✓
cheese	✗	✓	✓	✗

Work with a partner. Make questions and answers.
Examples: "Does Simon like ice cream?"
– "Yes, he does."
"Does Becky like fish fingers?"
– "No, she doesn't. (But she likes … .)"

Step B

At the boating lake

Grandma, David, Mark and Maxi are at the boating lake.

Grandma: Here we are. Do we want a boat for one hour?
David: Yes, we do! – Oh, does a boat really cost £5 for one hour?
Grandma: Yes, it does. It's a lot of money.
Mark: Have we got money for a boat *and* ice cream, Grandma?
Grandma: You and your ice creams, Mark. Yes, we have. It's OK. Now, do we buy the tickets over there?
David: Yes, we do. There's a little shop. Do we need a ticket for Maxi, too?
Grandma: I don't know. Does Maxi like boats?
Mark: Yes, she does! Of course she likes boats.

3 Questions at the boating lake

Example: Do they buy the tickets from the little shop? – Yes, they do.

Do Does	they buy the tickets from the little shop? a boat cost £4 for one hour? they need a ticket for Maxi? Maxi like boats? they want a boat for one hour? they take a big boat?

Yes, I/they do.
No, I/they don't.
Yes, he/she/it does.
No, he/she/it doesn't.
I/they don't know.

4 Who am I?

You are a person in the book (Becky, David, ...).
Your friends must ask questions.
You can only answer with short answers. Example:

"Do you go to Haywood School?"
– "Yes, I do".
"Do you play the guitar?"
– "No, I don't."
"Does your mother work for a computer firm?"
– "No, she doesn't."
"Does your father work for a bank?"
– "Yes, he does."
"Then you must be ... ." *Please go on.*

On the beach

Becky and Simon are on the beach.
They are looking at crabs.

Simon: Where do crabs live?
Becky: Under rocks, I think. Look, there's a crab.
Simon: What do they eat? Bread, maybe. Here, crab. Do you like bread?
Becky: No, it doesn't eat bread.
Simon: Why do crabs live under rocks, Becky?
Becky: Because the water is nice and quiet there, I think.
Simon: I like the water, too. Come on, let's go swimming.

5 What do crabs eat?

Put in the question words 'where', 'when', 'what', 'how', 'how much'.

1. *Grandma:* … do we buy the tickets?
   David: At the shop over there.
2. *David:* … do we meet the others?
   Grandma: At 3 o'clock.
3. *Simon:* … do crabs eat?
   Becky: Fish, maybe.
4. *Simon:* … does Mark like?
   David: He likes boats and ice creams.
5. *Simon:* … do we get to the beach?
   Becky: We can take this road.
6. *Becky:* … does the train to Nottingham go?
   Grandma: At 4.10.
7. *Grandma:* … does a boat cost for one hour?
   David: £5.
8. *Mark:* … do we eat?
   Grandma: We can eat at a snack bar.

Your turn 6 Where do you live?

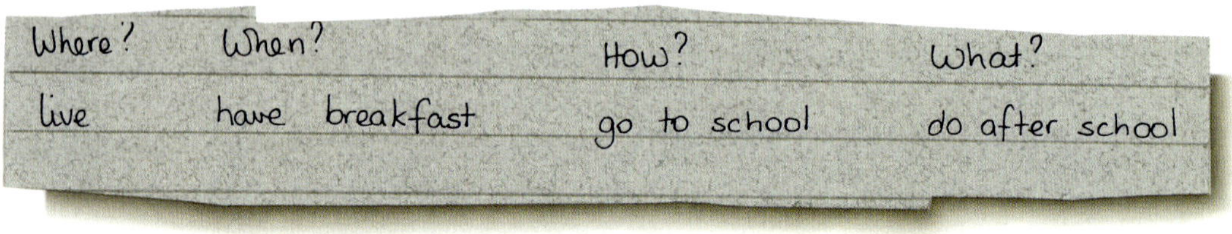

Make dialogues with your partner.
Example: "Where do you live?" – "I live in … ."

7 Sound practice

[ð] - [θ]

"It's **th**e ten**th**," says Mo**th**er,
"**Th**e dogs need a ba**th**."
"OK," says my bro**th**er.
"Put **th**em all in **th**e ba**th**."

Then in get **th**e **th**ree.
"**Th**ere's no room for me!"
says my bro**th**er.
"Well, I **th**ink," says Mo**th**er,
"It's your turn next mon**th**!"

LOOKING AT THE UK:

At Skegness

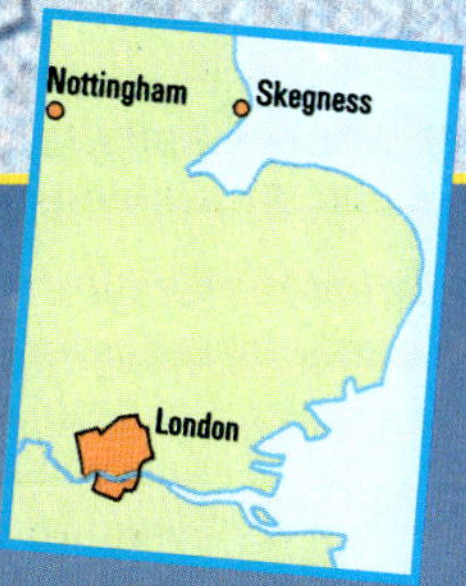

1 Look at the pictures

What can you do at Skegness?
You can go swimming.
Please go on.

Nottingham	0554	0803	0917	1004	1100	1200	1304
Netherfield	0600	——	——	1010	1106	——	1310
Radcliffe	0605	——	——	1015	1111	1209	1314
Bingham	0610	0817	——	1021	1116	1215	1320
Aslockton	0614	——	——	1025	1121	1219	1324
Elton & Orston	——	——	——	——	——	——	1328
Bottesford	0620	0825	——	1031	1127	1225	1332
Grantham	0635	0840	——	1048	1143	1242	1349
London Kings Cross	0812	1031	——	1232	——	1430	——
Sleaford	0716	——	1007	1116	1217	1317	1448
Boston	0740	——	1029	1139	1243	1341	1520
Skegness	0818	——	1104	1214	1319	1416	1555
Skegness	0921	1036	1147	1241	1330	1430	1610
Boston	1002	1109	1221	1316	1406	1504	1646
Sleaford	1023	1131	1247	1347	1428	1520	1718
London Kings Cross	0910	1110	——	1310	——	——	1620
Grantham	1056	1225	1322	1429	1505	1606	1748
Bottesford	1106	1234	1331	1439	1514	1616	1757
Elton & Orston	——	——	——	——	——	——	——
Aslockton	1112	1240	1337	1445	1520	1622	1803
Bingham	1115	1244	1341	1448	1524	1625	1807
Radcliffe	1120	1250	1346	1454	1529	1631	1812
Netherfield	——	1255	——	1458	——	1635	——
Nottingham	1135	1306	1401	1509	1544	1646	1827
Derby	1226	1342	1444	1544	1620	1725	1856

2 By train to Skegness

a) When does the first train to Skegness leave Nottingham?
When does the first train arrive in Skegness?
When does the second/third/next train …?

b) *You are at Nottingham station with your friends. Make dialogues.*
Example: "The first train to Skegness leaves at 5.54."
– "Oh no! That's too early."
"When does the next train leave?"
– "Er. At … ."

Unit 9

Step C

The sandcastle

Now Grandma and Mark are on the beach with Simon and Becky. David and Maxi are watching the friends from the promenade.

Mark: I want to make a sandcastle.
Simon: That's a good idea, Mark. Let's make a castle with water round it!
Becky: I want to get water for the castle. Can I have your bucket, please, Mark?
...
Grandma: Oh, it looks good now. That's a really big sandcastle.
Simon: Oh, look! It's Maxi. What's she doing here?
Mark: Ha, ha. She wants to make a sandcastle, too.
Becky: No, Maxi. This is a dog-free zone here.
Simon: Careful, Maxi. Our sandcastle!
Grandma: Too late! Now it's a very small castle.
Simon: Oh, Maxi! – I think a dog-free zone is a very good idea.

1 Beach activities

Make sentences with 'want to' or 'wants to'.
Example:
1. Mark – make a sandcastle.
Mark wants to make a sandcastle.
2. Simon and Becky – help Mark.
3. Becky – get water for the castle.
4. Maxi – make a sandcastle, too.
5. The friends – come to Skegness again.
6. Mark – eat more ice creams!

2 What can you say?

1. Your favourite group is on the radio. *You think*: I want to listen to the radio.
You ask your mother: Can I listen to the radio, please?
Your mother: Yes, of course./No, sorry. It's time for tea.
2. Your friend has got a new music magazine. *You think*: I want to... *Please go on.*
3. Your friends want to go to the seaside. You like the idea.
4. You and your friend see a chip shop. You're hungry.
5. You and your mother see a very nice blue sweatshirt. You like it.

Step C

At a souvenir shop

David, Mark and Grandma are at a souvenir shop at Skegness.

David: Let's buy two postcards. I want to write to Sarah and Robert from the seaside. How much do the postcards cost?
Grandma: Look, you can get two for 50p. OK. Let's get two. – What do you want, Mark?
Mark: Can I have that little red boat, please?
Grandma: Let's see, Mark.

3 In the shop

Make dialogues with a partner.

Let's get three postcards . → How much do they cost?
They cost 75 p. ← → OK. Let's get them .

a picture book · two bars of chocolate · a comic · does it · it · £1 · It costs · 80p

4 How much does it cost?

pint ***bottle*** ***pound*** ***bar*** ***packet***

Example: 1. How much does a pound of apples cost? – A pound of apples costs … . *Go on.*

5 WORD POWER

This is David's postcard to Sarah from Skegness.
Can you find the words?

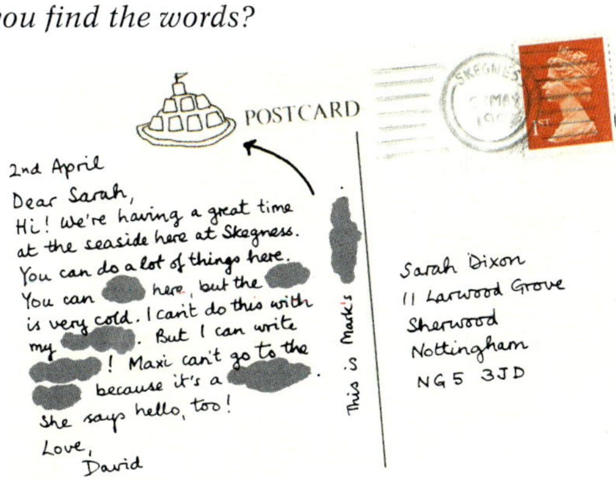

6 My English folder

Find words about the seaside and write them in your folder.

Unit 9

Step D

Maxi's day at the seaside

1. Hello, everyone! I'm at the seaside today with my pets, Simon and Becky and their friends. Poor Mini is at home because her leg hurts. But it's good for me because I get all the sandwiches.

2. Why do people lie on the beach for hours in their swimming things? Aren't they silly! I don't understand them. The beach is a dog-free zone – so I'm with David. I'm glad because I can help him with his ice cream.
And then I can sleep.

3. I'm with David, Mark and Grandma in a boat on the lake now. What do those silly ducks want? The sandwiches are for me, not for the ducks. I must bark at them. Oh, look at those people in the other boat. They're throwing all their rubbish from their lunch in the water. That's terrible. I must bark at them, too. We need a people-free zone on the lake.

4. What's that over there? Oh – my pets are making a sandcastle. I must help them.

5. No more sandwiches! So I'm taking my pets home. I've got the tickets for everyone. I'm showing them the way to the station so they can't get lost.

1 Answer the questions

1. Where is Maxi?
2. Why isn't Mini there?
3. What do people do at the seaside?
4. Why does Maxi like the dog-free zone?
5. Why doesn't Maxi like the ducks?
6. What does Maxi do in the boat?
7. Why doesn't Maxi like the people in the other boat?
8. What are the friends doing on the beach?
9. Why does Maxi show her pets the way to the station?

2 Maxi's day

Mark is asking Becky questions about Maxi and Mini.
Can you finish the questions?

Example: 1. … Maxi … (*get up*)? – She gets up very early.
When does Maxi get up? – She gets up very early.
2. … Maxi … in the morning (*do*)? – She plays with Mini.
3. … Maxi sometimes … (*bark*)? – Because we sometimes get angry with her.
4. … Maxi … (*sleep*)? – She usually sleeps in the kitchen.
5. … Mini … (*sleep*)? – She sleeps in the kitchen, too.
6. … Maxi … (*eat*)? – She eats everything.

3 In your beach bag

You are going to the seaside for the day.
What do you want to put in your beach bag?

– "I want to put a ball in my beach bag."
– "I want to put a ball and a book in my beach bag."
– "I want to put a ball and a book and … ."
Can you go on? Play this game in class.

4 Listening practice: The 4.10 train

a) *Tell the story. Can you find sentences for the pictures?*

Example: 1. The children are in a snack bar at the station and they're hungry.
2. Grandma is … . *Please go on.*

b) 1. What does David want to eat?
2. What does Mark want to eat? And Simon?
3. Why doesn't Becky want to eat?
4. Does David want to write a postcard to Jenny?
5. Why does Maxi go outside?
6. When does the train leave?
7. What does Mark want to do?
8. Where can Simon eat his chips?

Step E

Let's check

1 Questions for Jenny

Mrs Croft is asking Jenny a lot of questions.
Put in 'do' or 'does'. Can you find the answers, too?

1. … you come from Berlin?
2. … you like Nottingham?
3. … your mother speak English?
4. … Mrs Penrose speak German?
5. … David speak German?
6. … you like Haywood School?
7. … you often write to your friends in Berlin?

2 WORD POWER

You can make 'new' words from old words.
Can you find the 'new' words?

1. You buy it at the station.
2. You wear them in the water.
3. You play with it on the beach.
4. You can buy postcards here.
5. You can go in a boat here.

train		lake
boating		things
souvenir	+	ball
beach		shop
swimming		ticket

3 Your Saturday

Work with a partner.
Ask questions about your Saturdays.
Example:
"When do you get up on Saturdays?"
– "I get up at … ." *Go on, please.*

When Where What How	do you get up on Saturdays? do you often go on Saturdays? do you often do on Saturdays? do you get there? do you go to bed on Saturdays? do you do on Saturday evenings?

4 Maxi at home

Maxi can't speak, but you can understand her.
What does she want to do here?

go for a walk ✓ open the door sleep
get into the car eat go outside

Example: 1. She wants to go for a walk. *Please go on.*

⟨Revision 3⟩

1 At Cleethorpes for the day

It is a Sunday morning in June. The Dixons are at Cleethorpes for the day. Cleethorpes is their favourite seaside town.

Say what everyone in the picture is doing. Example: Sarah is making a big sandcastle.

2 Kim's postcard

It is Sunday afternoon Kim is writing a postcard to Debbie, her friend from the 'Just Jeans' shop.
Please put in the verbs.

Cleethorpes, June 6th

Dear Debbie,
We are ___ing a great time here!! ___ on the beach. (in the sun - it ___ (not) today!!). My sister ___ a magazine (my magazine, of course!). She ___ an ice cream at the same time. My parents ___ with our new beach ball. A man and a woman ___ with their children. They ___ their bags near our things. Now my parents ___ to them.

Love,
Kim

have read play eat rain lie put talk come

⟨Revision 3⟩

3 Sundays

The Dixons are talking to their new neighbours on the beach.

Mr Dixon says, "We often ... to Cleethorpes on a Sunday, because we ... the beach. We always ... home early, so we ... a nice long day. Our girls, Sarah and Kim, sometimes ... with us."

come like leave have go

Mrs Dixon says, "Sarah always ... with us, but Kim doesn't always ... to come. She often ... with her friends at home on Sundays. Sometimes they ... badminton, or they ... to the cinema together."

come go play go out want

Kim says, "I ... the seaside, but it's nice in Nottingham, too! I ... in a jeans shop on Saturdays. So usually I ... late on Sundays!"

like work sleep

4 Different people – different things

Cleethorpes is the Dixons' favourite seaside town – but the Penroses like Skegness best. They often go there when the weather is nice.
Ask questions about
– what they like best,
– what they always take to Skegness.

	what they like best	what they take to Skegness
Mr Penrose	the sea	a beach ball
Mrs Penrose	the promenade	a book
David	the boating lake	a camera
Mark	the beach	a bucket and spade

Examples: Does Mr Penrose like the boating lake best?
– No, he doesn't. He likes the sea best.
What does Mrs Penrose always take to Skegness?
– She always takes a book.

5 On the way home

On the way home to Nottingham, Sarah and Kim often play games in the car. Now they are playing "What's my job?" It is Kim's turn, so she thinks of a job, and Sarah asks the questions.

Kim is an assistant at a sweet shop. What are her answers?

Sarah: Do you work with other people? – *Kim:* Yes, I do.
Sarah: Do you work for a big firm? – *Kim:* No, I don't.

Go on. These are Sarah's next questions.

1. Do you work outside?
2. Do you work at a school?
3. Do you work in a hospital?
4. Do people come to you?
5. Ah! Do you work in a shop?
6. Does the shop sell clothes?
7. Does it sell things to eat?
8. Oh. Do you work in a supermarket then?
9. Hm. Do children often come to the shop?
10. Ah! Do you work in a sweet shop?

Play the game with your partner. Find other jobs.

On a Yorkshire farm

Step A

Springfield Farm

Robert and Mrs Croft are in Yorkshire for five days. They are staying at Springfield Farm, with Mr and Mrs Richards. The farm is also a guest house. Jack Richards is fourteen. He is showing Robert the farm.

Robert: What a lot of sheep!
Jack: Yes, this is a sheep farm really. We've got three hundred and fifty sheep. And that's Sam over there – one of our sheepdogs.
Robert: Oh, lambs, too! They're nice.
Jack: Yes, it's lambing time now. – This is Lenny. He's my special friend. – We've got more animals on the farm: eight cows and six pigs. – But let's go and see the hens now. Grandpa is just feeding them and collecting the eggs. – Grandpa! This is Robert.

one sheep – two sheep

Grandpa: Hello, Robert! – Do you like nice big eggs for breakfast?
Robert: Yes, I do.
Grandpa: That's good. We've got twenty-eight hens here, and they all lay good Yorkshire eggs.
Jack: Oh, Grandpa – you always say that!

1 On the farm

feed | collect | wash up | make | play

What are they doing now? Look at the pictures and say what you can see.
1. Grandpa is feeding the pigs. 2. Mrs Richards … . *Go on, please.*

2 WORD POWER

What animal is it? *Example:* It gives us milk. – It's a cow.
1. It gives us warm pullovers. 2. It has got a head and a long body – but it hasn't got legs. 3. It is at home in the water. 4. It is often black, and it has got feelers. 5. We get ham from this animal.

What can you say about these animals?

Step B

Jack's special friend

Robert: Hello, Mrs Richards. What's Jack doing?
Mrs Richards: He's feeding Lenny. Lenny's mother has got three lambs. But she hasn't got enough milk for them all.
Jack: So I feed him with a bottle. I feed him every day.
Robert: Oh, can I feed him?
Jack: Yes, that's OK. Here you are. – It's OK, Lenny. Robert is your friend.
Robert: Hey, he's drinking. Look, Jack!
Jack: Yes, he always drinks all his milk. He's always hungry.
Mrs Richards: Like his friend Jack!

1 In the evening

drink put ✔ feed lie listen

a) It is early evening.
Say what they are all doing.
1. Mrs Richards **is putting** … . *Go on.*

b) It's the same every evening!
1. At half past five Mrs Richards always **puts** … . 2. Jack is at home then, so he always … . 3. Lenny is always hungry, so he always … all … . 4. The cat always … at tea time. (She's hungry, too!) 5. And Grandpa … every evening.

2 Robert: at home and on the farm

walk home do his homework go to school listen to 'Tea and Talk' go to bed have lunch

a) *Say what Robert usually does.*

1. At 8.30 in the morning Robert usually **goes** to school.
2. At 1 o'clock he usually … at school.
3. At 4.30 he … from school.
4. At 5 o'clock he … on the radio.
5. At 6.30 he … for school the next day.
6. At 9 o'clock he … .

b) But Robert is on the farm now. So everything is different. *What is he doing now?*

1. It's 8.30 now. Robert **isn't going** to school. He**'s lying** in bed.
2. It's … now. Robert isn't … . He … with the Richards in their kitchen. *Go on, please.*

3 Mr Richards

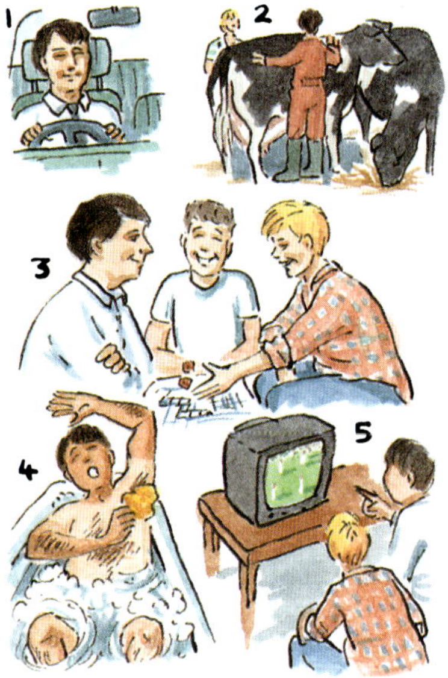

Jack's father works at the post office in Northallerton. He drives there every morning, and he comes home at half past five in the evening. So he can only work on the farm in his free time.

Put in the right forms.

1. (*drive*) Mr Richards is in his car now. He **is driving** to Northallerton. He **drives** there every day.
2. (*help*) Mr Richards usually … his father on the farm after tea. But this evening he … Mrs Richards.
3. (*play*) Jack and his father often … a game in the evening. Now they … a word game with Robert.
4. (*sing*) Now Mr Richards … in the bath. He often … in the car, too!
5. (*watch*) He and Jack sometimes … football on TV. But now they … cricket.

4 Can you tell me?

a) *Ask questions, and your partner must give the answers.*

Examples: Does Mrs Dixon work on a farm? – No, she doesn't. She works for a vet.
Does Mr Burton work in a shop? – Yes, he does. He works in a bike shop.

1. Mr Richards/in a shop? 2. Mrs Croft/for a doctor? 3. Mrs Penrose/in an office?
4. Mrs Dane/with children? 5. Mrs Burton/in a bank? 6. Mr Dixon/at home?

Your turn

b) *Make more questions – about you and your friends and family.*

Examples: Do you live in Berlin? – Yes, we do./No, I don't. I live in Neustadt.
Do your parents speak Italian? – No, they don't. But they speak Turkish.

you you and your friends you and your family your parents	live in Berlin/… play tennis listen to CDs speak Italian …

⟨5 A song: Old MacDonald had a farm⟩ (trad.)

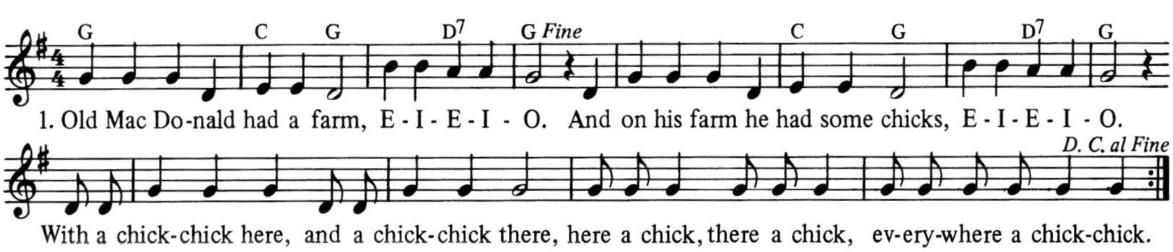

2. … some ducks (quack-quack)
3. … some sheep (baa-baa)
4. … a pig (oink-oink)
5. … a cow (moo-moo)

Unit 10

The tractor

Robert: Hey, a tractor! Who drives that?
Jack: Grandpa usually drives it. And my mum sometimes does. I often drive it, too.
Robert: You? But you can't drive a tractor, Jack.
Jack: Who says I can't? It's OK on the farm. But not on the roads. – And I must ask first, of course.
Robert: Who do you usually ask? Your mum?
Jack: No! I always ask Grandpa. Because he always says yes. – Come on, let's ask him now!

Who helps on the farm? – My dad helps.
Who does he help? – He helps Grandpa.

6 Jobs on the farm

People ↓ Jobs →	feed/pigs	collect/eggs	drive/tractor	work with/sheep
Jack	never	often	often	sometimes
Mrs Richards	sometimes	usually	sometimes	not often
Grandpa	usually	sometimes	usually	often

Ask questions about the jobs. Your partner must give the answers.
Example: Who feeds the pigs?
– Grandpa usually feeds them./Grandpa usually does that job. Mrs Richards sometimes feeds them, too. Jack never feeds them.

7 Jobs at home

Ask a partner questions about jobs at home.
Examples: Who makes the breakfast? – My mum usually does that. I sometimes help her.
Who takes the dog for a walk? – We haven't got a dog.

work in the garden | feed the cat | make the beds | do the washing-up

8 Problems

Example: You see a fire! – Who do you call? – The fire brigade! *Go on, please.*

1. Your dog's leg is broken.
2. You don't feel very well.
3. You see burglars in the next house.
4. You don't know the way to the station.
5. You're at a post office and you want to phone your parents in Germany.
6. You can't find the cornflakes on the shelves at the supermarket.

the vet
the fire brigade ✔
the doctor
the police
a person in the street
a shop assistant
a clerk at the post office

Unit 10

Step C

The seasons

ⓐ Mrs Richards is showing Mrs Croft her photos.

"This is Springfield Farm in the spring. There are always a lot of lambs on the farm then."

"A lot of guests come here for their holidays in the summer."

"Look! Here you can see the farm in the autumn. It's often very windy in Yorkshire then."

"Here's the farm in the winter. We sometimes get a lot of snow in Yorkshire. The nights are often very cold here, too."

1 Through the year

Talk about your activities at different times of the year. Here are some ideas:

In the	spring summer autumn winter	I we	sometimes often usually always	play outside. go to the seaside. play in the snow. play tennis/… . go for walks. …

ⓑ In the summer, Jack sometimes makes milkshakes.

Jack: "Mum! How much milk do we need?"
Mrs Richards: "Two pints of milk."
Jack: "And how many bananas do we need?"
Mrs Richards: "Four!"

When you can't count things: How much?/not much.
When you can count things: How many?/not many.

2 Dialogues

Put in 'much' or 'many'.

1. *Jack:* How … sugar do we need for the milkshakes?
   Mrs Richards: We don't need … sugar. Only two or three spoons.
2. *Mrs Croft:* How … lambs does a mother sheep usually have?
   Mrs Richards: Two. Sometimes only one. You don't see … sheep with three lambs.
3. *Grandpa:* How … guests are there this week?
   Mrs Richards: Not … . Two from Monday to Wednesday, and four from Friday to Sunday.
4. *Mr Richards:* How … tea do we need from the supermarket?
   Mrs Richards: We don't need … this week. One big packet is enough.
   Mr Richards: And how … packets of cornflakes?
   Mrs Richards: Three, please.

Step D

Problems on the farm

1. "Mary! We've got a problem. One of the sheep is in trouble. She's waiting for her lambs – but they aren't coming. I think there must be two or three in her, but I'm not sure." Grandpa comes into the kitchen, but he doesn't sit down.
"Let's phone the vet then," says Mrs Richards. "It's OK, Grandpa." She goes to the telephone.
"Don't go out again," she says to Grandpa. "You're tired. I can go to the lambing-shed now."
"Can Robert and I come, too?" asks Jack.
"Do you really want to come? You too, Robert? Well, OK, we can wait there together."

2. There is a lot of noise in the lambing-shed. Noise from all the sheep and their new lambs. But one sheep is very quiet.
"There she is," says Mrs Richards.
"Let's hope Mr Smith comes soon."

3. "He's coming! That's his car now."
Mrs Richards goes out and calls the vet.
"Alan! We're in the shed here."
Mr Smith comes in and examines the sheep.
"How many lambs are there?" asks Mrs Richards.
"Two," says Mr Smith. "Sorry, Mary, but the lambs inside her are dead. – Well, we must get them out and save the mother. – Jack, take your friend outside. This isn't a nice job."
But Robert wants to stay.

4. Soon the vet's work is finished. Robert is very quiet. He feels terrible.
"There's just one thing, Mary," says the vet. "This sheep doesn't feel very well yet. And she's got no lambs. Without lambs they sometimes die …"
"I know that, Alan," says Mrs Richards. "But we've got no baby lambs without mothers now."

5. "Hey – what about Lenny?" says Robert. He feels a bit better now. "His mother can't feed him!"
"Lenny is too old," says Jack. "He's three weeks old now. You can't trick a mother sheep like that."
"Well, wait a minute," says Mrs Richards. "Let's ask Grandpa. Maybe he's got an idea … ."

1 Grandpa's idea

"Yes, I've got an idea," says Grandpa. "It's an old trick. – Jack, give me one of the dead lambs. Right – we just need the skin … . Now you and Robert can go and get Lenny."

Find the right texts for the pictures.

a) It is a surprise for Lenny – but he likes the milk. And his new mother likes him!

b) Grandpa puts the dead lamb's skin round Lenny.

c) Robert and Jack find Lenny in the kitchen. They take him to the shed.

d) Then Mr Smith shows the sheep her new lamb. "Here you are!" he says.

2 Can you get it right?

1. There is a problem with one of the sheep, so
2. Mrs Richards goes to the lambing-shed because
3. Jack and Robert go with her, and
4. Mr Smith examines the sheep, but
5. Robert stays in the shed because
6. The mother sheep needs a lamb, but
7. Lenny's mother doesn't want him, so
8. But Jack thinks there is a problem because

- maybe the sheep can feed him.
- he wants to watch the vet.
- Lenny is three weeks old.
- Grandpa is tired.
- Mrs Richards phones the vet.
- he can't save her lambs.
- all the baby lambs have got mothers.
- they wait for the vet together.

3 Tell the story again

Can you tell the story again? Finish the sentences. (Can you do it without the text?)

There is trouble on the farm. One of the sheep is waiting …, but … . Mrs Richards phones … . Grandpa doesn't go … because … . But Jack and Robert go with … to … . There they wait … . Mr Smith can't save …, but he can … . Jack doesn't take Robert … because Robert wants … . The sheep really needs …, because sheep without … sometimes … . Robert has got an idea now: maybe the sheep can have …, because … . But Jack thinks it is too late for that because … . But maybe they can trick … . Maybe Grandpa … .

SB

4 Sound practice

[k] – [g]

We've **g**ot two ba**gs** of su**g**ar,
So what **c**an we ma**k**e?
We've **g**ot **c**hocolate and e**gg**s,
So let's ma**k**e a **c**a**k**e!

[p] – [b]

Bo**bb**y is in trou**b**le
And his **p**ro**b**lems never sto**p**.
He's got a jo**b** at 'Su**p**erFish'
But no cra**b** in the sho**p**!

[t] – [d]

Davi**d**, Mark and Rober**t**!
Don'**t** ea**t** all the brea**d**!
Toma**t**oes are much be**tt**er,
They're nice – an**d** goo**d** –
an**d** re**d**!

5 Dates and times

Can you answer these questions?

Example: When is the first day of spring this year?
– March the twentieth/The twentieth of March is the first day of spring this year.
– The first day of spring is on March the twentieth this year.

1. When is the first day of summer?
2. When is Mother's Day?
3. When do the next school holidays start?
4. When is the last day of the summer holidays?
5. When is your (your mother's/…'s) birthday?
6. What is the date next Saturday?

6 A new guest

me you her him it us them

1. *Mrs Richards:* We've got a new guest this evening: Mrs Walker. We can put … in Room 4. But the bed isn't ready yet.
   Mr Richards: I can make … .
   Jack: I can help …, Dad.
   Mr Richards: Thanks, Jack. But it's an easy job. I can do … without … really!
2. *Mrs Walker:* Hello! You must be Mrs Richards.
   Mrs Richards: Yes – and this is Jack. Give … your bags, Mrs Walker. Jack! Take Mrs Walker's bags upstairs for …, and show … the room.
   Jack: Right! Come with …, Mrs Walker.
3. *Mrs Walker:* What a nice room! – And I can see the sheep from here.
   Jack: Yes. Sam the sheepdog is with … . Can you see …?
   Mrs Walker: That big dog? Oh yes.
   Jack: We have tea at six. Do you want to have … with … today?
   Mrs Walker: Yes, please. And then maybe you can show … the farm.

7 Listening practice: Mrs Richards on the telephone

Can you get everything right?

1. The woman wants three rooms.
2. She wants the rooms for the last week in August.
3. The Greenwoods have got four children: a girl and three boys.
4. The Greenwoods' children are three, six and nine.
5. They have got three dogs. They want to bring them all.
6. Bed and breakfast costs £80. That's for one week.
7. The rooms are free for children.
8. Mrs Greenwood wants to take the rooms now.

Step E

Let's check

1 WORD POWER

Find the pairs. (Maybe you can make sentences with them, too.)
Example: take – photo
– Let's take a photo of the farm.

take ✔ feed call
drive answer lay
close play

police question door
photo ✔ football
egg tractor animals

2 Sunday afternoon *Put in the right forms.*

1. It is Sunday afternoon. Jack and his father … (*play*) football. They often … (*do*) things together on Sundays. They sometimes … (*go*) to the cinema in Northallerton.

2. Becky usually … (*go*) out with the dogs on Sunday. Now she and Mrs Burton … (*take*) them to the park. It is a nice day, and the sun … (*shine*).

3. It is 4.30. Sarah and her father … (*make*) tea together. Kim usually … (*help*) in the kitchen. But today she … (*lie*) down. She doesn't feel well.

3 Role play: Mr Penrose's list

two packets ✔
one pint two bars
three big bottles
three pounds
two boxes

Mr Penrose can't go to the shops today. He gives David his list.

David: How much sugar do we need, Dad?
Mr Penrose: Get two packets of sugar, please.

Go on, please. Ask questions with 'How much?' or 'How many?' Then find the right answers.

4 The people in this book

a) *What do you remember?*

1.

play ✔ read like sell take

1. Who plays the guitar? – David plays it. *Go on.*

2.

3.

4.

5.
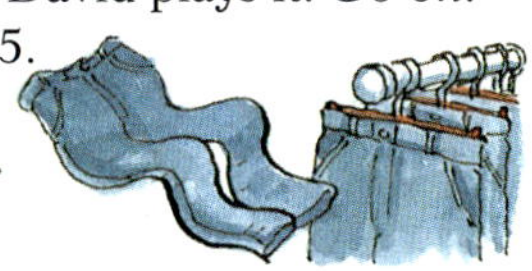

b) 1. Mrs Richards – phone – about a sheep?
Who does Mrs Richards phone about a sheep? – She phones the vet. *Go on, please.*
2. Grandma Penrose – take – to Skegness?
3. the friends – visit – in hospital?
4. Jenny and Robert – see – in a car near the 88 bus stop?
5. the Penroses – collect – at the airport?

⟨Extra line⟩

Christmas[1] in the UK

(after Unit 3)

It is Christmas Eve[2], and Mark and Jenny are upstairs.

Mark: Hey, Jenny, look! Here's my stocking[3].
It's for my presents from Father Christmas[4].
Jenny: A stocking? Oh, that's nice.
Mark: And here's a mince pie[5] for Father Christmas.
It's a long way[6] for him – so he's hungry.

It is Christmas Day[8]. Now they have all got their presents.

David: Christmas Dinner[9] – mmh! I'm hungry.
Jenny: What's for dinner?
Mr Penrose: Turkey[10]. And Christmas pudding[11].
Mark: Look, Jenny. Here are the crackers[12]. Let's pull[13] one.
David: No, Mark. We must wait[14] till[15] dinner.
Jenny: What's in the crackers?
Mark: A hat[16] and a present.

It is Boxing Day[17].

David: Can we go to the park?
Mrs Penrose: No! We've got tickets[18] for a pantomime[19] – 'Aladdin'[20].
Mark: Oh great!
Jenny: What's a pantomime?
David: A funny play[21]. With silly songs[22] and silly people. It's great fun[23].
Mrs Penrose: You can go to a pantomime at Christmas only.

SB

A song: We wish[24] you a Merry[25] Christmas (trad.)

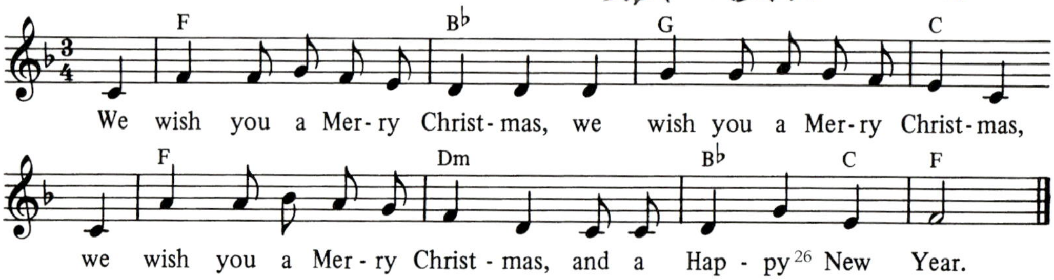

[1]Christmas ['krɪsməs] *Weihnachten* – [2]Christmas Eve [ˌkrɪsməs 'i:v] *Heiligabend* – [3]stocking ['stɒkɪŋ] *Strumpf* – [4]Father Christmas [ˌfa:ðə 'krɪsməs] *Weihnachtsmann* – [5]mince pie [ˌmɪns 'paɪ] *gefülltes Weihnachtsgebäck* – [6]a long way [ə 'lɒŋ 'weɪ] *langer Weg* – [7]December [dɪ'sembə] *Dezember* – [8]Christmas Day [ˌkrɪsməs 'deɪ] *Erster Weihnachtsfeiertag* – [9]dinner ['dɪnə] *Essen, Hauptmahlzeit* – [10]turkey ['tɜ:kɪ] *Truthahn* – [11]Christmas pudding [ˌkrɪsməs 'pʊdɪŋ] *kuchenartige Weihnachtssüßspeise* – [12]cracker ['krækə] *Knallbonbon* – [13]to pull [pʊl] *ziehen* – [14]to wait [weɪt] *warten* – [15]till [tɪl] *bis zum/zur* – [16]hat [hæt] *Hut* – [17]Boxing Day ['bɒksɪŋ ˌdeɪ] *Zweiter Weihnachtsfeiertag* – [18]ticket ['tɪkɪt] *Eintrittskarte* – [19]pantomime ['pæntəmaɪm] *Weihnachtsmärchen* – [20]Aladdin [ə'lædɪn] *Aladin* – [21]play [pleɪ] *Schauspiel* – [22]song [sɒŋ] *Lied* – [23]It's great fun. [ɪts ˌgreɪt 'fʌn] *Es macht viel Spaß* – [24]to wish [wɪʃ] *wünschen* – [25]merry ['merɪ] *fröhlich* – [26]happy ['hæpɪ] *glücklich*

⟨Extra line⟩

Wenn du auf unbekannte Wörter im Text stößt, schau nicht gleich unten auf die Erklärungen. Lies weiter und versuche, die Wörter aus dem Zusammenhang heraus zu verstehen. So macht dir das Lesen bestimmt noch mehr Spaß.

Nottingham castle caves[1]

(after Unit 7)

One Saturday afternoon Sarah, Jenny and Robert meet[2] in front of Nottingham castle. "What's the castle like?," Jenny asks. "There are great caves under the castle," Robert says. "I've got my torch[3] with me, so –". "Caves? Great! Let's go and explore[4] them!" says Jenny. The three friends buy their tickets[5] and walk to the castle. There are a lot of other people there. The next tour[6] is in half an hour[7]. At 4 o'clock the tour starts. The guide[8] counts thirty people. "Please keep together[9]," the guide says. He takes them through a door and down some stone steps[10]. The stone is cold and wet. The guide tells the group stories about the caves. Sarah and Jenny think it is very exciting, and they walk near the guide and ask him questions. They forget[11] about Robert. They walk up steps and down steps, round corners[12] and into big, cold caves. Robert is at the back[13] of the group. He thinks the stories are boring. "Good. I've got my torch with me. So I can go and see what's behind those steps over there. Maybe I can find a new cave or treasure[14]." Suddenly[15] Robert sees something[16] on the floor. It's a bracelet[17]. "Great!," he thinks. "My lucky day! It must be very old. Maybe I can find more treasure." Then Robert sees other steps. He goes up and round a corner. It is dark[18] and wet there. Robert suddenly trips and falls. He drops[19] the torch. He looks for it on the floor. At last[20] he finds it, but it is broken. It is very dark. "What can I do?" he thinks. "I can't see the way … ." It is the end of the tour now. The guide counts all the people. "Twenty-eight, twenty-nine … twenty-nine?" "Where is Robert?" Jenny asks. "Please, I think our friend is in the caves," Sarah says to the guide. "Oh no! Silly boy!" says the man. But he is worried. "I must go and look for[21] him." Sarah and Jenny are worried, too. There is only one other person with them, a woman. But she isn't very happy. "My bracelet," she says. "I can't find it. It must be down in the caves. It's a present from my grandma." At that moment the guide comes back with Robert. He has the broken torch in one hand, but he is smiling. "Hey, you two. Look what I've got! Old treasure: a very old bracelet." But Jenny, Sarah and the woman are smiling. "I'm sorry," says the woman. "It isn't treasure. It's my bracelet, you see." "Oh," Robert says. "No treasure for me today, only a broken torch. Here's your bracelet." "Thank you," the woman says. "Let's go and have tea together."

[1]cave [keiv] *Höhle* – [2]to meet [mɪt] *treffen, sich treffen* – [3]torch [tɔ:tʃ] *Taschenlampe* – [4]to explore [ɪk'splɔ:] *erforschen, erkunden* – [5]ticket ['tɪkɪt] *Eintrittskarte* – [6]tour [tʊə] *Führung* – [7]half an hour ['hɑ:f ən 'aʊə] eine halbe Stunde – [8]guide [gaɪd] *Führer* – [9]to keep together [ˌki:p tə'geðə] *zusammenbleiben* – [10]step [step] *Stufe* – [11]to forget [fə'get] *vergessen* – [12]corner ['kɔ:nə] *Ecke* – [13]at the back of [ət ðə 'bæk əv] *hinten* – [14]treasure ['treʒə] *Schatz* – [15]suddenly ['sʌdənlɪ] *plötzlich* – [16]something ['sʌmθɪŋ] *etwas* – [17]bracelet ['breɪslɪt] *Armband* – [18]dark [dɑ:k] *dunkel* – [19]to drop [drɒp] *fallen lassen* – [20]at last [ət 'lɑ:st] *endlich* – [21]to look for ['lʊk fɔ:] *suchen*

⟨Extra line⟩

The fun run[1]

(after Unit 9)

Dieses kleine englische Theaterstück könnt ihr gut aufführen, z. B. bei einem Schulfest. Ihr könnt dabei auch Ideen aus den Fächern Kunst oder Musik einbauen.

Viel Spaß!

Characters[2]: *Tracey, Tommy, Mrs Jones, Mr Jones, Sally, Mr Simpson, Mrs Simpson, Sam, Barry, Helen, Mr Clark, Starter, children*

Scene 1. *It is Saturday morning. Tracey, her little brother Tommy and her father are having breakfast. Her mother comes in.*

Mrs Jones: Hurry up[3], Tracey. We must go to the shops now.
Tracey: *(eating her cornflakes)* Mmm. OK. Just a minute. *(Mum goes out.)* Mum, can Tommy come to our fun run this afternoon?
Mrs Jones: Of course, dear. But come on, now.
Tracey: OK. Let's go. Bye!
Tommy: Bye. – Dad, what's a fun run?

Mr Jones: *(eating his cornflakes)* A fun run? Ah – er – well. Tracey's tutor group needs money for their school trip[4] to Austria[5]. So they run[6] round the playing fields[7] at school. They look for sponsors[8]. A sponsor gives two pounds for one time[9] round. And they give extra money for a funny costume[10].
Tommy: Are you a sponsor, Dad?
Mr Jones: Yes, I'm always a sponsor. They have a fun run every year. I give them a lot of money! But you can watch Tracey and her friends this afternoon. It's great fun … . *(They go out.)*

Scene 2. *In the afternoon. Mr and Mrs Jones, Tracey and Tommy are on the way to Tracey's school. They meet Sally in her wheelchair[11] with her parents.*

Tommy: What's your number for[12], Tracey?
Tracey: *(as a clown[13] with a big number 3 on her back.[14])* That's my number for the fun run. Hey look, there's Sally! She's got a number, too.
Mrs Jones: Hello Sally, are you in the run, too? Your wheelchair looks very nice today.
Sally: Thank you. Yes, I like our fun runs.
Tracey: But you can't go to Austria with us.
Sally: No, I can't *(she looks sad[15])*, but I want to help you and get a lot of money for your trip.

Tommy: Why can't Sally go to Austria?
Mrs Simpson: Well, she wants to do everything like the other children. But she can't ski[16] … .
Mr Simpson: And I haven't got a job now, so we haven't got much money.

Scene 3. *Starting point of the race[17]. The children and teachers are getting ready to run.*

Tracey: Hi Sam. Where's your saxophone[18]? Aren't you playing it today?
Sam: Of course I am. It's over there. I always play my saxophone. I get extra money for that!
Tracey: Hey, hi Barry. What are you?

[1]fun run ['fʌn rʌn] *Volkslauf* – [2]characters ['kærəktəz] *Personen* – [3]to hurry up [ˌhʌrɪ 'ʌp] *sich beeilen* – [4]school trip ['sku:l ˌtrɪp] *Schulausflug* – [5]Austria ['ɒstrɪə] *Österreich* – [6]to run [rʌn] *laufen* – [7]playing fields ['pleɪɪŋ fi:ldz] *Sportplatz* – [8]sponsor ['spɒnsə] *Förderer* – [9]one time [ˌwʌn 'taɪm] *einmal* – [10]costume ['kɒstju:m] *Kostüm* – [11]wheelchair ['wi:ltʃeə] *Rollstuhl* – [12]What's … for? [wɒts ... fɔ:] *Wozu ist … gut?* – [13]clown [klaʊn] *Clown* – [14]back [bæk] *Rücken* – [15]sad [sæd] *traurig* – [16]to ski [ski:] *Ski laufen* – [17]starting point of the race ['stɑ:tɪŋ pɔɪnt əv ðə 'reɪs] *Ausgangspunkt des Rennens* – [18]saxophone ['sæksəfəʊn] *Saxofon*

Barry: I'm a vet, like my dad. Look, this is my dad's bag, and this is my frog and this is my snake. *(He gets a red frog and a blue snake out of his pockets.)*

Sally: Who's that? *(A fireman is carrying[19] a ladder.)*

Barry: The fireman? That's Mr Clark, our German teacher.

Tracey: Hello, Mr Clark. Why are you carrying a ladder?

Mr Clark: A good fireman always carries his ladder with him. *(The children are laughing.)*

Barry: What a crazy teacher!

Starter: Everyone ready? Right … go!

Scene 4. *At the start/finish[20].*

Mr Jones: Look, Tommy, here's Tracey!

Tracey: Oh, Dad. I'm so tired. I *can't* go round again.

Mr Jones: Come on, Tracey. Look at Sally!

Sally: Come on Tracey!

Tracey: Oof! OK, here I come! *(Runs off[21] with Sally. Sam runs in with his saxophone.)*

Sam: Hello, Mr Jones, hello Tommy. Do you like my saxophone?

Tommy: Yes, I do. Play it, Sam.

Sam: OK. *(Sam plays 'Oh when the saints[22] …' and goes out. Tracey comes in again. She looks sad.)*

Mrs Jones: It's the break[23] now. Do you feel OK, Tracey?

Tracey: Oh yes. I'm just thinking about Sally. She really *wants* to go to Austria.

Mrs Jones: But she can't ski.

Tracey: Yes, but she can come with us on the plane[24]. And Austria is beautiful[25]! Sally can look at the mountains[26], at the snow[27] and talk to the people.

Mrs Jones: But the Simpsons haven't got much money just now … . *(They go out.)*

Scene 5. *After the run. The children come with lemonade.*

Barry: This is great. We've got a lot of money now from our sponsors.

Tracey: Hey, listen, everyone. *Sally* wants to go to Austria, too. What can we do?

Sam: Mm. Let's put all the money together and pay for[28] her ticket.

Children: Good idea./Oh yes, let's do that./I like Sally./Mm, I don't know.

Helen: But then there's no money for us, for extra trips … .

Tracey: Hey, that isn't fair[29]. We can collect[30] more money. We can wash cars for the neighbours or help in gardens … .

Barry: Or we can go for walks with neighbours' dogs.

Helen: OK, OK. You're right. Let's tell her then.

Tracey: Here, she comes. Sally! You can come to Austria with us! We can pay for your ticket! Can you ask your parents?

Sally: Really? Oh, that's great! *(Cheers[31], Sam plays his song again, the children sing.)*

Children: Oh when we go to Austr-i-a, oh when we go to Austr-i-a, Sally's one of our number, when we go to Austr-i-a.

[19]to carry ['kærɪ] *tragen* – [20]finish ['fɪnɪʃ] *Ziel, Ende* – [21]to run off [rʌn'ɒf] *loslaufen* – [22]saints [seɪnts] *Heilige* – [23]break [breɪk] *Pause* – [24]on the plane [ɒn ðə 'pleɪn] *im Flugzeug* – [25]beautiful ['bju:təfʊl] *schön* – [26]mountains ['maʊntɪnz] *Berge* – [27]snow [snəʊ] *Schnee* – [28]to pay for ['peɪ fɔ:] *(be)zahlen für* – [29]fair [feə] *gerecht, fair* – [30]to collect [kə'lekt] *sammeln* – [31]cheers [tʃɪəz] *Hurrageschrei, Jubel*

⟨Extra line⟩

A holiday[1] in Scotland[2]

(after Unit 10)

It is a Saturday afternoon in July. The Burtons arrive at a holiday house near Inverness[3] in Scotland. A woman is waiting for them.
"Hello, I'm Mrs McNeil[4]. You must be the Burtons."
"That's right," says Mrs Burton. "This farmhouse[5] looks very nice! What a lovely[6] garden!"
"Yes," says Mrs McNeil, "it *is* a lovely garden. This is our old farmhouse, Tulloch House[7], but it's too big for us."
"And where do you live now?" Mr Burton asks. "We live in a new, small house," Mrs McNeil says.
"Well, Tulloch House is just right for us," says Mrs Burton. "We want a quiet holiday and a lot of long walks." "Woof!" says Mini.
"You can get milk from the Duncan[8] farm. Please be careful with your dogs – the Duncans have a lot of sheep on the hills."
"Oh, our dogs are very good!" Becky says.
"Good," says Mrs McNeil. "Here are the keys[9] and here is our telephone number. Have a nice holiday."
"Thank you, Mrs McNeil. Goodbye."
They all look at the house and are very happy. Tulloch House is a big old farmhouse with apple trees and a stream[10] in the garden. A big tree stands near the back door. The hills are behind the house. Simon runs[11] round the garden; Becky climbs an apple tree. Mr and Mrs Burton go into the house with the bags. The dogs are excited[12] and sniff[13] all round outside the house.
"Come and look at the house, children," calls Mrs Burton. "Bring the dogs."
Mini and Maxi don't want to go into the house. They run round the garden and bark.
"Silly dogs!" says Mr Burton. "Simon, Becky, take them for a walk."
They go for a walk on the hills. The dogs are happy. Then they all run back to the house. Maxi sniffs round the apple trees, Mini goes to the stream.
"Mini, Maxi, come in," says Simon.
The dogs go into the kitchen, but they sit together near the door.
"Maybe they don't like it here," says Simon.
"Don't be silly," says Becky. "They want to go into the garden again. They are excited. They can sleep[14] in my room."
In the night Becky wakes up[15]. Maxi and Mini are barking. Mrs Burton comes into Becky's room and asks, "What's all this noise?"
"There's a noise at my window," says Becky.
Mrs Burton listens. "It must be the tree outside. It's very windy."
In the morning the children go to the Duncans' farm with Maxi and Mini for milk and eggs.
Mrs Duncan comes to the door.
"Are you staying at Tulloch House?"

[1]holiday ['hɒlɪdeɪ] *Ferien* – [2]Scotland ['skɒtlənd] *Schottland* – [3]Inverness [ˌɪnvə'nes] *Stadt in Schottland* – [4]McNeil [mək'niːl] *schottischer Familienname* – [5]farmhouse ['fɑːmhaʊs] *Bauernhaus* – [6]lovely ['lʌvlɪ] *hübsch, toll* – [7]Tulloch House [ˌtʌlək 'haʊs] *Name eines Hauses* – [8]Duncan ['dʌnkən] *schottischer Familienname* – [9]key [kiː] *Schlüssel* – [10]stream [striːm] *Bach* – [11]to run [rʌn] *rennen, laufen* – [12]excited [ɪk'saɪtɪd] *aufgeregt* – [13]to sniff [snɪf] *schnüffeln* – [14]to sleep [sliːp] *schlafen* – [15]to wake up [weɪk 'ʌp] *aufwachen*

she asks. “Do you like it?”

“Yes, we do,” says Simon.

“Do your dogs like it?”

Simon starts to speak, but Becky says, “Yes, they do.” What a funny question, she thinks.

In the afternoon the family goes for a long walk over the hills. The dogs run about[16] and are happy.

“What a great holiday,” Mr Burton says.

“The dogs must sleep in the kitchen tonight[17],” says Mrs Burton after tea. “I don’t want to wake up in the night again.”

But that night Becky wakes up. Everything is quiet. Maybe it is the tree again, she thinks, and soon goes to sleep[18] again.

The next day the Burtons go to Loch Ness[19]. Simon wants to see the Loch Ness monster[20]. They look at the lake all day, but they don’t see a monster.

“I don’t think there is a monster,” says Becky.

“But there are a lot of monsters – and ghosts[21] in Scotland,” says Simon.

“Don’t be silly, Simon,” Mrs Burton says. They all laugh. That evening they go to the farm again.

“Are you having a good holiday?” asks Mrs Duncan.

“Yes, thank you,” says Simon.

“People don’t usually stay long at Tulloch House,” Mrs Duncan tells them. “They think there’s a ghost, but that’s silly. It’s just windy here at night.” “Yes, that’s silly,” says Simon.

But that night Simon wakes up, too. The dogs are barking in the kitchen. There is a crash outside. Simon goes downstairs. He opens the front door, looks outside and finds a broken flowerpot.

“It’s OK,” he says to Becky and his parents, “just an accident.”

Mrs Burton looks worried, but she says nothing.

In the morning Mr Burton asks, “Can you get two pints of milk from the farm, Becky?”

But Becky doesn’t want to go. “Mrs Duncan always asks funny questions,” she says.

“Oh, she just wants to speak to someone[22],” says Mrs Burton. “There aren’t many people here.” “I can go,” says Simon.

He goes to the farm with the dogs. The door is open and he can see Mrs Duncan.

“Ah, the boy from Tulloch House,” she says. “A storm[23] is coming. You must look after[24] your dogs tonight.”

The night is very windy and nobody can sleep. At four o’clock in the morning there is a funny noise again. Maxi and Mini bark and the Burtons all run downstairs. The dogs are barking at the door. Mr Burton opens the door and they all look out. They see a big black shape[25]. It jumps[26] into the stream and then runs away. The dogs want to run after it, but nobody can see the shape now. They look round outside, but everything is quiet. It is not windy now.

“Ooh, it must be a ghost,” says Simon.

Mr and Mrs Burton look worried.

“What is it?” Mrs Burton asks.

They all go back to bed, but nobody can go to sleep again.

The next morning Mrs Burton phones Mrs McNeil and tells her about the black shape. “Maybe someone doesn’t like tourists? Someone with sheep on the hills?” Mrs Burton asks. “The children think it’s a ghost, and the dogs are always so excited … .”

Mrs McNeil laughs, “Oh, I’m sorry, listen. We’ve got a big black sheepdog. Sometimes he gets out and runs back to the old house. He likes the big garden. He’s here now but he’s very wet and dirty.”

Mrs Burton laughs now, too. “Oh dear[27],” she says, “I’m so glad it’s your dog!”

“Come and see us and bring the dogs. Maybe they want to play with him,” says Mrs McNeil.

“I must tell the children,” Mrs Burton says. “Thank you, Mrs McNeil. We can come and see you this afternoon.”

[16]to run about [rʌn əˈbaʊt] *herumrennen* – [17]tonight [təˈnaɪt] *heute nacht* – [18]to go to sleep [ˌgəʊ tə ˈsli:p] *einschlafen* – [19]Loch Ness [ˌlɒk ˈnes] *schottischer See* – [20]monster [ˈmɒnstə] *Ungeheuer* – [21]ghost [gəʊst] *Geist, Gespenst* – [22]someone [ˈsʌmwʌn] *jemand* – [23]storm [stɔ:m] *Sturm, Unwetter* – [24]to look after [ˌlʊk ˈɑ:ftə] *aufpassen auf* – [25]shape [ʃeɪp] *Gestalt, Figur* – [26]to jump [dʒʌmp] *springen* – [27]Oh dear! [əʊ ˈdɪə] *Oh! Oh je!*

Grammar

Hallo,
genauso wie im Straßenverkehr gibt es auch für jede Sprache Regeln. Diese Sprachregeln nennt man **Grammatik.** Die Regeln der englischen Sprache unterscheiden sich in manchen Punkten von den deutschen Regeln. Dieser Grammatikteil fasst die Sprachregeln zusammen, die du aus dem Unterricht kennst. Hier kannst du also nachschauen:

- wenn du Hausaufgaben machst,
- wenn du bei einer Aufgabe unsicher bist,
- wenn du etwas vergessen hast und es nochmals auffrischen möchtest,
- wenn du dich auf eine Klassenarbeit oder einen Test vorbereitest.

Ich will dir die Arbeit natürlich möglichst leicht machen. Deshalb habe ich mir einen Wegweiser für dich ausgedacht:

Wo die Taschenlampe leuchtet, musst du besonders aufpassen!

Auf einen Blick Hier siehst du auf einen Blick, was zusammengehört. Diese Zusammenfassungen helfen dir auch, wenn du später etwas nachschlagen willst. Gut, nicht wahr?

Wenn du bestimmte Regeln finden möchtest, dann schlage einfach die Seite 143 auf. Dort ist die Grammatikliste.

Let's start

1 Nottingham / 2 Hello

1 "I'm . . . ."

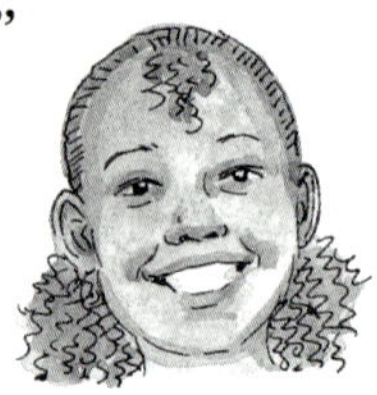

Mit *I'm* kannst du dich selbst vorstellen.

2 "He's . . .", "She's . . . ."

Mit *he's* und *she's* kannst du eine dritte Person vorstellen und etwas über sie sagen. Für eine weibliche Person (z. B. Sarah) steht *she*, für eine männliche Person (z. B. Robert) steht *he*. Deshalb heißen *he* und *she* persönliche Fürwörter (Personalpronomen).

He **is** in my class.

He **'s** in my class.

She **is** from Nottingham.

She **'s** from Nottingham.

Beim Sprechen lässt man das *i* von *is* meistens weg. Wenn du diese **Kurzform** schreiben willst, dann markierst du das ausgelassene *i* mit einem Auslassungszeichen. Dieses nennt man auch Apostroph.

3 "Is she ...?" "Is he ...?"

Mit *Is she ...?* und *Is he ...?* kannst du Fragen über eine dritte Person stellen.
Bei diesen Fragen steht das Verb (hier: *is*) am Anfang, genauso wie im Deutschen.
Im Englischen braucht man immer die **Langform,** um diese Fragen zu bilden.
Mehr über die Kurzformen und Langformen findest du bei Punkt 11.

3 School!

4 "Am I ...?"

Wie bei Fragen mit *is* (vergleiche Punkt 3) braucht man hier die Langform *(am)*, um Fragen zu bilden.
Das Wort *I* wird immer groß geschrieben.

5 "You're ... ."

Wenn du einer anderen Person etwas über sie sagen willst, kannst du *you're* benutzen. *You're* ist die Kurzform von *you are.* Hier wird das *a* in *are* weggelassen.

6 "Are you ...?"

Mit *Are you ...?* kannst du eine andere Person etwas über sie fragen. Du brauchst die Langform *are,* um Fragen zu bilden.

4 Tutor group 7MD

7 'My', 'your', 'his', 'her'

I'm	twelve.	**My**	friend David is eleven.
You're	in class ten.	**Your**	teacher is Mr Cooper.
He's	from London.	**His**	name is Robert.
She's	a tutor.	**Her**	group is 7 MD.

Die Wörter *my*, *your*, *his* und *her* zeigen, wer etwas besitzt oder zu wem etwas gehört. Sie heißen deshalb besitzanzeigende Fürwörter (Possessivpronomen).

You're klingt sehr ähnlich wie *your*:

You're ten. (*Du* bist zehn.)
Your comic is nice. (*Dein* Comic ist nett.)

8 "We're …", "You're …", "They're … ."

We, *you* und *they* stehen für mehrere Personen (= Mehrzahl).
You kann *du* heißen (Einzahl), oder *ihr* (Mehrzahl), oder *Sie* (höfliche Anrede).

Beispiele: *David, you're late. (du)*
Sarah and Robert, you're my friends. (ihr)
Mr Cooper, you're my new teacher. (Sie)

9 "Are we …?", "Are you …?", "Are they …?"

We're in 7 MD. → Are we in 7 MD?

Becky and Sarah, you're in 7 MD, too. → Becky and Sarah, are you in 7 MD, too?

They're our teachers. → Are they our teachers?

Wie bei Punkt 6 werden hier die Fragen gebildet, indem man *are* an den Anfang stellt.

10 "It's … ."

David: Where's my pencil? — *Robert:* It's on the desk.

David: And my folder? — *Robert:* It's under the desk.

David: And my book? — *Robert:* It's in your bag.

Wenn du über Sachen reden willst, gebrauchst du *it*. *It* steht für Sachen und kann sowohl *er* als auch *sie* und *es* heißen. Man benutzt *it* außerdem für unbekannte Tiere. Wenn ein Tier einen Namen hat, wird es mit *he* oder *she* bezeichnet.

Beispiele: *That's a dog. It's nice.* Aber: *That's my dog Mini. She's funny.*

5 Haywood School

11 'To be': Kurzformen und Langformen

Jetzt hast du alle Formen des Verbs *to be* kennengelernt. *To be* ist die Grundform (der Infinitiv) und entspricht dem deutschen Wort *sein*. Der Infinitiv wird in bestimmten Fällen mit *to* und in anderen Fällen ohne *to* gebraucht. Bei Überschriften und in Vokabellisten wird er mit *to* angegeben.

Auf einen Blick

	Langformen (long forms)		Kurzformen (short forms)	
Einzahl (Singular)	**I am**	from London.	**I'm**	from London.
	You are	nice.	**You're**	nice.
	He is	in my tutor group.	**He's**	in my tutor group.
	She is	late.	**She's**	late.
	It is	my bag.	**It's**	my bag.
Mehrzahl (Plural)	**We are**	from Nottingham.	**We're**	from Nottingham.
	You are	my friends.	**You're**	my friends.
	They are	English.	**They're**	English.

Die Langformen verwendet man:
- beim Schreiben, z. B. bei Aufsätzen
- bei Briefen an Fremde.

Die Kurzformen verwendet man:
- beim Sprechen
- wenn man Gespräche aufschreibt
- bei Briefen an Freunde.

Beim Sprechen lässt man oft Buchstaben weg, z. B. hier das *a* von *am* und *are* und das *i* von *is*. Beim Aufschreiben der Kurzformen markiert man diese Stelle immer mit einem Apostroph (Auslassungszeichen).

12 Aussagen und Fragen mit dem Verb 'to be'

Auf einen Blick

	Aussagesatz		Fragesatz	
Einzahl (Singular)	**I'm**	late.	**Am I**	late?
	You're	my friend.	**Are you**	my friend?
	He's	from London.	**Is he**	from London?
	She's	nice.	**Is she**	nice?
	It's	a new ball.	**Is it**	a new ball?
Mehrzahl (Plural)	**We're**	late.	**Are we**	late?
	You're	English.	**Are you**	English?
	They're	at Haywood School.	**Are they**	at Haywood School?

Die Frage wird gebildet, indem man die Langformen des Verbes *to be* an den Anfang stellt. Diese Langformen sind *am*, *are* und *is*. Schau auch nach bei den Punkten 3, 4, 6 und 9.

13 Die Verneinung von 'to be'

Auf einen Blick

I'm not	English.
You aren't	late.
He isn't	German.
She isn't	at Haywood school.
It isn't	on your desk.
We aren't	in tutor group 7 MD.
You aren't	the teacher.
They aren't	in London.

Nur bei *I am* wird *not* in ungekürzter Form verwendet. Ansonsten wird *not* verkürzt *(n't)* und an die Form von *be* angehängt *(isn't, aren't)*.

Unit 1

Unit 1 Step A

14 Die Pluralform der Substantive (regelmäßige Formen)

The plural of nouns (regular forms)

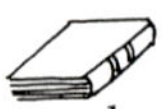
one book
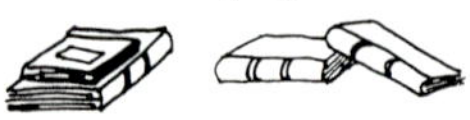
four book**s**
a girl

two girl**s**

Um über mehrere Dinge oder Personen zu sprechen, verwenden wir die Pluralform des Substantives (= Mehrzahlform des Hauptwortes). Diese Form ist im Englischen ganz einfach zu bilden: Man hängt ein *-s* an das Hauptwort.

one box

three box**es** [ɪz]

one pencil cas**e**

two pencil cas**es** [ɪz]

Bei einem Wort wie *box,* das schon auf einen *s*-Laut endet [bɒks], hängen wir ein *-es* an. Wenn ein Wort schon auf *-e* endet, genügt das einfache *-s,* z.B. *pencil case – pencil cases.*

Die Aussprache des Mehrzahl-*s*/*-es*

book	–	book**s**	[s]	dog	–	dog**s**	[z]	box	–	box**es**	[ɪz]
comic	–	comic**s**	[s]	girl	–	girl**s**	[z]	case	–	cas**es**	[ɪz]
group	–	group**s**	[s]	boy	–	boy**s**	[z]				

Bei der Aussprache des Mehrzahl-*s* musst du aufpassen. Nach hart gesprochenen Mitlauten wie 'p' und 'k' wird das Mehrzahl-*s* scharf ausgesprochen: [s].
Nach weich gesprochenen Mitlauten wie 'g' und 'l' und nach den Vokalen 'a, e, i, o, u' und deren Verbindungen mit -y, z. B. *boy,* wird das Mehrzahl-*s* weich ausgesprochen: [z].
-es wird immer als [ɪz] ausgesprochen.

Unit 1 Step B

15 Die Possessivpronomen 'our', 'your', 'their'

The possessive determiners 'our', 'your', 'their'

Mit *our, your, their* kannst du ausdrücken, was zu mehreren Personen gehört oder was diese besitzen. Deshalb heißen sie besitzanzeigende Fürwörter oder Possessivpronomen. Für die Einzahl kennst du schon *my, your, his* und *her* (siehe Punkt 7).

Weißt du's noch? *You* kann *du, ihr* oder *Sie* heißen! (Siehe Punkt 8.) Mit *your* ist es genau so: es kann *dein, euer* oder *Ihr* bedeuten. Das ist doch eigentlich ganz praktisch.

Mrs Dane: Becky, that's your book. *(dein)*
Mrs Dane: Becky and Sarah, Robert is in your tutor group. *(euer)*
Becky: Mrs Dane, here's your book. *(Ihr)*

16 Die Possessivpronomen The possessive determiners

Auf einen Blick

Einzahl (Singular)	Here's	**my**	school.	I	→	my
	Here's	**your**	pencil case.	you	→	your
	That's	**his**	bike.	he	→	his
	That's	**her**	computer.	she	→	her
Mehrzahl (Plural)	Here's	**our**	school.	we	→	our
	Here's	**your**	teacher.	you	→	your
	That's	**their**	tutor group.	they	→	their

Wenn man sagt, zu wem etwas gehört oder wer etwas besitzt, verwendet man besitzanzeigende Fürwörter (Possessivpronomen).

17 'has got'

Sarah has got a bike.

Has she got a football?

Simon has got a football.

Has he got a computer?

Wenn man sagen will, dass jemand etwas hat, benutzt man *she has got* oder *he has got.* Bei *has got* gibt es genau wie bei *is* und *are* eine Langform und eine Kurzform.

she has got	he has got
▼	▼
she's got	he's got

Hier brauchst du wieder einen Apostroph.

Wenn du wissen willst, wann man Lang- oder Kurzform verwendet, sieh bei Punkt 11 nach.

Die Frage, ob jemand etwas hat, drückt man durch *Has he got …?/Has she got …?* aus. Dafür brauchst du immer die Langform. *Has* wird an den Anfang der Frage gestellt. Das *got* dagegen bleibt hinter dem Personalpronomen *she* oder *he*.

Mit *she hasn't got/he hasn't got* kann man sagen, dass jemand etwas nicht hat. Hier wird die Kurzform genauso gebildet wie bei *isn't* und *aren't* (siehe Punkt 13). *Has not* wird zu *hasn't* zusammengezogen. Dabei wird das *not* zu *n't*.

18 'have got'

Wie du bei Punkt 17 gesehen hast, verwendet man *has got* nur bei *he* und *she* (und *it*). Bei allen anderen Personen gebraucht man *have got*. Die Kurzformen von *have got* lauten: *I've got, you've got, we've got, you've got, they've got.*

Die Fragen bildet man genauso wie bei *has got* (Punkt 17).

Die verneinte Form von *have got* ist *haven't got.*

19 'have got'/'has got'

Auf einen Blick

	Aussage (statement)	Frage (question)	Verneinung (negation)
Einzahl (Singular)	I've got you've got he's got she's got	have I got? have you got? has he got? has she got?	I haven't got you haven't got he hasn't got she hasn't got
Mehrzahl (Plural)	we've got you've got they've got	have we got? have you got? have they got?	we haven't got you haven't got they haven't got

Unit 1 Step C

20 Der unbestimmte Artikel The indefinite article

a [ə]	an [ən]
Is this **a b**all?	Have you got **an a**pple?
Yes, that's **a g**ood idea.	Oh, that's **an o**ld dog biscuit.
That's **a c**razy example.	This is **an e**asy example.
Our English teacher has got **a G**erman car.	The Burtons have got **an E**nglish car.

Der unbestimmte Artikel (deutsch: ein oder eine) heißt im Englischen *a* oder *an*.
Beispiel: *Have you got an apple?* – Hast du einen Apfel?
Vor einem Konsonanten (**b**all, **g**ood, **c**razy, **G**erman) verwendet man *a* [ə].
Vor einem Vokal (**a**pple, **o**ld, **e**asy, **E**nglish) verwendet man *an* [ən].

21 'This' und 'that'

This weist auf etwas hin, was in der Nähe ist, *that* dagegen auf etwas, das weiter entfernt ist. Deshalb heißen *this* und *that* hinweisende Fürwörter (Demonstrativpronomen). *This* wird oft zusammen mit *here* verwendet, *that* mit *over there.* Nach *this* wird die Langform *is* gebraucht, nach *that* meistens die Kurzform *'s.*

Unit 2

Unit 2 Step A

22 Die Pluralform der Substantive (unregelmäßige Formen)

The plural of nouns (irregular forms)

a man – four men
one woman – three women
a child – five children

Einige Substantive haben eine unregelmäßige Form im Plural. Da es nur wenige sind, kann man sich diese Formen leicht merken.

Unit 2 Step B

23 Die Pluralform der Substantive (Besonderheiten)

The plural of nouns (special forms)

one knife [f] – two knives [vz]
a shelf [f] – shelves [vz]

Auch bei einigen Mehrzahlformen mit *-s* ändert sich die Aussprache – und die Schreibweise. Substantive mit der Endung *-f* oder *-fe* haben im Plural oft die Endung *-ves*.

 family – families
boy – boys

Substantive, die auf einen Mitlaut (=Konsonanten) und *-y* enden, haben im Plural die Endung *-ies.* Endet ein Substantiv auf einen Selbstlaut (=Vokal) und *-y,* hängt man ein *-s* an. Das *y* bleibt.

24 Das Possessivpronomen 'its' The possessive determiner 'its'

The CD is in its box.
(... in ihrer Hülle.)

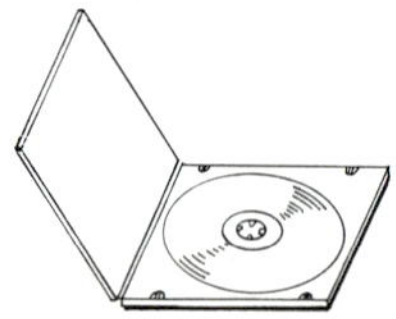

The frog is in its pond.
(... in seinem Teich.)

Mit *its* kann man angeben, was zu einer Sache oder zu einem Tier gehört. *Its* ist ein besitzanzeigendes Fürwort (Possessivpronomen), wie z.B. *my, your, her, him* (siehe Punkt 7). *Its* kann sowohl *sein* als auch *ihr* bedeuten.

Its klingt genauso wie *it's* (=it is). Du darfst die beiden Wörter beim Schreiben nicht verwechseln.

25 Kurzantworten auf Fragen mit 'to be' Short answers with 'to be'

Auf einen Blick

	YES, ...	NO, ...
Are you Robert Croft?	Yes, I am.	No, I'm not.
Am I in your tutor group?	Yes, you are.	No, you aren't.
Is Mr Dixon a bank clerk?	Yes, he is.	No, he isn't.
Is Sarah in her room?	Yes, she is.	No, she isn't.
Is my pump in the garage?	Yes, it is.	No, it isn't.
Are you from London?	Yes, we are.	No, we aren't.
Are we late?	Yes, you are.	No, you aren't.
Are they in the kitchen?	Yes, they are.	No, they aren't.

Anstatt nur mit *Yes* oder *No* zu antworten, benutzt man im Englischen oft eine *Kurzantwort* mit einem Verb. Kurzantworten klingen höflicher als nur *Yes* oder *No*. Sie setzen sich aus einem Personalpronomen (z.B. *she*) und einem Verb (z.B. *is*) zusammen.

26 Kurzantworten auf Fragen mit 'have got' Short answers with 'have got'

Auf einen Blick

	YES, ...	NO, ...
Have you got a cat?	Yes, I have.	No, I haven't.
Have I got my lunch box?	Yes, you have.	No, you haven't.
Has he got a knife?	Yes, he has.	No, he hasn't.
Has she got a red bike?	Yes, she has.	No, she hasn't.
Has it got a pump?	Yes, it has.	No, it hasn't.
Have you got our telephone number?	Yes, we have.	No, we haven't.
Have we got the bag?	Yes, you have.	No, you haven't.
Have they got a car?	Yes, they have.	No, they haven't.

Wie bei den Kurzantworten mit *to be* (Punkt 25) sind diese Kurzantworten mit *have got* höflicher als nur *Yes* oder *No*. Du kannst auch hier das Verb aus der Frage für die Kurzantwort übernehmen. *Got* fällt in der Antwort weg.

Unit 2 Step C

27 'These' und 'those'

These ist der Plural von *this*, und *those* ist der Plural von *that* (vergleiche mit Punkt 21).
Mit *these* kannst du auf Sachen oder Personen, die in deiner Nähe sind, hinweisen.
Mit *those* weist du auf Sachen oder Personen hin, die weiter entfernt sind.
Deshalb nennt man *these* und *those* hinweisende Fürwörter (Demonstrativpronomen).

Unit 3

Unit 3 Step A

28 "There is …", "There are …"

There is a girl from Berlin in our tutor group.	In unserer Klasse ist ein Mädchen aus Berlin.
There are two big airports in Berlin.	In Berlin gibt es zwei große Flughäfen.

Mit *there is/there's* oder *there are* kannst du Sätze einleiten, um auf Dinge oder Personen hinzuweisen (ähnlich wie mit *es gibt, es ist, es sind* im Deutschen).
Wenn es sich um *eine* Person oder *einen* Gegenstand handelt, wird *there is (short form: there's)* verwendet. Bei *mehreren* Personen oder Dingen steht *there are*. Um Fragen zu bilden, stellst du wieder um: *Is there …?, Are there …?*

Unit 3 Step B

29 Das Hilfsverb 'can' (Aussage und Verneinung)
The modal auxiliary 'can' (statement and negation)

I	can	play football.
Mark	can	draw a house.
We	can	speak English and German.

Mit *can* drückst du aus, dass jemand etwas kann – also eine Fähigkeit. Das Hilfsverb *can* ist in allen Personen gleich. Direkt nach *can* steht das Verb (z. B. *play, draw, speak*) in der Grundform (dem Infinitiv) ohne *to*.

I	can't	do this exercise.
She	can't	draw people.
We	can't	see my Dad in the picture.

Die verneinte Form von *can* [kæn] heißt *can't* [kɑːnt]. Die Langform heißt *cannot* ['kænɔt] und wird in einem Wort geschrieben. Auch die Formen *can't* und *cannot* sind in allen Personen gleich.

30 Das Hilfsverb 'can' (Frage und Kurzantwort)
The modal auxiliary 'can' (question and short answer)

Becky can play football.

Can Becky play football?

Um Fragen mit *can* zu bilden, stellst du das Hilfsverb *can* an den Anfang des Satzes.

Frage		Kurzantwort	
Can	you draw a cat?	Yes, I can.	No, I can't.
Can	Becky play football?	Yes, she can.	No, she can't.
Can	they speak Turkish?	Yes, they can.	No, they can't.
Can	you help me with my homework?	Yes, I can.	Sorry, I can't.

Zu den Kurzantworten vergleiche Punkt 25 und 26. Das Verb im Infinitiv fällt bei den Kurzantworten weg.

31 Die Fragewörter 'who', 'what', 'where', 'how'
The question words 'who', 'what', 'where', 'how'

Who's	in the living-room?	Mark.
What's	in your bag?	My books and my folder.
Where's	my English book?	On the table in the kitchen.
How old	is Robert?	He's eleven.

Mit *who* fragt man nach Personen, mit *where* fragt man nach einem Ort.

32 Der s-Genitiv   The s-genitive

Becky's mother has got a green bike.	Beckys Mutter …
The girl's bike is red.	Das Fahrrad des Mädchens …
The Penroses' house is in Arndale Road.	Das Haus der Penroses …
The boys' room is untidy.	Das Zimmer der Jungen …

Um auszudrücken, dass etwas oder jemand zu einer Person gehört, benutzt man den s-Genitiv. Im Singular hängt man zuerst einen Apostroph (') und dann ein *s* an das Substantiv. Bei regelmäßigen Pluralformen mit der Endung *-s* hängt man im Genitiv Plural nur einen Apostroph (') an. Die Aussprache ändert sich nicht.

the girl's room – das Zimmer des Mädchens
the girls' room – das Zimmer der Mädchen

Bei Hauptwörtern mit unregelmäßigen Pluralformen (Punkt 22) wird *'s* angehängt; z. B. *the children's teacher, the men's folders, the women's cars.*
Vergleiche die unterschiedliche Schreibung im Deutschen:
Mr Dixon's car is green. = Herr Dixons Auto ist grün.

33 Die Objektform der Personalpronomen: 'me', 'him', 'her'

The object form of the personal pronouns: 'me', 'him', 'her'

Subjektform		Objektform		
I	Please tell	**me**	about your school.	(mir)
	You can speak to	**me**	in English.	(mit mir)
	You can phone	**me**	at my aunt's house.	(mich)
he	Give	**him**	this pencil, please.	(ihm)
	Let's talk to	**him.**		(mit ihm)
	Can you see	**him?**		(ihn)
she	You can help	**her**	in the garage.	(ihr)
	Let's play with	**her.**		(mit ihr)
	Can you see	**her?**		(sie)

Im Deutschen haben die Personalpronomen *ich*, *er* und *sie* **zwei** Objektformen, nämlich *mir/mich*; *ihm/ihn* und *ihr/sie*. Im Englischen gibt es dagegen für die Objektform von *I*, *he* und *she* nur je *eine* Form: *me*, *him* und *her*.

34 Das Hilfsverb 'must' The modal auxiliary 'must'

I	must	do my homework now.
She	must	be in the picture, Robert.
We	must	work in the garden this afternoon.

Mit *must* drückst du eine Notwendigkeit oder eine Verpflichtung aus. Das Hilfsverb *must* ist in allen Personen gleich. Direkt nach *must* steht das Verb im Infinitiv ohne *to*.

Unit 4

Unit 4 Step B

35 Die Verlaufsform des Präsens

The present progressive

David is reading a comic. Mark is playing a game. And Becky and Sarah are playing a game, too.

Wenn du ausdrücken willst, was jemand gerade macht, verwendest du die Verlaufsform des Präsens (Gegenwart). Die Verlaufsform (present progressive) wird so gebildet:

Form von 'to be'	Grundform (Infinitiv) eines Verbes	ing-Endung
is **are**	**play**	**ing**

Im Deutschen gibt es die Verlaufsform nicht.
Die Bedeutung dieser Form wird deshalb oft mit *gerade, im Augenblick* oder *jetzt* ausgedrückt.
Beispiel: *She's doing her homework.*
= Sie macht gerade ihre Hausaufgaben.
Um Fragen mit der Verlaufsform zu bilden, stellst du die Form von *to be* (hier: *is*) an den Satzanfang.

36 Die Verlaufsform des Präsens (Aussage und Verneinung)

The present progressive (statement and negation)

Auf einen Blick

I'm repair**ing**	my bike.	I'm not read**ing**	a comic.
You're play**ing**	with my game.	You aren't do**ing**	your homework.
He's work**ing**	in the garage.	He isn't watch**ing**	TV.
She's read**ing**	a book.	She isn't listen**ing**	to music.
It's rain**ing.**		It isn't rain**ing.**	
We're watch**ing**	TV.	We aren't help**ing**	Mum.
You're play**ing**	with my computer.	You aren't watch**ing**	TV.
They're work**ing**	in the garden.	They aren't work**ing**	in the kitchen.

37 Die Verlaufsform des Präsens (Frage und Kurzantwort)

The present progressive (question and short answer)

Are you doing	your homework, Simon?	– Yes, I am.	
Are you working	together?	– Yes, we are.	
Is David playing	a game?	– Yes, he is.	
Are you reading	a comic, Becky?	– No, I'm not.	I'm reading a book.
Are you doing	your homework, boys?	– No, we aren't.	We're playing a game.
Is she listening	to the radio?	– No, she isn't.	She's watching TV.
Are they playing	football?	– No, they aren't.	They're playing tennis.

Bei den Antworten verwendet man meist die Kurzantworten mit *to be.*

38 Die Objektform der Personalpronomen The personal pronouns (object form)

Auf einen Blick

You can phone	me.		I → me
This biscuit is for	you.		you → you
Can we play with	him?		he → him
Can you see	her?		she → her
The frog is in the garden. Can you see	it?		it → it
In this photo, you can see	us	in the kitchen.	we → us
These biscuits aren't for	you,	Maxi and Mini.	you → you
Where are the children? I can't find	them.		they → them

Unit 5

Unit 5 Step B

39 Die Verlaufsform des Präsens (unregelmäßige Formen)
The present progressive (irregular forms)

Die Verlaufsform des Präsens hast du schon unter Punkt 35 kennengelernt.
Hier geht es um einige unregelmäßige Formen.

Sarah	is making	a poster.	→ mak~~e~~ + ing
Jenny	is writing	a letter.	→ writ~~e~~ + ing
Robert	is getting	the tea ready.	→ get + t + ing
Mini	is sitting	under the bed.	→ sit + t + ing
Mark	is lying	on the floor.	→ l~~ie~~ + y + ing

Um die Verlaufsform bestimmter Verben zu bilden, fällt das stumme *-e* am Ende des Verbes weg. Verben mit einem kurzen, betonten Vokal vor dem Endkonsonanten verdoppeln den Endkonsonanten; *ie* am Ende eines Verbes wird zu *y*.

40 Die Ordnungszahlen 1.–100. The ordinal numbers

first	1st	eleventh	11th	twenty-first	21st	tenth	10th
second	2nd	twelfth	12th	twenty-second	22nd	twentieth	20th
third	3rd	thirteenth	13th	twenty-third	23rd	thirtieth	30th
fourth	4th	fourteenth	14th	twenty-fourth	24th	fortieth	40th
fifth	5th	fifteenth	15th	twenty-fifth	25th	fiftieth	50th
sixth	6th	sixteenth	16th	twenty-sixth	26th	sixtieth	60th
seventh	7th	seventeenth	17th	twenty-seventh	27th	seventieth	70th
eighth	8th	eighteenth	18th	twenty-eighth	28th	eightieth	80th
ninth	9th	nineteenth	19th	twenty-ninth	29th	ninetieth	90th
tenth	10th	twentieth	20th	thirtieth	30th	one hundredth	100th

Erster, zweiter, dritter usw. sind Ordnungszahlen. Im Deutschen bildest du sie, indem du -ter an die Zahl anhängst (z. B. vierter, fünfter, sechster).
Im Englischen hängt man in der Regel *-th* an (z. B. *fourth, fifth, sixth*). Dabei ändert sich in einigen Fällen die Schreibweise der Zahl.
First, second und *third* haben andere Endungen, die auch für zusammengesetzte Zahlen gelten (*thirty-first, forty-second, fifty-third*).

41 Das Datum The date

Man schreibt:	Man spricht:
31st December oder December 31st	"The thirty-first of December" oder "December the thirty-first"

Unit 5 Step C

42 Die Uhrzeit The time

It's 5 o'clock – time for tea! (fünf Uhr)
It's half past 8. Jenny is going to school. (halb neun)
It's 3 minutes to 9. Mr Dixon is late. (drei Minuten vor neun)

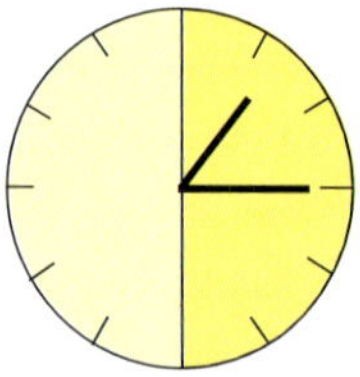

quarter past

quarter to

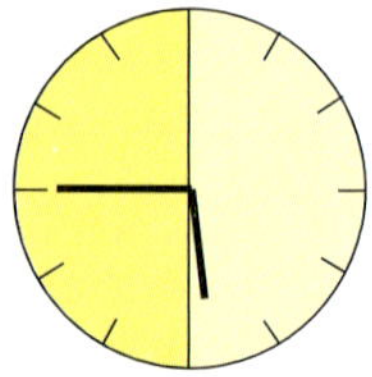

Im Englischen benutzt man *past* bei Zeitangaben für die ersten 30 Minuten nach der vollen Stunde, z. B.:
5.05 = *five past five*
5.10 = *ten past five*
5.15 = *quarter past five*
5.30 = *half past five* (halb sechs)

Nach *half past* zählt man zur nächsten Stunde hin:

5.35 = *twenty-five to six*
5.45 = *quarter to six*
5.55 = *five to six*

o'clock wird nur bei vollen Stunden verwendet: *5 o'clock*, *8 o'clock* etc.

Bei Fünferzahlen (5, 10, 15 usw.) fehlt gewöhnlich das Wort *minutes.* Bei anderen Minutenangaben musst du *minutes* hinzufügen, z. B.:
5.16 = *sixteen minutes past five*
5.48 = *twelve minutes to six*

43 Der bestimmte Artikel
The definite article

Während es im Deutschen **der, die** und **das** gibt, wird im Englischen immer *the* verwendet (also für männliche und weibliche Personen und für Sachen im Singular und im Plural).

the [ðə]	the [ði:]
the banana	the apple
the tidy room	the untidy room
the unit	
the uniform	

The kann man [ðə] oder [ði:] aussprechen.
Die Aussprache von *the* richtet sich nach der Aussprache des Anfangslauts des folgenden Wortes.
Das Wort *uniform* beginnt zwar mit einem Vokal, wird aber [ju:nɪfɔ:m] ausgesprochen.
In diesem Fall wird *the* als [ðə] ausgesprochen.
Vor allen anderen Vokalen wird es zu [ði:].

Das Gleiche gilt auch für *a* und *an* (s. Punkt 20).
Es heißt a**n** **u**ncle [ən 'ʌŋkl], aber **a** **u**nit [ə 'ju:nɪt].

Unit 6

Unit 6 Step B

44 Der of-Genitiv The of-genitive

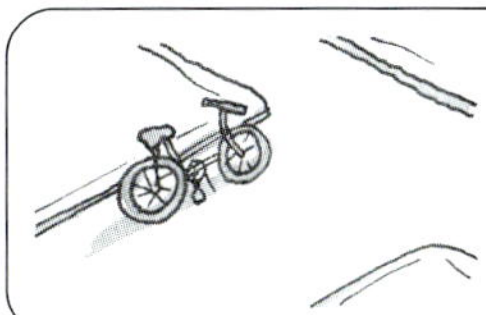

There is a bike at the **end of the road.**

It is **Robert's** bike.

Monday is the first **day of the week.**

Jenny's birthday is on Monday.

Der of-Genitiv gibt an, welcher *Sache* etwas zugeordnet ist. Der s-Genitiv gibt an, welcher *Person* oder welchen *Personen* etwas gehört oder zugeordnet ist (siehe auch Punkt 32).

Unit 7

Unit 7 Step B

45 Die einfache Form des Präsens The simple present

Auf einen Blick

I	play	football.
You	play	badminton.
He	play**s**	tennis.
She	play**s**	tennis, too.
The dog	play**s**	with the balloon.
We	play	cricket at school.
You	play	football.
They	play	in a team.

Bei *I, you, we* und *they* hat die einfache Form des Präsens die gleiche Form wie der Infinitiv (ohne *to*).

Bei *he, she, it* wird ein -*s* angehängt.

Die Aussprache und Schreibung der Verben nach *he, she, it* (3. Person Singular) folgen den gleichen Regeln wie die Pluralform der Substantive (vergleiche mit Punkt 14).

Es gibt aber Besonderheiten:

I go [gəʊ] – she goes [gəʊz]

I do [du:] – he does [dʌz]

I say [seɪ] – she says [sez]

Das *simple present* benutzt man, um über Gewohnheiten zu sprechen.
Außerdem wird es verwendet, um Geschichten zu erzählen, in denen eine Sache nach der anderen passiert.

Beispiel: It is Saturday morning.
First, Simon **goes** into the kitchen. Then he **comes** into the living-room with his cornflakes. After that he **reads** his comic. Then he **goes** to bed again.

46 Die Wortstellung in Aussagesätzen Word order in statements

Subjekt	Verb	Objekt
David	plays	the guitar.
Becky	has got	a computer.
We	are making	a cake.
They	can repair	the bike.

Die Wortstellung im englischen Aussagesatz lautet:

Subjekt – Verb – Objekt (**S** – **V** – **O**).

Im Gegensatz zum Deutschen kann man diese Reihenfolge nicht umstellen.

Auch Zeitangaben wie zum Beispiel *every morning, every day* ändern die Reihenfolge nicht. Sie stehen am Anfang oder am Ende des Satzes. Beispiel:

	S	V	O	
	Simon	plays	football	every week.
Every week	Simon	plays	football.	

Vergleiche mit dem Deutschen:
Simon spielt jede Woche Fußball.
Jede Woche spielt Simon Fußball.

47 Adverbien der Häufigkeit
Adverbs of frequency

Subjekt	Adverb	Verb	Objekt
Robert	sometimes	reads	comics.
Jenny	often	writes	letters.
Kim and Sarah	never	do	the washing-up.
Mr Penrose	always	makes	tea.

Beim *simple present* stellst du die Adverbien der Häufigkeit (zum Beispiel *sometimes, often, never, always*) meistens zwischen Subjekt und Verb. Verb und Objekt bilden nämlich eine feste Einheit, und man darf keine anderen Satzteile dazwischenstellen.

Vergleiche mit dem Deutschen: Mr Penrose always makes the breakfast.
Mr Penrose macht immer das Frühstück.

Unit 7 Step C

48 Mengenangaben mit 'of' Expressions of quantity with 'of'

a	bottle	of	lemonade	eine Flasche Limonade
two	bars	of	chocolate	zwei Tafeln Schokolade
a	pound	of	bananas	ein Pfund Bananen
one	packet	of	cornflakes	eine Packung Cornflakes

Mengenangaben werden im Englischen mit Hilfe des Wortes *of* gemacht.

Unit 8

Unit 8 Step B

49 Verneinte Sätze mit 'do' Negative sentences with 'do'

	Hilfsverb	Vollverb		Hilfsverb	Vollverb	
I	can	speak	German, but I	can't	speak	Turkish.
I		like	ice cream, but I	don't	like	milk.

Wenn du etwas verneinen willst, brauchst du dafür meistens ein Hilfsverb (z. B. *can*) und ein Vollverb (z. B. *speak*) im Infinitiv. Gibt es im Aussagesatz kein Hilfsverb (zum Beispiel *I like ice cream*), so musst du bei der Verneinung *don't* (= *do* + *not*, verkürzt zu *n't*) verwenden.

50 Fragen und Kurzantworten mit 'do'
Questions and short answers with 'do'

You can play the guitar.

They read comics.

Can you play the guitar?

Do they read comics?

Wenn du eine Frage bilden willst und kein Hilfsverb im Aussagesatz hast, setzt du das Hilfsverb *do* ein. Kurzantworten auf Fragen mit *do* sind *Yes, I do.* oder *No, I don't.*

Beispiel: *Do you like ice cream? – Yes, I do./No, I don't.*

Do und *don't* benutzt du bei den Personalpronomen *I, you, we, they.*

Unit 8 Step C

51 Der verneinte Imperativ The negative imperative

Wenn du jemandem sagen willst, dass er oder sie etwas nicht machen soll, benutzt du *don't* + Vollverb im Infinitiv (= verneinte Befehlsform oder verneinter Imperativ).

Don't make a noise.	Mach/Macht/Machen Sie keinen Lärm.
Don't go in.	Geh/Geht/Gehen Sie nicht hinein.

Die Form des verneinten Imperativs ist im Englischen immer dieselbe, ganz gleich, ob eine oder mehrere Personen angesprochen werden.

Unit 9

Unit 9 Step B

52 Verneinte Sätze mit 'doesn't' Negative sentences with 'doesn't'

	Hilfsverb	Vollverb	
Mrs Penrose		**works**	for a computer firm.
Mr Penrose	doesn't	work	for a computer firm. He works at home.

Du kennst die Verneinung mit dem Hilfsverb *do* schon aus Unit 8, z. B. *I don't like ice cream.*
Sie setzt sich zusammen aus *don't* + Vollverb im Infinitiv.
In der dritten Person Singular (bei *he, she, it*) heißt die Form von *do: does.*
Für die Verneinung musst du also *does not* = *doesn't* [dʌznt] verwenden.

She works.
↓
She doesn't work.

53 Fragen und Kurzantworten mit 'does' Questions and short answers with 'does'

Hilfsverb	Subjekt	Vollverb	
Does	Mark	like	ice cream? Yes, he does.
Does	Maxi	like	chocolate? No, she doesn't.

Fragen und Kurzantworten in der dritten Person Singular bildest du genauso wie für die anderen Personen (z. B. *Do you like chocolate?* Siehe Punkt 50). Du musst aber die Form *does* statt *do* nehmen.

54 Fragen mit Fragewörtern und 'do'/'does'

Questions with question words and 'do'/'does'

Fragewort	Hilfsverb	Subjekt	Vollverb	
What	does	Mrs Penrose	do?	She works for a computer firm.
Where	do	the Penroses	live?	In Arndale Road.
When	do	the Penroses	get up?	At half past seven.
How	does	Mark	get to nursery school?	He walks with his father.
Why	does	Mr Penrose	walk with him?	Because Mark is only four.

Du stellst das Fragewort an den Anfang der Frage.
Die anderen Wörter stehen in derselben Reihenfolge wie bei den Fragen unter Punkt 53.

55 'do'/'does' in Fragen, Kurzantworten und verneinten Sätzen

'do'/'does' in questions, short answers and negative sentences

Auf einen Blick

	Do you like fish?	Yes, I do, but I don't like fish fingers.
	Does Mark go to school?	No, he doesn't, but he goes to nursery school.
	Do the Dixons live in Arndale Road?	No, they don't. They live in Larwood Grove.
Where	does Jenny live?	She lives in Nottingham now.
What	do the dogs eat?	They eat dog biscuits.

Unit 10

Unit 10 Step B

56 Gegenüberstellung: Present Progressive – Simple Present

contrast: present progressive – simple present

Mrs Richards feeds the hens every day. Jack often drives the tractor.

= present progressive

= simple present

Das Präsens wird im Englischen durch zwei verschiedene Formen ausgedrückt:
present progressive und *simple present.*

Wenn du sagen willst, was jemand gerade macht, benutzt du das *present progressive.* Dabei kommen oft Signalwörter wie zum Beispiel *just, now* vor.
Wenn du über Gewohnheiten sprechen willst, benutzt du das *simple present,* oft mit Signalwörtern wie *always, sometimes, often, never, every day, every morning* usw.
Außerdem kann man das *simple present* verwenden, um Geschichten zu erzählen.
Auch hier gibt es typische Signalwörter wie *first, then, after that.* Vergleiche mit den Punkten 35, 39 und 45.

57 Das Fragewort 'who' als Subjekt und Objekt
The question word 'who' as subject and object

Mit *who* kann man nach dem Subjekt oder nach dem Objekt im Satz fragen.

Objekt	Hilfsverb	Subjekt	Vollverb	Objekt	
		David	asks	Grandpa.	
		Who	asks	Grandpa?	– David.
Who	does	David	ask?		– He asks Grandpa.

Wenn du mit *who* nach dem Subjekt fragst, kommt das Verb direkt nach *who.*
Wenn du mit *who* nach dem Objekt fragst, musst du ein Hilfsverb (zum Beispiel *does*) verwenden. Nach dem Hilfsverb stehen Subjekt und Vollverb.

Auf einen Blick

Objekt	Hilfsverb	Subjekt	Hilfsverb	Vollverb	Objekt	
		Who		asks	Mrs Croft?	Wer fragt Mrs Croft?
		Who	can	phone	the vet?	Wer kann den Tierarzt anrufen?
		Who	must	call	the police?	Wer muss die Polizei rufen?
Who	does	she		ask?		Wen fragt sie?
Who	must	the boys		phone?		Wen müssen die Jungen anrufen?
Who	can	the police		help?		Wem kann die Polizei helfen?

Unit 10 Step C

58 Mengenangaben mit 'How much', 'How many' und 'not much', 'not many'
Expressions of quantity with 'How much', 'How many', and 'not much', 'not many'

How much milk do you want? – Not much.	How many biscuits do you want? – Not many. Only two or three.

Bei Mengenangaben verwendet man *how much* oder *how many* in Fragen, *not much* oder *not many* in negativen Sätzen. Dabei werden *how much* und *not much* für nicht zählbare Mengen verwendet. *How many* und *not many* dagegen werden für zählbare Mengen verwendet.

⟨Grammar list⟩

Deutsch/Lateinisch	*Englisch*	*Englisches Beispiel*	*Punkt in der Grammatik*
Adverb	adverb		
Adverb der Häufigkeit	adverb of frequency	sometimes, often, etc.	**47**
Apostroph (Auslassungszeichen)	apostrophe	That's Sarah.	**2**
Artikel	article		
bestimmter Artikel	definite article	the [ðə, ðiː]	**43**
unbestimmter Artikel	indefinite article	a, an	**20**
Aussagesatz	statement	Robert is from London.	**12**
Befehlsform (Imperativ)	imperative	Sit down.	
verneinte Befehlsform	negative imperative	Don't eat that.	**51**
Datum	date	1st April	**41**
Einzahl (Singular)	singular	one house	**14**
Fragen und Kurzantworten	questions and short answers		
mit 'to be'	with 'to be'	Are you …? Yes, I am.	**25**
mit 'can'	with 'can'	Can she …? Yes, she can.	**30**
mit 'do'	with 'do'	Do you …? Yes, I do.	**50, 53**
mit 'have/has got'	with 'have/has got'	Have you …? No, I haven't.	**26**
mit der Verlaufsform des Präsens	with the present progressive	Are you reading? No, I'm not.	**37**
Fragesatz → Gegenwart	question		
Fragewort	question word	Where? What? Who? etc.	**31**
Fürwort	pronoun		
besitzanzeigendes Fürwort	possessive determiner	my, your, his, her, etc.	**7, 15, 16**
hinweisendes Fürwort	demonstrative pronoun	this, that, these, those	**21, 27**
persönliches Fürwort	personal pronoun	I, you, she, he, etc.	**11**
Gegenwart (Präsens)	present tense		
einfache Form	simple present	I go to the shops.	**45**
einfache Form (Frage und Verneinung)	simple present (question and negation)	Do you play tennis? She doesn't play tennis.	**50** **52**
Verlaufsform	present progressive	I'm going to the shops.	**35, 39**
Genitiv	genitive		
of-Genitiv	of-genitive	the end of the road	**44**
s-Genitiv	s-genitive	Sarah's bike	**32**
Grundform (Infinitiv)	infinitive	to be	**11**

Grammar list

Deutsch/Lateinisch	*Englisch*	*Englisches Beispiel*	*Punkt in der Grammatik*
Hauptwort (Substantiv)	noun	cat, man, school, etc.	**14**
Hilfsverb	modal auxiliary	can, must	**29, 34**
Kurzantwort	short answer	Yes, I am.	**25**
Kurzform	short form	he's, she's, etc.	**11**
Langform	long form	he is, she is, etc.	**11**
Mehrzahl (Plural)	plural	four houses	**14**
Mitlaut (Konsonant)	consonant	b, k, l, p, etc.	**14**
Mengenangaben	expressions of quantity		
Mengenangaben mit 'How much', 'How many'		How much sugar do you want?	**58**
Mengenangaben mit 'of'		a packet of biscuits	**48**
Objektform	object form	me, him, her, etc.	**38**
Ordnungszahl	ordinal number	first, second, third, etc.	**40**
Person	person		
dritte Person	third person	he, she, it; they	**2**
Plural → Mehrzahl			
Präposition (Verhältniswort)	preposition	in, on, under, etc.	**10**
Präsens → Gegenwart			
Pronomen → Fürwort			
Satz	sentence	He reads his comic.	**46**
Selbstlaut (Vokal)	vowel	a, e, i, o, u	**14**
Singular → Einzahl			
Subjektform (der Personalpronomen)	subject form	I, you, he, she, etc.	**11**
Uhrzeit	time	It's half past four.	**42**
Verb (Tätigkeitswort)	verb	to go, to play	**46**
Verneinung	negation	It isn't on your desk.	**13**
Wortstellung	word order	He often plays tennis.	**46**

Vocabulary

a) Aufbau des Vokabulars

Im Unterricht erklärt dir deine Lehrerin oder dein Lehrer die neuen Wörter. Du musst sie aber auch lernen. Dabei hilft dir diese Liste der neuen Vokabeln.
In der linken Spalte findest du die englischen Wörter in der Reihenfolge, in der sie in der Unit vorkommen. Dahinter steht die Lautschrift in eckigen Klammern. Sie zeigt, wie das Wort ausgesprochen wird und wie es betont wird. Wie du die Lautschrift lesen musst, steht unten auf dieser Seite.
In der mittleren Spalte stehen Beispielsätze oder kleine Zeichnungen sowie wichtige Hinweise, die dir beim Lernen helfen.
In der rechten Spalte findest du eine deutsche Übersetzung des englischen Wortes. Oft lassen sich aber Wörter aus einer Sprache nicht einfach in die andere übersetzen. Deshalb stehen manchmal mehrere Wörter in der rechten Spalte, die dir zeigen, wie das englische Wort benutzt wird.
Tipps zum Vokabellernen findest du in den Kästchen vor jeder Unit.

b) Abkürzungen und Zeichen

(pl) Plural, Mehrzahl
(sg) Singular, Einzahl

= ist gleich
⟷ ist das Gegenteil von

c) Lautschrift

Wie die englischen Wörter ausgesprochen werden, lernst du im Unterricht. Die Lautschrift im Vokabular hilft dir, die Aussprache und Betonung eines Wortes nachzusehen. Sie benutzt einige normale Buchstaben und einige besondere Zeichen. Die Aussprache der einzelnen Zeichen kannst du dir anhand eines einfachen Wortes merken. Die Betonung eines Wortes wird durch einen Betonungsstrich **vor** der betonten Silbe gezeigt: [ˈ] zeigt den Hauptakzent des Wortes, [ˌ] den Nebenakzent. Der Bindebogen [‿] zeigt, dass zwei Wörter in der Aussprache miteinander verbunden werden.

Konsonanten		**Vokale**		**Doppellaute**	
[ŋ]	morni**ng**	[ɑː]	f**a**ther	[aɪ]	**I**, m**y**
[r]	**r**ed	[ʌ]	b**u**t, **u**nder	[aʊ]	n**ow**, h**ou**se
[s]	cla**ss**	[e]	p**e**n	[eə]	th**ere**, p**air**
[z]	i**s**	[ə]	**a** sist**er**	[eɪ]	n**a**me, th**ey**
[ʒ]	televi**sion**	[ɜː]	g**ir**l	[ɪə]	h**ere**, id**ea**
[dʒ]	**G**ermany, pa**ge**	[æ]	**a**pple	[ɔɪ]	b**oy**
[ʃ]	**sh**e	[ɪ]	**i**t	[əʊ]	**o**ld, hell**o**
[tʃ]	**ch**air, lun**ch**	[iː]	**ea**sy, sh**e**	[ʊə]	**you're**
[ð]	**th**e	[ɒ]	g**o**t, **o**n		
[θ]	**th**anks	[ɔː]	b**a**ll		Alle anderen Zeichen werden genauso ausgesprochen, wie sie im Deutschen geschrieben werden [j, k, ...].
[v]	**v**ideo, ha**v**e	[ʊ]	b**oo**k		
[w]	**w**ord, **o**ne	[uː]	t**oo**, t**wo**		

Vocabulary

Let's start

Mit dem Lernen fängst du an, indem du das Wort, das Beispiel und die deutsche Entsprechung liest. Danach kannst du z.B. die mittlere und die rechte Spalte abdecken und ausprobieren, ob du noch die deutsche Übersetzung zum englischen Wort weißt.
Das geht natürlich auch umgekehrt, indem du versuchst, vom deutschen Begriff aus, dich an das englische Wort zu erinnern.
Auch das Aufschreiben und das laute Vorsagen der englischen Wörter können dir beim Lernen helfen. Mehr darüber steht in den Lerntipps, die vor jeder Unit im Vokabelverzeichnis zu finden sind.

Let's start. [ˌlets ˈstɑːt]		Lasst uns anfangen.

1 In Nottingham

in [ɪn]		in
Nottingham [ˈnɒtɪŋəm]	 Kannst du Nottingham auf der Karte vorne im Buch finden?	*Stadt in Mittelengland*
Hello. [həˈləʊ]		Hallo., Guten Tag.
I'm (= I am) [aɪm]		ich bin
I [aɪ]		ich
Sarah [ˈseərə]	 Hello, I'm *Sarah*.	*weiblicher Vorname*
Robert [ˈrɒbət]	Hello, I'm *Robert*. 	*männlicher Vorname*

2 Hello

ⓐ **Becky** [ˈbekɪ]	Wenn ich mich vorstelle, kann ich sagen: „I'm Monny" oder „My name is Monny". 	*weiblicher Vorname*
My name is … [ˈmaɪ neɪm‿ɪz]		Ich heiße …
my [maɪ]		mein/meine
name [neɪm]	Im Englischen werden innerhalb eines Satzes nur Namen und das kurze Wort *I* groß geschrieben.	Name
is [ɪz]		ist
Burton [ˈbɜːtn]		*Familienname*
Croft [krɒft]		*Familienname*
new [njuː]		neu
yes [jes]		ja
from [frɒm]		aus, von
London [ˈlʌndən]	Robert is from *London*.	*Hauptstadt von Großbritannien*
ⓑ **Woof!** [wʊf]		Wau! *(Hundebellen)*
oh [əʊ]	 Woof, woof.	oh
dog [dɒg]		Hund

Vocabulary

What's your name? [ˌwɒts jɔː ˈneɪm] — Wie heißt du?/Wie heißen Sie?

Man kann nicht immer einfach Wort für Wort übersetzen. Vergleiche: *What's your name?*–Wie heißt du?

what's (= what is) [wɒts] — was ist …

your [jɔː] — dein/deine, Ihr/Ihre

my ⟷ *your*

Maxi [ˈmæksɪ] — *Hundename*

and [ænd] — und

that's (= that is) [ðæts] — das ist

Mini [ˈmɪnɪ] — *Hundename*

1 **Your turn.** [ˈjɔː tɜːn] — Du bist an der Reihe.

Monny [ˈmɒnɪ] — *Name eines Maskottchens*

⟨3⟩ a [ə] — ein/eine

song [sɒŋ] — Lied

Dixon [ˈdɪksn] — *Familienname*

ⓒ **I'm at Haywood School.** [ˈaɪm‿ət ˈheɪwʊd ˈskuːl] — Ich bin an der Haywood-Schule.

at [æt], [ət] — an

at wird [æt] ausgesprochen, wenn es betont wird. Unbetont spricht man es [ət] aus.

Haywood School [ˈheɪwʊd ˈskuːl] — *Name einer Gesamtschule in Nottingham*

school [skuːl] — Schule

Is she … ? [ˈɪz ˈʃiː] — Ist sie … ?

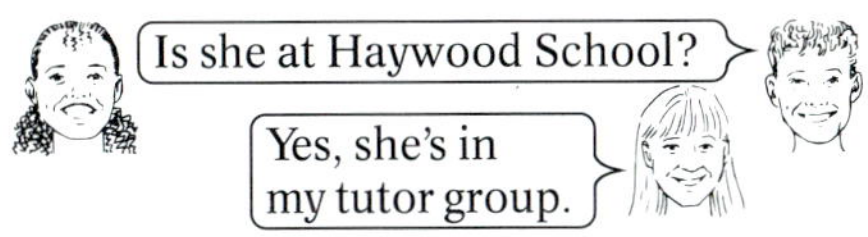

she's (= she is) [ʃiːz] — sie ist

she [ʃiː] — sie

tutor group [ˈtjuːtə ˌgruːp] — Klasse (*in einer englischen Schule*)

tutor [ˈtjuːtə] — Klassenlehrer/in, Betreuungslehrer/in

group [gruːp] — Gruppe

ⓓ **Look.** [lʊk] — Sieh mal./Seht mal.

to **look** [lʊk] — sehen, anschauen

Am vorangestellten Wörtchen *to* kann man erkennen, dass es sich um eine Grundform (Infinitiv) handelt.

David [ˈdeɪvɪd] — *männlicher Vorname*

Penrose [ˈpenrəʊz] — *Familienname*

he's (= he is) [hiːz] — er ist

he [hiː] — er

too [tuː] — auch

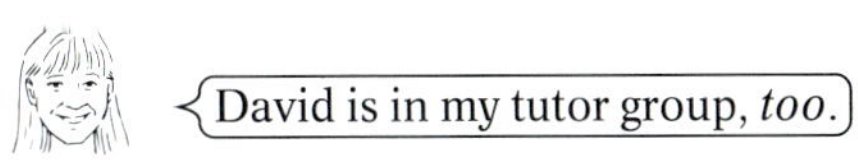

Is he … ? [ˈɪz ˈhiː] — Ist er … ?

nice [naɪs] — nett, schön

a [ə] — ein/eine

friend [frend] — Freund/in

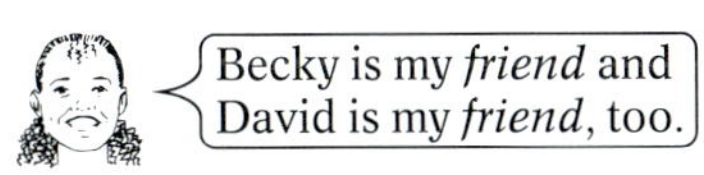

Please, look at page … [ˈpliːz ˌlʊk‿ət peɪdʒ] — Bitte schau/schaut auf Seite …

please [pliːz] — bitte

to **look at** [ˈlʊk‿ət] — anschauen

page [peɪdʒ] — Seite

4 **class** [klɑːs] — Klasse (*in einer deutschen Schule*)

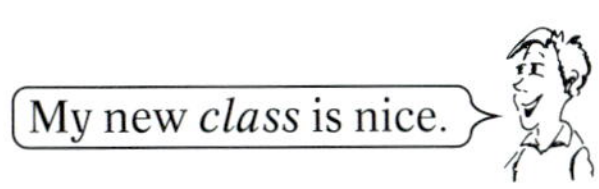

6 **poster** [ˈpəʊstə] — Poster, Plakat

Make a poster. [meɪk‿ə ˈpəʊstə] — Mach/Macht ein Poster.

to **make** [meɪk] — machen

Vocabulary

3 School!

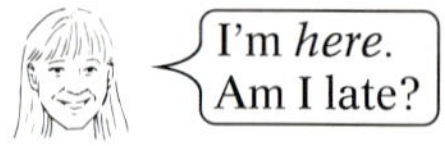

ⓐ	**here** [hɪə]		hier
	Am I … ? ['æm‿aɪ]		Bin ich … ?
	late [leɪt]		spät, zu spät
	Goodbye. [gʊd'baɪ]	Hello. ⟷ *Goodbye.*	Auf Wiedersehen, Tschüs.
	no [nəʊ]	yes ⟷ *no*	nein
	you [juː]	I ⟷ *you*	du, Sie
	crazy ['kreɪzɪ]		verrückt
	bag [bæg]		Tasche

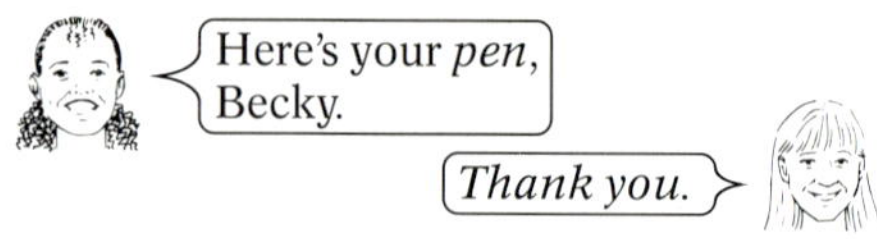

1	**here's (= here is)** [hɪəz]		hier ist
	pen [pen]		Füller
	Thank you. ['θæŋk‿jʊ]		Danke schön.
	Please go on. [ˌpliːz gəʊ‿'ɒn]		Bitte mach/macht weiter.
	to **go on** [gəʊ‿'ɒn]		weitermachen
	book [bʊk]		Buch
	folder ['fəʊldə]		Mappe, Hefter
	pencil case ['pensl keɪs]		Federmäppchen
	pencil ['pensl]		Bleistift
	case [keɪs]		Etui, Hülle
	comic ['kɒmɪk]		Comic
	ball [bɔːl]		Ball
	lunch box ['lʌntʃ bɒks]		*Dose für belegte Brote zum Mittagessen*

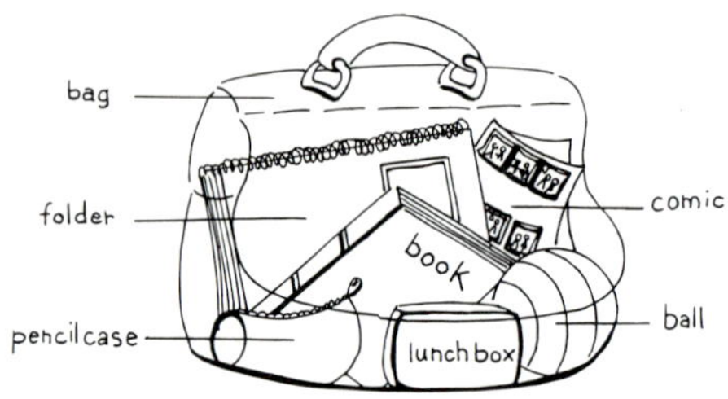

	lunch [lʌntʃ]		Mittagessen
	box [bɒks]		Schachtel, Kiste, Dose
2	**teacher** ['tiːtʃə]	That's my *teacher*. She's my tutor, too.	Lehrer/in
	What's that in English? [ˌwɒts ðæt‿ɪn‿'ɪŋglɪʃ]		Wie heißt das auf Englisch?
	English ['ɪŋglɪʃ]	Wörter für Staatsangehörigkeit werden immer groß geschrieben.	englisch, Englisch
	biro ['baɪrəʊ]		Kugelschreiber
4	**sound practice** ['saʊnd ˌpræktɪs]		Ausspracheübung
	practice ['præktɪs]		Übung, Training
	Listen. ['lɪsn]		Hör/Hört zu.
	to **listen** ['lɪsn]		zuhören
	Say. [seɪ]		Sag/Sagt es.
	to **say** [seɪ]		sagen

ⓑ	**twelve** [twelv]	12	zwölf
	Are you … ? [ɑː juː]	*Are you* twelve? – No, I'm *eleven*.	Bist du … ?/Sind Sie … ?
	eleven [ɪ'levn]	11	elf
	How old are you? [haʊ‿'əʊld‿ɑː ˌjuː]	*How old are you?* – I'm twelve.	Wie alt bist du?
	how [haʊ]		wie
	old [əʊld]		alt
	not [nɒt]		nicht
	Sorry! ['sɒrɪ]		Entschuldigung./Tut mir Leid.
	you're (= you are) [jʊə]		du bist/Sie sind
	ten [ten]	10	zehn
	girl [gɜːl]		Mädchen

Vocabulary

4 Tutor group 7MD

Das Vokabellernen geht einfacher, wenn du dir eine Vokabelkartei machst. Dazu brauchst du einen Karton und viele Kärtchen aus dünner Pappe oder dickem Papier. Den Karton unterteilst du mit einer Pappwand quer in zwei Fächer.
Wenn ihr Vokabeln zum Lernen aufhabt, schreibst du das englische Wort auf die eine Seite der Karteikarte und die deutsche Übersetzung auf die Rückseite.
Dann stellst du die Karten in den vorderen Teil deines Kartons. Später überprüfst du beim Durchblättern der Karten, ob du die Übersetzung des Wortes noch weißt und zwar deutsch – englisch und englisch – deutsch. Zwischendurch solltest du die Reihenfolge der Karten neu mischen. Wenn du ganz sicher bist, dass du ein Wort kannst, stellst du die Karte in das hintere Fach.

ⓐ **seven** [sevn]	7	sieben
7MD [ˌsevn emˈdiː]		*Name der Klasse mit den Anfangsbuchstaben ihrer Lehrerin Margaret Dane*
your *(pl)* [jɔː]		euer/eure; Ihr/Ihre
her [hɜː]	That's my teacher. I'm in *her* tutor group.	ihr/ihre
Mrs [ˈmɪsɪz]		Frau *(Anrede für verheiratete Frauen)*
Dane [deɪn]		*Familienname*
Good morning. [gʊd ˈmɔːnɪŋ]		Guten Morgen.
good [gʊd]		gut
morning [ˈmɔːnɪŋ]		Morgen
the [ðə]		der/die/das
boy [bɔɪ]		Junge
his [hɪz]		sein/seine
ⓑ **you're (= you are)** *(pl)* [jʊə]		ihr seid/Sie sind
you [juː]		ihr/Sie
right [raɪt]		richtig
we're (= we are) [wɪə]		wir sind
we [wiː]		wir
teachers *(pl)* [ˈtiːtʃəz]		Lehrer/innen
OK [əʊˈkeɪ]		OK, in Ordnung
they're (= they are) [ðeə]		sie sind
they [ðeɪ]		sie *(Pl)*
Mr [ˈmɪstə]		Herr *(Anrede für Männer)*
Cooper [ˈkuːpə]		*Familienname*
girls and boys [ˌgɜːlz‿n ˈbɔɪz]		Mädchen und Jungen
German [ˈdʒɜːmən]	Mr Cooper is a *German* teacher.	deutsch, Deutsch

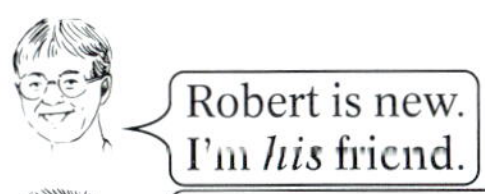

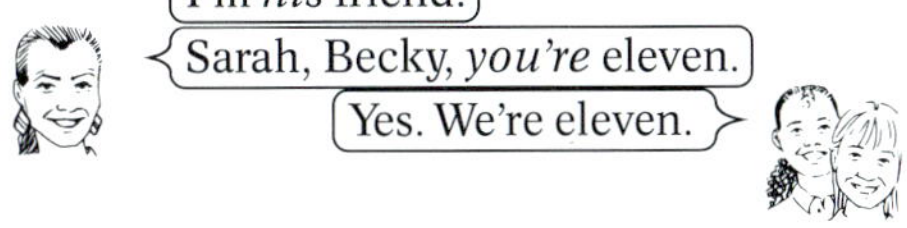

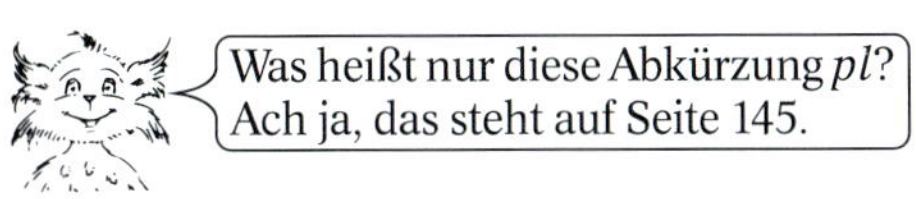

Vocabulary

2 **answer** ['ɑːnsə] — Antwort
3 **questions** *(pl)* ['kwestʃənz] — Fragen
Greenwood ['griːnwʊd] — *Name einer Schule*

ⓒ **Hey!** [heɪ] — He!
where [weə] — wo
on [ɒn] — auf
desk [desk] — Schreibtisch, Pult
under ['ʌndə] — unter
on ⟷ *under*
chair [tʃeə] — Stuhl
Aaah! [ɑː] — Oh! Huch!
it's (= it is) [ɪts] — es ist, er ist, sie ist
it [ɪt] — es/er/sie

Sneaky Snake ['sniːkɪ ˌsneɪk] — *Name eines Spielzeugs*
snake [sneɪk] — Schlange
4 **where's (= where is)** [weəz] — wo ist

5 **game** [geɪm] — Spiel
to **play** [pleɪ] — spielen
Is it … ? [ɪs‿ɪt] — Ist es … ?

5 Haywood School

Du behältst die neuen Wörter besser, wenn du sie dir nur 5 Minuten anschaust, aber dafür nach einer halben Stunde wiederholst und am Ende deiner Hausaufgaben noch einmal 5 Minuten überprüfst.

ⓐ **picture** ['pɪktʃə] — Bild
year [jɪə] — Jahr, Jahrgang
or [ɔː] — oder

in the morning [ɪn ðə 'mɔːnɪŋ] — morgens, am Vormittag
in the afternoon [ɪn ðiː‿ɑːftə'nuːn] — nachmittags, am Nachmittag
the [ðiː] — der/die/das
afternoon [ɑːftə'nuːn] — Nachmittag
morning ⟷ *afternoon*

1 **sentences** *(pl)* ['sentənsɪz] — Sätze
3 **Let's learn words.** [ˌlets lɜːn 'wɜːdz] — Lasst uns Wörter lernen.

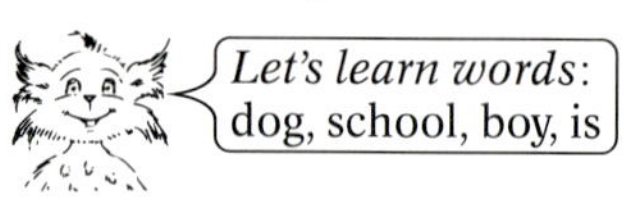

Let's [lets] — Lasst uns
to **learn** [lɜːn] — lernen
word [wɜːd] — Wort
easy ['iːzɪ] — einfach, leicht
pair [peə] — Paar
Maxi and Mini are a crazy *pair*!
Write the pairs in your folder. [raɪt ðə 'peəz‿ɪn jɔː 'fəʊldə] — Schreibt die Paare in eure Mappe.

to **write** [raɪt]		schreiben
question ['kwestʃən]	answer ←→ *question*	Frage
	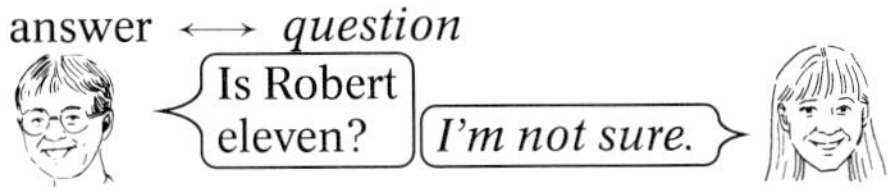	
(b) **I'm not sure.** [aɪm nɒt 'ʃɔː]		Ich bin mir nicht sicher.
sure [ʃɔː]		sicher
she isn't (= she is not) [ʃiː‿'ɪznt]	she is ←→ *she isn't*	sie ist nicht
they aren't (= they are not) [ðeɪ‿'ɑːnt]	they are ←→ *they aren't*	sie sind nicht
playground ['pleɪgraʊnd]		Schulhof, Spielplatz
Hmm.		Hm./Tja.
chocolate ['tʃɒklət]		Schokolade
5 to **find** [faɪnd]		finden
6 **listening practice** ['lɪsnɪŋ ˌpræktɪs]		Hörverstehensübung

6 The lesson

lesson [lesn]	My English *lesson* is in the morning.	Unterrichtsstunde
classroom ['klɑːsrʊm]		Klassenzimmer
Dixon ['dɪksn]		*Familienname*
funny ['fʌnɪ]		lustig, komisch
Sit down. [sɪt 'daʊn]		Setz dich./Setzt euch.
to **sit down** [sɪt 'daʊn]		sich hinsetzen
now [naʊ]		jetzt, nun
homework ['həʊmwɜːk]		Hausaufgaben
to **bring** [brɪŋ]		bringen
quiet ['kwaɪət]	Please *be quiet*!	still, ruhig
Good afternoon. [gʊd ˌɑːftə'nuːn]	Good morning. ←→ *Good afternoon.*	Guten Tag. (*Anrede am Nachmittag*)
1 **wrong** [rɒŋ]	right ←→ *wrong*	falsch
to **correct** [kə'rekt]		korrigieren, verbessern

7 Let's check

to **check** [tʃek]		überprüfen, kontrollieren

Unit 1 At home with the Burtons

Auch die „alten" Wörter solltest du dir noch mal vornehmen.

Hast du schon eine Vokabelkartei angelegt? Dann sind die Karten bestimmt schon alle im hinteren Fach.
Aber denk daran: Alle paar Wochen solltest du auch diese Karten einmal durchschauen. Wenn du ein Wort nicht mehr kannst, wandert die Karte wieder ins vordere Fach zurück und wird mit den neuen Wörtern wiederholt.
(Auf S. 164 in Unit 5 findest du einen Vorschlag für ein Spiel mit diesen Karteikärtchen.)

unit [ˈjuːnɪt] — Lektion, Kapitel
At home with the Burtons. [ət ˈhəʊm wɪð‿ðə ˌbɜːtnz] — Zu Hause bei den Burtons.
at home [ət ˈhəʊm] — zu Hause
with [wɪð] — bei, mit

Step A **Superdogs**

ⓐ **step** [step] — Schritt, Stufe
superdogs *(pl)* [ˈsuːpədɒgz] — Superhunde
brother [ˈbrʌðə] — Bruder
one [wʌn] — ein/eine/eins
Simon [ˈsaɪmən] — *männl. Vorname*
clever [ˈklevə] — intelligent, klug
two [tʊː] — zwei
Wow! [waʊ] — *Ausruf*

That's Becky and her brother *Simon*.

one [wʌn]	eins	**five** [faɪv]	fünf	**nine** [naɪn]	neun
two [tuː]	zwei	**six** [sɪks]	sechs	**ten** [ten]	zehn
three [θriː]	drei	**seven** [ˈsevn]	sieben	**eleven** [ɪˈlevn]	elf
four [fɔː]	vier	**eight** [eɪt]	acht	**twelve** [twelv]	zwölf

1 **example** [ɪgˈzɑːmpl] — Beispiel
2 **for Superkids** [fə ˈsuːpəkɪdz] — für Superkinder
for [fɔː], [fə] — für

Weißt du noch? Kurze Wörter wie *at* und *for* werden [ət], [fə] ausgesprochen, wenn sie unbetont sind.

ⓑ **biscuit** [ˈbɪskɪt] — Keks
car [kɑː] — Auto
but [bʌt] — aber

The *biscuits* are for Becky.

Step B **The Burtons**

kitchen [ˈkɪtʃɪn] — Becky and Simon are in the *kitchen*. — Küche
their [ðeə] — ihr/ihre *(Pl)*
mother [ˈmʌðə] — Their *mother* is in the garden. — Mutter
father [ˈfɑːðə] — mother ⟷ *father* — Vater

Vocabulary

hungry ['hʌŋgrɪ] — hungrig
our ['aʊə] — unser/unsere
Thanks! [θæŋks] — Danke!
dog biscuit ['dɒg ˌbɪskɪt] — Hundekuchen

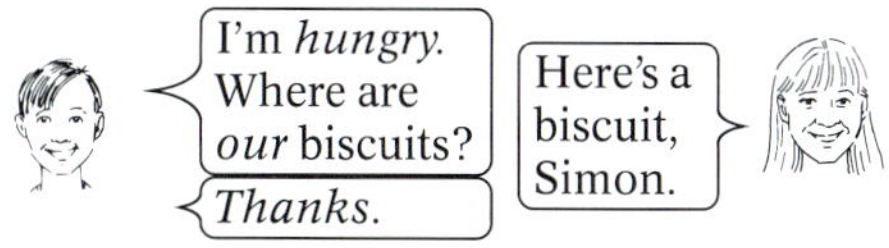

Dad [dæd] — Vati, Papa

Dad wird nur groß geschrieben, wenn das Wort als Name verwendet wird.

⟨2⟩ Say it to the beat. [ˌseɪ‿ɪt tə ðə 'bi:t] — Sag/t es im Rhythmus.

Clap your hands. [ˌklæp jɔ: 'hændz] — Klatsch/t mit den Händen.
to clap [klæp] — klatschen
hand [hænd] — Hand
Stamp your feet. [ˌstæmp jɔ: 'fi:t] — Stampf/t mit deinen/euren Füßen.
to stamp [stæmp] — stampfen
feet *(pl)* [fi:t] — Füße
together [tə'geðə] — zusammen

all the way [ˌɔ:l ðə 'weɪ] — *hier:* den ganzen Weg

Step B **Two rooms**

ⓐ **room** [ru:m] — Raum, Zimmer
Simon has got ... ['saɪmən hæz gɒt] — Simon hat ...
football ['fʊtbɔ:l] — Fußball
skateboard ['skeɪtbɔ:d] — Skateboard
radio ['reɪdɪəʊ] — Radio
CD player [si: 'di: pleɪə] — CD-Spieler
CD [si: 'di:] — CD

ⓑ **computer** [kəm'pju:tə] — Computer
she hasn't got ... [ʃi: 'hæznt gɒt] — sie hat nicht/kein ...

\+ she has got ... — *she hasn't got ...*

Step B **Good idea!**

ⓐ **idea** [aɪ'dɪə] — Idee
I haven't got ... [aɪ 'hævnt gɒt] — ich habe nicht/kein ...
Have you got ... ? ['hæv ju: gɒt] — Hast du ... ?

Have you got an idea? – Yes, *I've got* a good idea.

I've got ... ['aɪv gɒt] — Ich habe ...
Oops! [u:ps] — Hoppla!
garden ['gɑ:dən] — Garten

8 **sister** ['sɪstə] — Schwester
to **work** [wɜ:k] — arbeiten
partner ['pɑ:tnə] — Partner/in

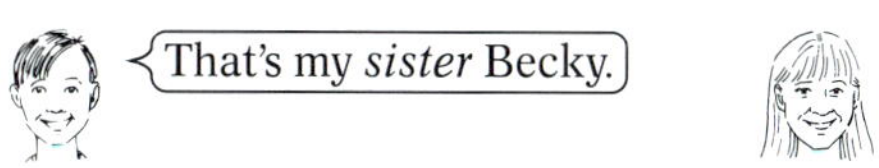

Vocabulary

ⓑ **big** [bɪg] — groß
tree [triː] — Baum

bad [bæd] — schlimm, schlecht
hole [həʊl] — Loch
pond [pɒnd] — Teich

to **ask** [ɑːsk] — fragen

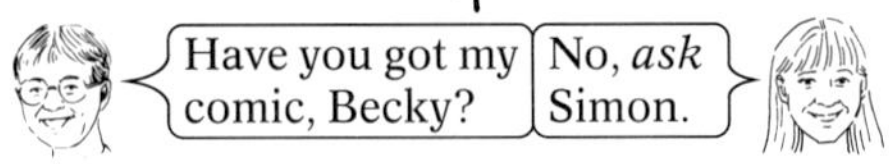

Mum [mʌm] — Dad ⟷ *Mum* — Mama, Mutti

Looking at the UK: Nottingham

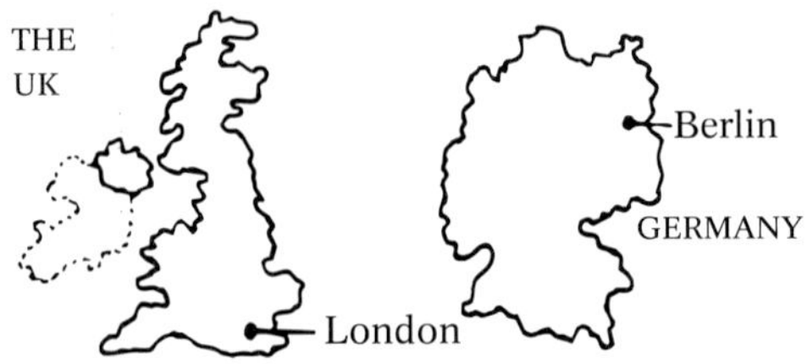

Looking at the UK [ˌlʊkɪŋ‿ət ðə juː ˈkeɪ] — Ein Blick auf das Vereinigte Königreich!
The UK (= The United Kingdom) [juː ˈkeɪ], [juːˈnaɪtɪd ˈkɪŋdəm] — Vereinigtes Königreich von Großbritannien und Nordirland
this [ðɪs] — dies/dieser/diese/dieses
England [ˈɪŋglənd] — England
Germany [ˈdʒɜːmənɪ] — Deutschland
Berlin [bɜːˈlɪn] — Berlin
Sherwood [ˈʃɜːwʊd] — *Bezirk in Nottingham*
Arndale Road [ˈɑːndeɪl ˈrəʊd] — *Straße in Nottingham*
road (= Rd.) [rəʊd] — Straße
1 **house** [haʊs] — Haus
2 **home** [həʊm] — Heim, Zuhause
flat [flæt] — The teacher has got three rooms in her *flat*. — Wohnung

Step C **Look!**

ⓐ **there** [ðeə] — Becky is in the garden. Simon is *there*, too. — da, dort
an [ən] — ein/eine
apple [ˈæpl] — Apfel

egg [eg] — Ei
broken [ˈbrəʊkən] — kaputt, zerbrochen

2 **Word power** [ˈwɜːd ˌpaʊə] — Die Kraft der Wörter

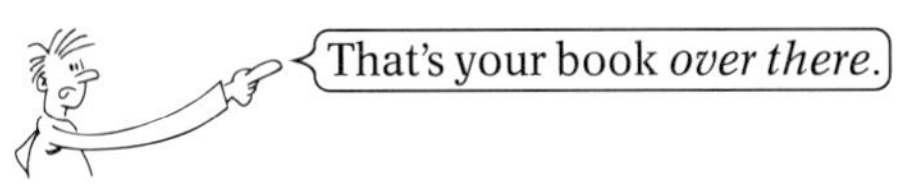

ⓑ **bed** [bed] — Bett
over there [əʊvə ˈðeə] — da drüben, dort

4 **role play** [ˈrəʊl pleɪ] — Rollenspiel
together [təˈgeðə] — zusammen
6 **What is it?** [wɒt‿ˈɪz ɪt] — Was gibt's?
7 **telephone** [ˈtelɪfəʊn] — Telefon
number [ˈnʌmbə] — Nummer, Zahl
o [əʊ] — *hier:* null (*bei Telefonnummern*)
double three [ˈdʌbl θriː] — *hier:* zweimal die 3
8 **that's** [ðæts] — *hier:* also (*wenn man etwas zum besseren Verständnis wiederholt*)

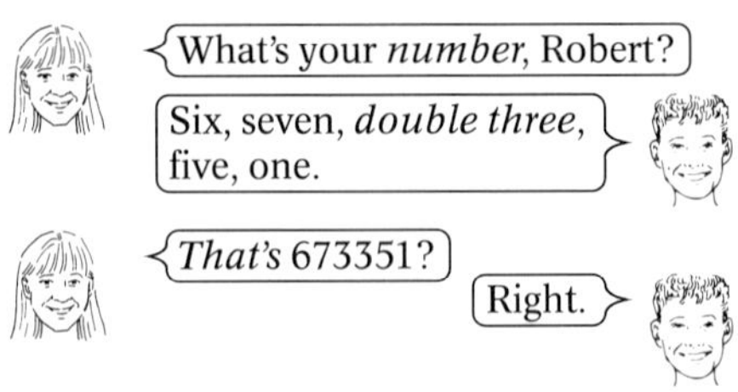

Margaret [ˈmɑːgrɪt] — *weibl. Vorname*
Tim [tɪm] — *männl. Vorname*

Step D **The frog**

	frog [frɒg]		Frosch
	bike [baɪk]		Fahrrad
	Arnot Hill Park [ˌɑːnət hɪl ˈpɑːk]		*Park in Nottingham*
	park [pɑːk]		Park
	Hi! [haɪ]		Hallo!
	table [ˈteɪbl]		Tisch
	ready [ˈredɪ]		fertig, bereit
	not … yet [nɒt … jet]	The pond is*n't* ready *yet*.	noch nicht
	poor [pɔː]		arm
	more [mɔː]	An apple. – Here are *more* apples.	mehr, weitere
⟨2⟩	At the door. [ət ðə ˈdɔː]		An der Tür.
	door [dɔː]		Tür
	to come in [kʌm‿ˈɪn]		hereinkommen
5	**thing** [θɪŋ]	*things:* ball ~~dog~~ bag ~~girl~~ bike ~~frog~~	Ding, Sache

Step E **Let's check**

1	to **put in** [ˈpʊt‿ɪn]		einsetzen, hineintun

Unit 2 The Dixons

Wörter lernen sich einfacher und schneller, wenn man sie sich päckchenweise vornimmt. Am besten lernt man nur 10–15 Wörter in einem Päckchen.

Step A **Sarah and her family**

ⓐ	**family** [ˈfæməlɪ]	The Dixons are a *family.*	Familie
	man [mæn]	Mr Burton is a *man*. Simon is a boy.	Mann
	men *(pl)* [men]		Männer
	Eddy [ˈedɪ]		*männl. Vorname*
	bank clerk [ˈbæŋk‿klɑːk]		Bankangestellte/r
	bank [bæŋk]		Bank
	clerk [klɑːk]		Büroangestellte/r
	woman [ˈwʊmən]	man ⟷ *woman*	Frau
	women *(pl)* [ˈwɪmɪn]		Frauen
	Janet [ˈdʒænɪt]		*weibl. Vorname*

	vet's assistant ['vets‿ə'sɪstənt]		Tierarzthelfer/in
	vet [vet]		Tierarzt/Tierärztin
	assistant [ə'sɪstənt]		Helfer/in, Assistent/in
	cat [kæt]		Katze
	Tabby ['tæbɪ]		*Name einer Katze*
	Kim [kɪm]		*weibl. Vorname*
	child [tʃaɪld]		Kind
	children *(pl)* ['tʃɪldrən]	Becky and Simon are *children*.	Kinder
ⓑ	**red** [red]		rot
	black [blæk]		schwarz
	green [gri:n]		grün
	yellow ['jeləʊ]		gelb
	blue [blu:]		blau
	brown [braʊn]		braun
	crayon ['kreɪən]		Buntstift
	colour ['kʌlə]		Farbe
	Here you are. ['hɪə jʊ‿ˌɑ:]		Hier, bitte schön.
3	to **draw** [drɔ:]	Let's *draw* frogs with our green crayons.	zeichnen

Step B **What a crazy family!**

ⓐ	**What a ...** ['wɒt‿ə]		Was für ein/e ...
	knife [naɪf]		Messer (*Sg*)
	knives *(pl)* [naɪvz]		Messer (*Pl*)
	spoon [spu:n]		Löffel
	today [tə'deɪ]	We've got English *today.*	heute
	shelf [ʃelf]		Regal
	shelves *(pl)* [ʃelvz]		Regale
	families *(pl)* ['fæmɪlɪz]	The Dixons and the Burtons are *families*.	Familien
2	**Wood** [wʊd]		*Familienname*
	Miller ['mɪlə]		*Familienname*
	That's great! [ˌðæts 'greɪt]		Das ist toll/großartig!
ⓑ	**parents** *(pl)* ['peərənts]	Your mother and father are your *parents*.	Eltern
	very ['verɪ]		sehr
	untidy [ʌn'taɪdɪ]		unordentlich
	its [ɪts]		sein, seine/ihr, ihre

Step B **In the garage**

garage ['gærɑ:dʒ]		Garage
flat tyre [ˌflæt 'taɪə]		platter Reifen, Platten
flat [flæt]		flach, platt
tyre ['taɪə]		Reifen
pump [pʌmp]		Luftpumpe
to **go** [gəʊ]		gehen, fahren

6 **dice** *(sg + pl)* [daɪs] — Würfel
to **throw** [θrəʊ] — werfen

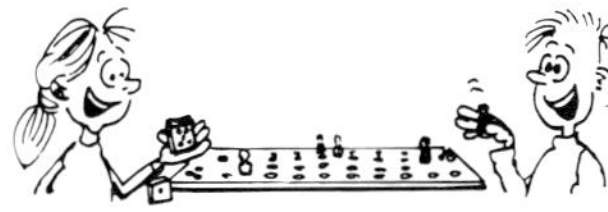

Step B **In Larwood Grove**

Larwood Grove ['lɑ:wʊd 'grəʊv] — *Straße in Nottingham*
shop [ʃɒp] — a book *shop*, a bike *shop*, a computer *shop* — Geschäft, Laden
other ['ʌðə] — andere, weitere

9 **Nosy** ['nəʊzɪ] — *hier: Familienname*
nosy ['nəʊzɪ] — neugierig
neighbour ['neɪbə] — Nachbar/in

Mrs A and Mr B are *neighbours.*

Step C **Is that my new CD, Sarah?**

little [lɪtl] — big ⟷ *little* — klein
those [ðəʊz] — die da drüben
these [ði:z] — diese hier

1 to **act** [ækt] — spielen, nachspielen
dialogue ['daiəlɒg] — Dialog, Gespräch
2 to **talk about** ['tɔ:k‿əˌbaʊt] — reden über, sprechen über

Step D **The ring**

ring [rɪŋ] — Ring
living-room ['lɪvɪŋru:m] — Wohnzimmer
to **see** [si:] — sehen
Be careful! [bɪ 'keəfʊl] — Pass auf! Vorsicht!
again [ə'gen] — wieder, noch einmal
silly ['sɪlɪ] — dumm, albern
Come on! [kəm‿'ɒn] — Komm schon!/Kommt schon!

to **get** [get] — *hier:* holen
outside [ˌaʊt'saɪd] — draußen
at the top of [ət ðə 'tɒp‿əv] — ganz oben
to **put** [pʊt] — setzen, stellen, legen
What's all this noise? [ˌwɒts‿ɔ:l ðɪs 'nɔɪz] — Was soll der Lärm?
noise [nɔɪz] — Lärm, Krach, Geräusch
nothing ['nʌθɪŋ] — nichts
everything ['evrɪθɪŋ] — alles

⟨5⟩ on the hillside [ˌɒn ðə 'hɪlsaɪd] — am Hang
ticky tacky ['tɪkɪ 'tækɪ] — *hier:* billiges Material

all the same [ˌɔːl ðə 'seɪm]		alle gleich
there's ['ðeəz]		es gibt, es ist
a green one [ə 'griːn wʌn]		eine grüne
pink [pɪŋk]		rosa
made out of [ˌmeɪd 'aʊt‿əv]		gemacht aus, hergestellt aus
to look [lʊk]		*hier:* aussehen
just the same [ˌdʒʌst ðə 'seɪm]		*hier:* genau gleich

Unit 3 The new girl from Germany

Lerne Vokabeln in Ruhe zu Hause, möglichst immer am gleichen Arbeitsplatz. Versuche einen Arbeitsplatz zu finden, an dem du immer ohne Störung arbeiten kannst.
Wenn du mit Musik lernen kannst, dann versuche, zum Lernen eine ruhige Musik zu finden.
An deinem Arbeitsplatz solltest du auch zu Beginn der Arbeit alles zur Hand haben: Schreibzeug, Hefte, Bücher, Karteikasten usw.

Step A **At the airport**

(a)	**airport** ['eəpɔːt]		Flughafen
	people *(pl)* ['piːpl]	The Burtons are nice *people.*	Leute
	Heathrow [ˌhiːθ'rəʊ]		*Name eines Londoner Flughafens*
	there are [ðeər‿'ɑː]	*There are* three airports in Berlin.	es gibt, es sind
	there is [ðeər‿'ɪz]	*There is* a very big airport in Frankfurt.	es gibt, es ist
(b)	**Jenny** ['dʒenɪ]		*weibl. Vorname*
	Her father is German. [hɜː ˌfɑːðər‿ɪz 'dʒɜːmən]		Ihr Vater ist Deutscher.
	British ['brɪtɪʃ]		britisch
	aunt [ɑːnt]	Mrs Penrose is my *aunt*, Mr Penrose is my *uncle* and David and Mark are my *cousins.*	Tante
	uncle ['ʌŋkl]		Onkel
	cousin ['kʌzn]		Cousin/e
	Mark [mɑːk]		*männl. Vorname*
	Welcome to … ['welkəm tʊ]		Willkommen in …
	to **help** [help]		helfen
2	**Italian** [ɪt'æljən]		italienisch, Italienisch
	Spanish ['spænɪʃ]		spanisch, Spanisch
	Greek [griːk]		griechisch, Griechisch
	Turkish ['tɜːkɪʃ]		türkisch, Türkisch
	Poland ['pəʊlənd]	*Poland* und andere Länder findest du auf der Karte hinten im Buch.	Polen
	to **start** [stɑːt]		anfangen, beginnen
	to **ask for** ['ɑːsk fɔː]		bitten um

Vocabulary

Step B In the car

	You're lucky. [jɔː ˈlʌkɪ]	Du hast Glück.
	to be **lucky** [bɪ ˈlʌkɪ]	Glück haben
	can [kæn]	können
	to **speak** [spiːk]	sprechen
	can't [kɑːnt]	nicht können
	to **do** [duː]	tun, machen
	What about ... ? [wɒt‿əˈbaʊt]	Was ist mit ... ?
	who [huː]	wer
3	**quiz** [kwɪz]	Quiz, Ratespiel
4	to **tell** [tel]	erzählen

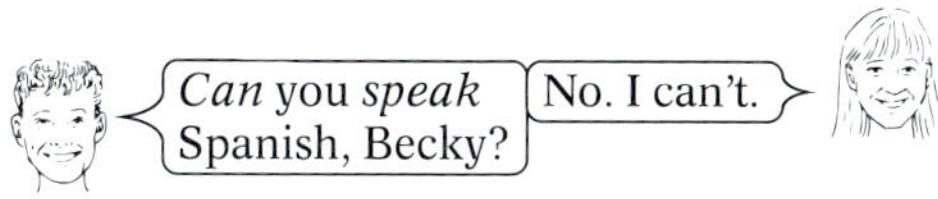

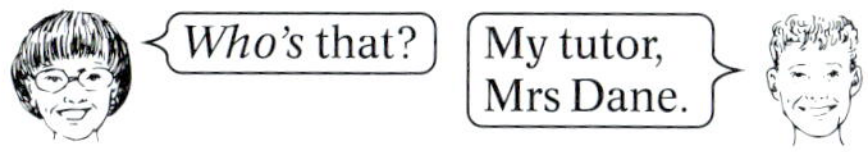

Step B At home in Sherwood

ⓐ	**Aunty** [ˈɑːntɪ]	*Anrede für eine Tante*
	so [səʊ]	also
	present [ˈprezənt]	Geschenk
6	**Pat** [pæt]	*weibl. Vorname*
	Colin [ˈkɒlɪn]	*männl. Vorname*
ⓑ	**Edward's Lane** [ˈedwədz ˌleɪn]	*Straße in Nottingham*
	Mansfield Road [ˈmænsfiːld ˈrəʊd]	*Straße in Nottingham*
8	**form** [fɔːm]	Form
	houses *(pl)* [ˈhaʊzɪz]	Häuser

A *present* for Becky.

Vorsicht bei der Aussprache: house [haʊs], houses [ˈhaʊzɪz]

Step B Let's say hello

ⓐ	**her** [hɜː]	ihr/sie
	to **give** [gɪv]	geben
	me [miː]	mir/mich
	him [hɪm]	ihm/ihn
	to [tuː]	*hier:* mit, zu
	terrible [ˈterəbl]	schrecklich, furchtbar
	maybe [ˈmeɪbiː]	vielleicht
	to **phone** [fəʊn]	anrufen
10	**on the telephone** [ɒn ðə ˈtelɪfəʊn]	am Telefon
ⓑ	**this afternoon** [ðɪs‿ɑːftəˈnuːn]	heute Nachmittag
	must [mʌst]	müssen
	to **go to the shops** [gəʊ tə ðə ˈʃɒps]	einkaufen gehen
	uniform [ˈjuːnɪfɔːm]	Uniform

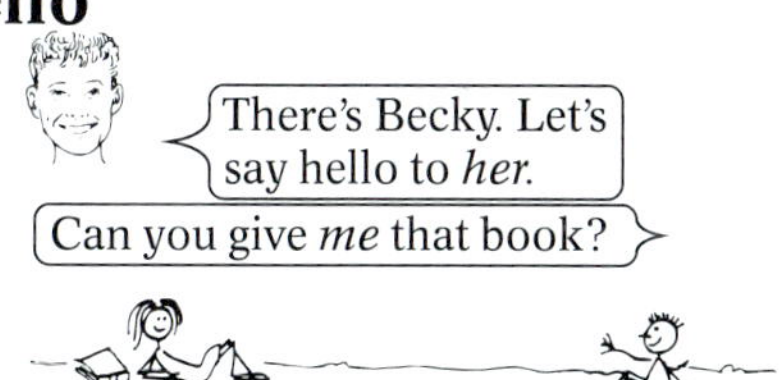

Vocabulary

Looking at the UK: How can you get there?

	How can you get there? [ˌhaʊ kən jʊ ˈget ðeə]	Wie kannst du/kann man dort hinkommen?
	to **get there** [ˈget ðeə]	hinkommen
	by [baɪ]	*hier:* mit
	plane [pleɪn]	Flugzeug
	ferry [ˈferɪ]	Fähre
	hovercraft [ˈhɒvəkrɑːft]	Luftkissenboot
	train [treɪn]	Zug
	through [θruː]	durch
	Channel Tunnel [ˈtʃænl ˈtʌnl]	*Tunnel unter dem Ärmelkanal*
	The Channel [ðə ˈtʃænl]	Ärmelkanal
	tunnel [ˈtʌnl]	Tunnel
2	**map** [mæp]	Landkarte
	from ... to [frəm ... tə]	*hier:* von ... nach
	Belgium [ˈbeldʒəm]	Belgien
	the Netherlands [ðə ˈneðələndz]	die Niederlande
	France [frɑːns]	Frankreich
	North Sea [nɔːθ ˈsiː]	Nordsee
	sea [siː]	Meer
3	**photo** [ˈfəʊtəʊ]	Foto

Diese Länder findest du auch auf der Karte hinten im Buch.

Step C **Tea**

	tea [tiː]	*hier: Mahlzeit am frühen Abend*
	ham [hæm]	gekochter Schinken
	cheese [tʃiːz]	Käse
2	**What's for tea?** [wɒts fə ˈtiː]	Was gibt es zum Abendbrot?
	salad [ˈsæləd]	gemischter Salat
	bread [bred]	Brot
	butter [ˈbʌtə]	Butter
	milk [mɪlk]	Milch
	tea [tiː]	Tee
	sugar [ˈʃʊgə]	Zucker
3	to **pass** [pɑːs]	reichen, weitergeben
	to **have** [hæv]	haben
	of [ɒv], [əv]	von

Step D **The photo**

	camera [ˈkæmərə]	Fotoapparat, Kamera
	right away [ˈraɪt‿əˈweɪ]	sofort
	to **take a photo of** [teɪk‿əˈfəʊtəʊ‿əv]	ein Foto machen von
	all [ɔːl]	alle/alles
	cannot [ˈkænɒt], [kɑːnt]	nicht können
	only [ˈəʊnlɪ]	nur, erst
	leg [leg]	Bein

Cannot wird in einem Wort geschrieben.

1 **story** ['stɔːrɪ] — Mark can tell the *story* about the frog. — Geschichte, Erzählung
5 **like** [laɪk] — (so) wie

Step E **Let's check**

5 **different** ['dɪfrənt] — unterschiedlich, anders

⟨Revision 1⟩

revision [rɪ'vɪʒn] — Wiederholung

Unit 4 Free time

a [eɪ]	e [iː]	i [aɪ]	m [em]	q [kjuː]	u [juː]	
b [biː]	f [ef]	j [dʒeɪ]	n [en]	r [ɑː]	v [viː]	
c [siː]	g [dʒiː]	k [keɪ]	o [əʊ]	s [es]	w ['dʌbljuː]	y [waɪ]
d [diː]	h [eɪtʃ]	l [el]	p [piː]	t [tiː]	x [eks]	z [zed]

free [friː] — frei
time [taɪm] — Zeit

Step A **The alphabet**

alphabet ['ælfəbət] — Alphabet
ABC book [eɪbiː'siː ˌbʊk] — ABC-Fibel
letter ['letə] — The alphabet has got 26 *letters.* — Buchstabe
rhyme [raɪm] — Reim
then [ðen] — dann
to **count** [kaʊnt] — zählen
of course [əv‿'kɔːs] — natürlich, selbstverständlich

shoe [ʃuː] — Schuh
last [lɑːst] — Z is the *last* letter in the alphabet. — letzter/letzte/letztes
It's time for … [ɪts‿'taɪm fə] — Es ist Zeit für …

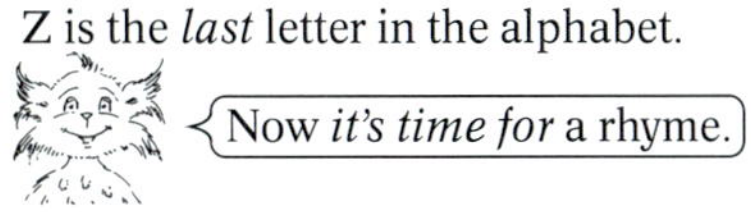

to **watch** [wɒtʃ] — (zu)schauen, gucken
TV ['tiː'viː] — Fernsehen
boring ['bɔːrɪŋ] — langweilig
to **read** [riːd] — lesen

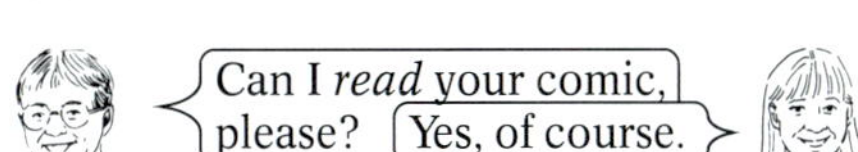

kite [kaɪt] — Drachen
well [wel] — gut, nun, na ja
to **repair** [rɪ'peə] — reparieren

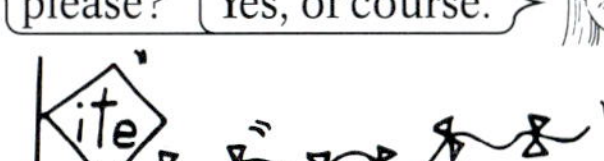

2 to **spell** [spel] — buchstabieren
to **think** [θɪŋk] — denken, glauben

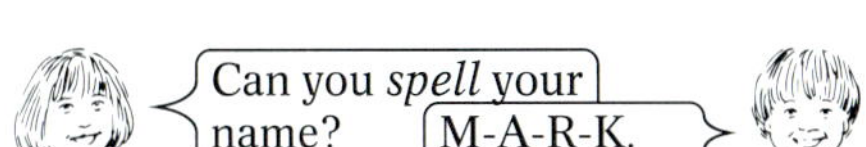

Step B **In the living-room**

	to **be on** [bɪ‿'ɒn]	Listen! The radio *is on.*	eingeschaltet sein
	nobody ['nəʊbədɪ]		niemand, keiner
2	**in the evening** [ɪnðiː‿'iːvnɪŋ]	in the morning ⟷ *in the evening*	abends, am Abend
	evening ['iːvnɪŋ]		Abend

Step B **Mrs Croft**

	to **come** [kʌm]		kommen
	In a minute. [ɪn‿ə 'mɪnɪt]		Augenblick noch! Warte/t mal einen Moment.
	minute ['mɪnɪt]		Minute
	just [dʒʌst]	I'm *just* repairing my kite. Can you help me? – Yes, *in a minute.*	eben, gerade, nur
	to **wash up** [wɒʃ‿'ʌp]		abwaschen, (Geschirr) spülen
	Ugh! [ɜːh]		*Ausruf des Abscheus*
	to **work late** ['wɜːk leɪt]		länger arbeiten
	on (the radio) [ɒn]		*hier:* im (Rundfunk)
	job [dʒɒb]	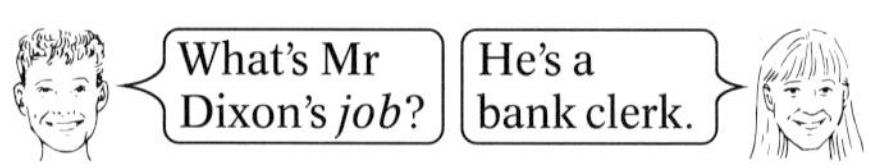	Beruf, Arbeit
	exciting [ɪk'saɪtɪŋ]		aufregend, spannend
4	to **think of** ['θɪŋk‿əv]		ausdenken
	activity [æk'tɪvɪtɪ]		Tätigkeit
	to **find out** [faɪnd‿'aʊt]		herausfinden

Step B **The idea**

them [ðem]	The boys are working in the garden.Let's help *them.*	sie/ihnen
stone [stəʊn]		Stein
round [raʊnd]		um … herum
it [ɪt]		ihn/sie/es; ihm/ihr
to **get** [get]		bekommen
out [aʊt]	in ⟷ *out*	draußen, heraus
us [ʌs]	We are in the garden. Can you see *us*?	uns
you [jʊ]		dich/euch/Sie; dir/euch/Ihnen
spade [speɪd]		Spaten

Looking at the UK: Free time

	tennis ['tenɪs]	 This ball is for *tennis.*	Tennis
	cricket ['krɪkɪt]	It isn't for *cricket.*	*englischer Rasensport*
	pop music ['pɒp 'mjuːzɪk]		Popmusik
	music ['mjuːzɪk]		Musik
3	**same** [seɪm]	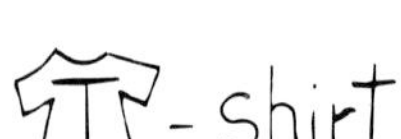	gleich
	T-shirt ['tiːʃɜːt]		T-Shirt

	sweatshirt ['swetʃɜːt]		Sweatshirt
	badminton ['bædmɪntən]		Federballspiel

Step C **What's the weather like?**

	What's … like? [wɒts … laɪk]		Wie ist … ?
	weather ['weðə]		Wetter
	warm [wɔːm]		warm
	sunny ['sʌnɪ]		sonnig
	windy ['wɪndɪ]		windig
	to **go for a walk** [ˌgəʊ fər‿ə 'wɔːk]		spazieren gehen
	walk [wɔːk]		Spaziergang
	to **rain** [reɪn]		regnen
	cold [kəʊld]		kalt
	wet [wet]		nass
1	to **sit** [sɪt]		sitzen
⟨2⟩	to sail [seɪl]		segeln
	'cross [krɒs]		über
	stormy ['stɔːmɪ]		stürmisch
	waters *(pl)* ['wɔːtəz]		Gewässer
	near [nɪə]		nahe

Step D **The flowerpot**

	flowerpot ['flaʊəpɒt]		Blumentopf
	Saturday ['sætədɪ]		Samstag, Sonnabend
	no [nəʊ]		kein/keine
	team [tiːm]		Mannschaft
	door [dɔː]		*hier:* (Garagen-)Tor
	goal [gəʊl]		Tor *(beim Sport)*
	to **be good at …** [bɪ 'gʊd‿ət]	Sarah *is good at* football.	gut sein in …
	to **kick** [kɪk]		treten, mit dem Fuß stoßen
	Crash! [kræʃ]		Rums!
	floor [flɔː]		Boden
	Audrey ['ɔːdrɪ]		*weibl. Vorname*
	to **laugh** [lɑːf]	Monny is *laughing*.	lachen
	angry ['æŋgrɪ]		böse, verärgert
3	**exercise** ['eksəsaɪz]		Übung, Aufgabe

Step E **Let's check**

2	**opposite** ['ɒpəzɪt]	Yes ⟷ No, little ⟷ big are *opposites.*	Gegenteil

Unit 5 Jenny's birthday

„Remember"

Schreib die englischen Wörter, die du lernen willst, auf kleine Zettel.
Auf die Rückseite jedes Zettels schreibst du in einer anderen Farbe die deutsche Bedeutung. (Wenn du eine Kartei führst, kannst du auch die Karteikarten nehmen.)
Breite die Karten mit der deutschen Bedeutung nach oben aus. Wenn du den englischen Begriff nennen kannst, darfst du die Karte einsammeln.
Wenn du beim Überprüfen feststellst, dass deine Antwort nicht richtig war, musst du die Karte wieder hinlegen.
Das Spiel geht natürlich auch umgekehrt.

Step A **A surprise party**

birthday ['bɜːθdeɪ]		Geburtstag
surprise [sə'praɪz]		Überraschung
party ['pɑːtɪ]		Party, Feier
in ... days [ɪn ... deɪz]		in ... Tagen
day [deɪ]		Tag
invitation [ˌɪnvɪ'teɪʃn]		Einladung
to **invite** [ɪn'vaɪt]		einladen
cake [keɪk]		Kuchen, Torte
problem ['prɒbləm]		Problem
guitar [gɪ'tɑː]	David can play the *guitar.*	Gitarre
to **sing** [sɪŋ]		singen
to **dance** [dɑːns]		tanzen

ten [ten]	zehn	**twenty** ['twentɪ]	zwanzig
eleven [ɪ'levn]	elf	**twenty-one** [ˌtwentɪ'wʌn]	einundzwanzig
twelve [twelv]	zwölf	**thirty** ['θɜːtɪ]	dreißig
thirteen [ˌθɜː'tiːn]	dreizehn	**forty** ['fɔːtɪ]	vierzig
fourteen [ˌfɔː'tiːn]	vierzehn	**fifty** ['fɪftɪ]	fünfzig
fifteen [ˌfɪf'tiːn]	fünfzehn	**sixty** ['sɪkstɪ]	sechzig
sixteen [ˌsɪks'tiːn]	sechzehn	**seventy** ['sevntɪ]	siebzig
seventeen [ˌsevn'tiːn]	siebzehn	**eighty** ['eɪtɪ]	achtzig
eighteen [ˌeɪ'tiːn]	achtzehn	**ninety** ['naɪntɪ]	neunzig
nineteen [ˌnaɪn'tiːn]	neunzehn	**a hundred** [ə'hʌndrəd]	hundert

2 **over** ['əʊvə]	under ⟷ *over*	über

Step A **Jenny's letter**

letter ['letə]	 a letter	Brief
dear [dɪə]	3 letters 	liebe/lieber/liebes
How are you? [haʊ‿'ɑ: ju:]		Wie geht es dir/euch/ Ihnen?
I'm fine. [aɪm 'faɪn]	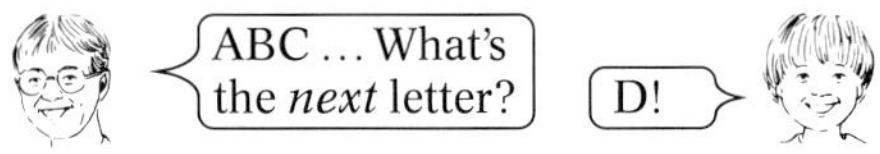	Mir geht's gut.
next [nekst]		nächste/nächster/ nächstes
month [mʌnθ]	There are 12 *months* in a year.	Monat
first [fɜ:st]		erste/erster/erstes
without [wɪð'aʊt]	You can't write *without* a pen.	ohne
February ['februərɪ]		Februar
That's all for now. [ðæts 'ɔ:l fə ˌnaʊ]		Das wär's für heute.
love [lʌv]		*hier:* alles Liebe *(als Briefschluss)*

January ['dʒænjʊərɪ]	Januar	**July** [dʒʊ'laɪ]	Juli
February ['februərɪ]	Februar	**August** ['ɔ:gəst]	August
March [mɑ:tʃ]	März	**September** [sep'tembə]	September
April ['eɪprɪl]	April	**October** [ɒk'təʊbə]	Oktober
May [meɪ]	Mai	**November** [nəʊ'vembə]	November
June [dʒu:n]	Juni	**December** [dɪ'sembə]	Dezember

3 to **remember** [rɪ'membə] — behalten, sich merken, sich erinnern

Step B **Everyone is very busy**

everyone ['evrɪwʌn]	*Everyone* is here.	jede/jeder, alle
busy ['bɪzɪ]	The children are very *busy.*	beschäftigt
to **get ready** [get 'redɪ]	They are *getting ready* for school.	(sich) vorbereiten
shopping list ['ʃɒpɪŋ lɪst]	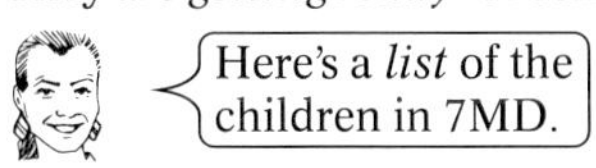	Einkaufsliste
list [lɪst]		Liste
to **lie** [laɪ]		liegen
she is lying [ʃɪ:z 'laɪɪŋ]		sie liegt im Augenblick
balloon [bə'lu:n]		Luftballon

Step B **What is the date?**

date [deɪt]	Datum
on the seventh of [ɒn ðə 'sevnθ‿əv]	am siebten
at ... o'clock [ət ... ə'klɒk]	um ... Uhr
3 **when** [wen]	wann

first [fɜ:st]	erste/r/s	**sixteenth** [ˌsɪksˈti:nθ]	sechzehnte/r/s
second [ˈsekənd]	zweite/r/s	**seventeenth** [ˌsevnˈti:nθ]	siebzehnte/r/s
third [θɜ:d]	dritte/r/s	**eighteenth** [ˌeɪˈti:nθ]	achtzehnte/r/s
fourth [fɔ:θ]	vierte/r/s	**nineteenth** [ˌnaɪnˈti:nθ]	neunzehnte/r/s
fifth [fɪfθ]	fünfte/r/s	**twentieth** [ˈtwentɪəθ]	zwanzigste/r/s
sixth [sɪksθ]	sechste/r/s	**twenty-first** [ˈtwentɪfɜ:st]	einundzwanzig-ste/r/s
seventh [ˈsevnθ]	siebte/r/s		
eighth [eɪtθ]	achte/r/s	**thirtieth** [ˈθɜ:tɪəθ]	dreißigste/r/s
ninth [naɪnθ]	neunte/r/s	**fortieth** [ˈfɔ:tɪəθ]	vierzigste/r/s
tenth [tenθ]	zehnte/r/s	**fiftieth** [ˈfɪftɪəθ]	fünfzigste/r/s
eleventh [ɪˈlevnθ]	elfte/r/s	**sixtieth** [ˈsɪkstɪəθ]	sechzigste/r/s
twelfth [twelfθ]	zwölfte/r/s	**seventieth** [ˈsevntɪəθ]	siebzigste/r/s
thirteenth [ˌθɜ:ˈti:nθ]	dreizehnte/r/s	**eightieth** [ˈeɪtɪəθ]	achtzigste/r/s
fourteenth [ˌfɔ:ˈti:nθ]	vierzehnte/r/s	**ninetieth** [ˈnaɪntɪəθ]	neunzigste/r/s
fifteenth [ˌfɪfˈti:nθ]	fünfzehnte/r/s	**hundredth** [ˈhʌndrətθ]	hundertste/r/s

Step C **What time is it?**

What time is it? [ˌwɒt ˈtaɪm‿ɪz‿ɪt]	Wie spät ist es? Wie viel Uhr ist es?
quarter [ˈkwɔ:tə]	Viertel
past [pɑ:st]	nach *(bei Uhrzeiten)*
1 **half** [hɑ:f]	halb; Hälfte
to [tʊ], [tə]	*hier:* vor
2 to **tell the time** [ˈtel ðə ˈtaɪm]	die Uhrzeit angeben
4 **tomorrow** [təˈmɒrəʊ]	morgen

Da muss man aufpassen: "halb vier" heißt "*half* past three".

Looking at the UK: A British house

upstairs [ˌʌpˈsteəz]	oben (im Gebäude)
bedroom [ˈbedrʊm]	Schlafzimmer
bathroom [ˈbɑ:θrʊm]	Badezimmer
toilet [ˈtɔɪlɪt]	Toilette
downstairs [ˌdaʊnˈsteəz]	unten (im Gebäude)
1 **hall** [hɔ:l]	Diele, Flur
bath [bɑ:θ]	Bad, Badewanne
to **have a bath** [hæv‿ə ˈbɑ:θ]	baden
breakfast [ˈbrekfəst]	Frühstück
2 **plan** [plæn]	Plan

Step D **A great birthday**

candle [ˈkændl]	Kerze
another [əˈnʌðə]	noch einen/eine/eins
happy [ˈhæpɪ]	fröhlich, glücklich
Happy birthday! [ˌhæpɪ ˈbɜ:θdeɪ]	Herzlichen Glückwunsch zum Geburtstag!
video [ˈvɪdɪəʊ]	Video
Helen [ˈhelɪn]	*weibl. Vorname*

⟨Revision 2⟩

camcorder ['kæmkɔ:də]		Videokamera
scene [si:n]		Szene

Unit 6 In town

Es führt kein Weg daran vorbei:
Die Schreibweise der Wörter
prägt sich am besten durch Schreiben ein.

Das Aufschreiben der Wörter für deine Lernkartei oder in dein Vokabelheft hilft dir schon, die Schreibweise zu behalten. Besonders schwierige Wörter kannst du auf einen Haftzettel schreiben, dabei die Buchstaben, die du sonst immer falsch schreibst, in einer stärkeren Farbe hervorheben. Diese Zettel heftest du z.B. in der Nähe deines Arbeitsplatzes oder am Bett an. So prägen sie sich gut ein.

Step A **In Nottingham**

town [taʊn]		Stadt
Robin Hood ['rɒbɪn 'hʊd]		*Figur einer englischen Sage*
statue ['stætʃu:]		Statue, Denkmal
in front of [ɪn 'frʌnt əv]		vor
castle ['kɑ:sl]	Neuschwanstein is a *castle* in Germany.	Burg
Old Market Square [əʊld 'mɑ:kɪt 'skweə]		*Platz in Nottingham*
market ['mɑ:kɪt]		Markt
square ['skweə]		Platz
centre ['sentə]		Mitte, Zentrum
city ['sɪtɪ]		(Groß-)Stadt
shopping centre ['ʃɒpɪŋ ˌsentə]		Einkaufszentrum
Victoria [vɪk'tɔ:rɪə]		*weibl. Vorname*
a lot of [ə'lɒt əv]	 *a lot of* boxes	viel/viele, eine Menge
restaurant ['restərɔnt]	I'm hungry. Let's go to that *restaurant.*	Restaurant
street [stri:t]		Straße
St Peter's Church [snt ˌpi:təz 'tʃɜ:tʃ]		Sankt-Peter-Kirche
church [tʃɜ:tʃ]		Kirche
near [nɪə]	The Crofts' house is *near* the Dixons' house in Larwood Grove.	in der Nähe von

Step B **Days of the week**

ⓐ **week** [wi:k]	There are seven days in a *week.*	Woche
Friday ['fraɪdeɪ]		Freitag
Saturday ['sætədeɪ]		Samstag
into ['ɪntʊ]		in, hinein

cinema ['sɪnɪmə]		Kino
too [tuː]	 *Why* can't Mark get the biscuits from the shelf?	allzu, zu
why [waɪ]		warum
because [bɪ'kɒz]	*Because* he's too little. 	weil
to **get the bus** [ˌget ðə 'bʌs]		den Bus nehmen
bus [bʌs]	Vorsicht bei der Pluralform: *buses*!	Bus
end [end]		Ende
double decker ['dʌbl 'dekə]		Doppeldecker
at the bottom of [ət ðə 'bɒtəm‿əv]	at the top of ⟷ *at the bottom of*	unten, am unteren Ende
to **walk** [wɔːk]		(zu Fuß) gehen
bus stop ['bʌs stɒp]		Bushaltestelle

Monday ['mʌndeɪ]	Montag	**Friday** ['fraɪdeɪ]	Freitag
Tuesday ['tjuːzdeɪ]	Dienstag	**Saturday** ['sætədeɪ]	Samstag
Wednesday ['wenzdeɪ]	Mittwoch	**Sunday** ['sʌndeɪ]	Sonntag
Thursday ['θɜːzdeɪ]	Donnerstag		

(b) **best** [best]	 Mrs Dane is the *best* English teacher at our school. She's my *favourite* teacher, too.	beste/bester/bestes
favourite ['feɪvərɪt]		Lieblings-
3 **calendar** ['kælɪndə]		Kalender

Step C **At the Victoria shopping centre**

to **try on** [traɪ‿'ɒn]	 Can I *try* your sweatshirt *on*, please David?	anprobieren
clothes *(pl)* ['kləʊðz]		Kleider
jeans *(pl)* [dʒiːnz]	These *jeans* are red. They're nice.	Jeans
pullover ['pʊlˌəʊvə]		Pullover
to **wear** [weə]	 I'm *wearing* my yellow *trousers* today with a green T-shirt.	tragen, anhaben
trousers *(pl)* ['traʊzəz]		Hose/Hosen
anorak ['ænəræk]		Anorak
shirt [ʃɜːt]		Hemd(bluse)
3 to **answer** ['ɑːnsə]	Please *answer* the question. Give me an answer please.	(be)antworten

Step C **Excuse me, please**

Excuse me, please. [ɪk'skjuːz mɪ pliːz]		Entschuldigung. Entschuldigen Sie bitte.
to **tell** [tel]		sagen, mitteilen
way [weɪ]		Weg
down [daʊn]	up ⟷ *down*	herunter, hinunter
Friar Lane ['fraɪə 'leɪn]		*Straßenname*

straight on [streɪt‿'ɒn] to **turn** [tɜːn]	 Don't *turn left.* Go *straight on.* 	geradeaus abbiegen
left [left]		(nach) links
Maid Marian Way [ˌmeɪd 'mærɪən 'weɪ]		*Straßenname*
right [raɪt]	left ⟷ *right*	(nach) rechts
Castle Gate ['kɑːsl 'geɪt]		*Straßenname*
on the left/right [ɒn ðə 'left], [ɒn ðə 'raɪt]	 That's Becky, *on the right.* 	links/rechts, auf der linken/rechten Seite
Angel Row ['eɪndʒəl 'rəʊ]		*Straßenname*
Mount Street ['maʊnt ˌstriːt]		*Straßenname*
Beastmarket Hill ['biːstmɑːkɪt 'hɪl]		*Straßenname*
hill [hɪl]	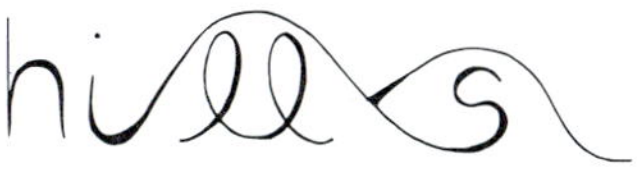	Hügel
Parliament Street ['pɑːləmənt ˌstriːt]		*Straßenname*
South Parade ['saʊθ pə'reɪd]		*Straßenname*
Exchange Walk [ɪks'tʃeɪndʒ 'wɔːk]		*Straßenname*
6 **behind** [bɪ'haɪnd]	in front ⟷ *behind*	hinter

Step C **David's grandma**

grandma ['grænmɑː]		Oma
Twinning Office ['twɪnɪŋ ˌɒfɪs]		Städtepartnerschaftsbüro
office ['ɒfɪs]		Büro, Amt
to **eat** [iːt]		essen
hot [hɒt]	cold ⟷ *hot*	heiß
potato, *(pl)* potatoes [pə'teɪtəʊ]		Kartoffel
special ['speʃl]		besondere/r/s; *hier:* Spezialität des Hauses
tomato, *(pl)* tomatoes [tə'mɑːtəʊ]		Tomate
person ['pɜːsn]	 Für die Pluralform von *person* verwendet man normalerweise *people.*	Person
twin town ['twɪn 'taʊn]		Partnerstadt
twin [twɪn]		Zwilling

Step D **Robert and Jenny in town**

Beeston ['biːstən]		*Bezirk von Nottingham*
driver ['draɪvə]		Fahrer/in
Bestwood ['bestwʊd]		*Bezirk von Nottingham*
long [lɒŋ]		lang
back [bæk]		zurück
worried ['wʌrɪd]		besorgt, beunruhigt
to **stand** [stænd]		stehen
to **stop** [stɒp]	start ⟷ *stop*	anhalten
to **give ... a lift** [lɪft]		... im Auto mitnehmen

Unit 7 School days

Die neuen Vokabeln kann man immer. Aber Wörter, die länger zurückliegen, fallen einem nicht mehr ein.

Dass man nicht alles behält, ist doch normal.
Dagegen hilft Wiederholung.
Nimm dir zusammen mit Freunden Vokabeln aus einer früheren Unit vor.
Ihr könnt sie euch gegenseitig ganz durcheinander abfragen oder das Remember-Spiel damit machen.

Step A **Lunch time**

ⓐ	**competition** [kɒmpəˈtɪʃn]		Wettbewerb, Preisausschreiben
	healthy living [ˈhelθɪ ˈlɪvɪŋ]		gesunde Lebensweise
	prize [praɪz]	The first *prize* in the competition is a bike.	Preis, Gewinn
	to **lend** [lend]		leihen, verleihen
	p [piː]		*Abkürzung für* penny, pence *(kleinste britische Münze)*
	sausage [ˈsɒsɪdʒ]		Würstchen, Wurst
	chips *(pl)* [tʃɪps]		Pommes frites
	How much? [haʊ ˈmʌtʃ]	*How much* are the chips? – They're 60p.	Wie viel?
	£1 [wʌn ˈpaʊnd]	£1 = 100p	*britisches Geld*
	to **buy** [baɪ]		kaufen
	packet [ˈpækɪt]	 A packet of *crisps*.	Päckchen
	crisps *(pl)* [krɪsps]		Kartoffelchips
ⓑ	**money** [ˈmʌnɪ]		Geld
	pence *(pl)* [pens]	 Say "sixty p" or "sixty *pence*".	Pfennige *(britisches Geld)*
	pound (= £) [paʊnd]	£1.20: say "one *pound* twenty".	Pfund *(britisches Geld)*
	reduced in size [rɪˌdjuːst‿ɪn ˈsaɪz]		verkleinert
	size [saɪz]		Größe
1	**White** [waɪt]		*Familienname*
	white [waɪt]		weiß

Step B **Jenny's day**

	to **get up** [get‿ˈʌp]		aufstehen
	every [ˈevrɪ]		jede/jeder/jedes
	to **finish** [ˈfɪnɪʃ]		beenden, aufhören
	to **come home** [kʌm ˈhəʊm]		nach Hause kommen
1	**after** [ˈɑːftə]		nach
	to **go to bed** [gəʊ tə ˈbed]	to get up ⟷ *to go to bed*	ins Bett gehen, schlafen gehen

Step B **Mark's day**

early ['ɜ:lɪ]	late ⟷ *early*	früh
cornflakes *(pl)* ['kɔ:nfleɪks]		Cornflakes
nursery school ['nɜ:sərɪ ˌsku:l]	Mark is only 4. He goes to *nursery school.*	Kindergarten
to **collect** [kə'lekt]		abholen
irregular [ɪ'regjʊlə]		unregelmäßig

Step B **A busy day**

ⓐ **sometimes** ['sʌmtaɪmz]		manchmal
never ['nevə]		nie
often ['ɒfn]		oft
always ['ɔ:lweɪz]	never ⟷ *always*	immer
to **take home** [teɪk 'həʊm]		nach Hause bringen
5 **word order** ['wɜ:d ˌɔ:də]		Satzstellung
ⓑ to **do the washing-up** ['dʊ ðə ˌwɒʃɪŋ'ʌp]		spülen, abwaschen
washing-up [ˌwɒʃɪŋ'ʌp]		Abwasch
Oh dear! [əʊ 'dɪə]		Oh je!
mess [mes]		Unordnung
to **tidy up** ['taɪdɪ‿ʌp]		aufräumen
tidy ['taɪdɪ]	untidy ⟷ *tidy*	ordentlich, aufgeräumt
door [dɒ:]		Tür
Well done! [wel 'dʌn]		Gut gemacht! Bravo!
housework ['haʊswɜ:k]		Hausarbeit

Looking at the UK: Haywood School

assembly [ə'semblɪ]		Versammlung
pupil ['pju:pl]	There are 630 *pupils* at Haywood School.	Schüler/in
drama group ['drɑ:mə gru:p]		Theatergruppe
hockey ['hɒkɪ]		Rasenhockey

Step C **The poster**

Get out! [get 'aʊt]		Hinaus mit dir!/Hinaus mit euch!
dirty ['dɜ:tɪ]		schmutzig, dreckig
head [hed]		Kopf
arm [ɑ:m]		Arm
hand [hænd]		Hand
eye [aɪ]		Auge
mouth [maʊθ]		Mund
2 **beetle** ['bi:tl]		Käfer
body ['bɒdɪ]		Körper
exercise book ['eksəsaɪz ˌbʊk]		Heft

	winner ['wɪnə]	Gewinner/in
	feeler ['fi:lə]	Fühler
⟨3⟩	shoulder ['ʃəʊldə]	Schulter
	knee [ni:]	Knie
	toe [təʊ]	Zeh
	ear [ɪə]	Ohr
	nose [nəʊz]	Nase

Step C **At the shops**

ⓐ	**pound** [paʊnd]	Pfund *(Gewicht)*
	banana [bə'nɑ:nə]	Banane
	Anything else? ['enɪθɪŋ 'els]	Sonst noch etwas?
	pint [paɪnt]	*etwa 0,5l*
ⓑ	**bottle** ['bɒtl]	Flasche
	lemonade [lemə'neɪd]	Limonade
	bar [bɑ:]	Tafel
4	to **go together** [gəʊ tə'geðə]	zusammenpassen
	lb = pound [paʊnd]	*Abkürzung für* pound (*Gewicht*)
6	**supermarket** ['su:pəˌmɑ:kɪt]	Supermarkt

Step D **The healthy living prize**

	Benson ['bensn]	*Familienname*
	headteacher [ˌhed'ti:tʃə]	Schuldirektor/in
	to **take** [teɪk]	nehmen
	lucky ['lʌkɪ]	glücklich, Glücks-
	Peter ['pi:tə]	*männl. Vorname*
	Wall [wɔ:l]	*Familienname*
	Annabel ['ænəbel]	*weibl. Vorname*
	Barker ['bɑ:kə]	*Familienname*
	Suvina [sə'vi:nə]	*weibl. Vorname*
	Adib [ə'dɪb]	*Familienname*
	extra ['ekstrə]	zusätzlich
	soap [səʊp]	Seife
	bubble bath ['bʌbl ˌbɑ:θ]	Schaumbad
	to **trip** ['trɪp]	stolpern
	to **fall over** [fɔ:l‿'əʊvə]	hinfallen
	all over ['ɔ:l‿ˌəʊvə]	überall auf
3	**verb** [vɜ:b]	Verb

Step E **Let's check**

5	**mascot** ['mæskət]	Maskottchen

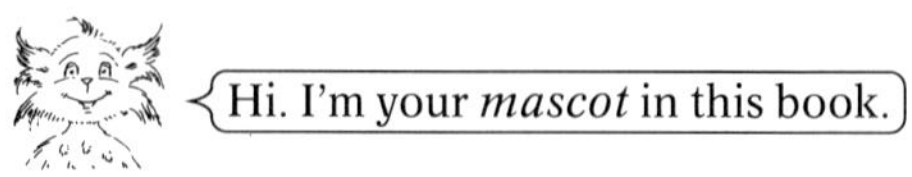

Unit 8 The accident

Manchmal hilft es beim Wiederholen, Wörter in eine ganz neue Reihenfolge zu bringen. Du könntest z.B. die Wörter deines Lernpäckchens in alphabetischer Reihenfolge oder nach Wortgruppen zusammenstellen. Wenn du einen Karteikasten angelegt hast, kannst du die Wörter aus dem hinteren Fach jetzt alphabetisch ordnen. Dazu musst du nicht nur auf den ersten, sondern auch auf die folgenden Buchstaben achten. Beispiel: Unter „s" kommt das Wort *shop* vor *soap*, weil das „h" im Alphabet vor dem „o" kommt.

accident ['æksɪdənt]		Unfall

Step A **Money and jobs**

ⓐ **pocket money** ['pɒkɪt ˌmʌnɪ]		Taschengeld
pocket ['pɒkɪt]		Tasche (*bei Kleidung*)
sweet [swi:t]		Bonbon
magazine [ˌmægə'zi:n]		Zeitschrift
to **save** [seɪv]		sparen
ⓑ to **sell** [sel]		verkaufen
to **like** [laɪk]		mögen, gern haben
to **want** [wɒnt]		(haben) wollen
to **need** [ni:d]		brauchen, benötigen
shop assistant ['ʃɒp‿əˌsɪstənt]		Verkäufer/in
to **know** [nəʊ]	Wie bei *knife* wird das *k* nicht gesprochen, so dass *know* genau wie *no* klingt.	wissen, kennen
mechanic [mɪ'kænɪk]		Mechaniker/in

Step B **Saturday morning**

song [sɒŋ]	"Happy Birthday to you" is a song.	Lied
'n' [n]	Two 'n' Two = Two and Two	und (*kurze gesprochene Form von* and)
I don't like … [aɪ dəʊnt 'laɪk]	Achtung bei der Aussprache von *don't* [dəʊnt]!	ich mag nicht …
Bye. [baɪ]		Tschüs! (*kurze gesprochene Form von* Goodbye.)

Step B **In Edward's Lane**

popular ['pɒpjʊlə]		beliebt
to **go home** [gəʊ 'həʊm]		nach Hause gehen

Step C **In hospital**

	hospital ['hɒspɪtl]		Krankenhaus
	It's good to see you. [ɪts ˌgʊd tə 'siː jʊ]		Schön, dich/euch zu sehen.
	to **hurt** [hɜːt]		weh tun, schmerzen
	a bit [a'bɪt]		etwas, ein bisschen
	I hope you're better soon. [aɪ 'həʊp jʊə ˌbetə 'suːn]		Ich hoffe, es geht dir bald besser.
	to **hope** [həʊp]		hoffen
	soon [suːn]		bald
	nurse [nɜːs]	A *nurse*. She works in a hospital.	Krankenschwester/ Krankenpfleger
	cupboard ['kʌbəd]		Schrank
4	**card** [kɑːd]		Karte
	Get well soon! ['get wel 'suːn]	*Get well soon* = I hope you're better soon.	Gute Besserung!
6	**request** [rɪ'kwest]		Bitte, Wunsch
	Anna ['ænə]		*weibl. Vorname*
	Hunt ['hʌnt]		*Familienname*
	Michael ['maɪkəl]		*männl. Vorname*
	Hilton ['hɪltən]		*Familienname*
7	to **use** [juːz]	My pen's broken. I can't *use* it.	benutzen

Looking at the UK: Help!

	Help! [help]		Hilfe!
	to **call** [kɔːl]		rufen, anrufen
	fire brigade ['faɪə brɪˌgeɪd]		Feuerwehr
	ambulance ['æmbjʊləns]		Krankenwagen
	police [pə'liːs]		Polizei
2	to **take** [teɪk]		*hier:* bringen
	fireman ['faɪəmən]		Feuerwehrmann
	police officer [pə'liːs ˌɒfɪsə]		Polizist/in
	doctor ['dɒktə]		Arzt/Ärztin

Step D **Fish fingers and ice cream**

	fish finger [fɪʃ 'fɪŋgə]		Fischstäbchen
	fish [fɪʃ]	 one *fish* – three *fish*	Fisch
	ice cream [ˌaɪs 'kriːm]		Eiskrem
	give my love to ... [ˌgɪv maɪ 'lʌv tə]		grüß/grüßt ... recht herzlich
	usually ['juːʒʊəlɪ]		gewöhnlich, normalerweise
	firm [fɜːm]		Firma
	to **open** ['əʊpən]		öffnen, aufmachen
	front door ['frʌnt 'dɔː]		Haustür
	to **close** [kləʊz]	to open – *to close*	schließen, zumachen

	back door ['bæk 'dɔː]		Hintertür
	locked [lɒkt]		abgeschlossen
	to **wait for** ['weɪt fɔː]		warten auf
	window ['wɪndəʊ]		Fenster
	open ['əʊpən]		offen, geöffnet
	ladder ['lædə]	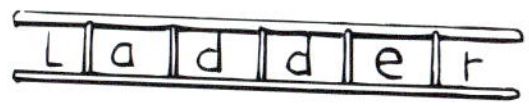	Leiter
1	**text** [tekst]		Text
2	**ending** ['endɪŋ]		Ende, Schluss *(bei Geschichten)*
	to **climb up** [ˌklaɪm 'ʌp]	Achtung: das *b* in *climb* wird nicht gesprochen.	hochklettern, erklettern
	burglar ['bɜːglə]		Einbrecher/in
	to **get stuck** [get 'stʌk]		stecken bleiben

Step E **Let's check**

5	**fun** [fʌn]		Spaß

Unit 9 A day at the seaside

Du behältst Vokabeln besonders gut, wenn du sie zusätzlich vor dem Einschlafen noch einmal ansiehst.

at the seaside [ət ðə 'siːsaɪd]	am Meer, an der See

Step A **On the train**

	Skegness [skeg'nes]		*englischer Seebadeort*
	seat [siːt]	There are four *seats* there, let's sit down.	Sitz, Sitzplatz
	ticket ['tɪkɪt]		Fahrkarte
	beach [biːtʃ]		Strand
	to **go swimming** [gəʊ 'swɪmɪŋ]		schwimmen gehen
	Never mind. ['nevə ˌmaɪnd]		Mach dir nichts daraus./ Macht euch nichts daraus.
	boating lake ['bəʊtɪŋ leɪk]		Bootsteich
	lake [leɪk]		(der) See, Teich
	boat [bəʊt]		Boot
⟨2⟩	sun [sʌn]		Sonne
	to have on [hæv‿'ɒn]		anhaben, tragen
	hat [hæt]		Hut
	hip, hip, hurray [hɪp hɪp hʊ'reɪ]		hipp, hipp, hurra!

	everybody ['evrɪbɒdɪ]	= everyone	jede/jeder
	gay [geɪ]		fröhlich
	holiday ['hɒlədɪ]		Urlaub(stag)

Step B **At Skegness**

	station ['steɪʃn]	Look, the train is coming into the *station.*	Bahnhof
	the High Street ['haɪ stri:t]	Bei diesem Straßennamen verwendet man ausnahmsweise *the.*	*Straßenname, etwa "Hauptstraße"*
	dog-free zone ['dɒgfri: 'zəʊn]		hundefreie Zone
	to **meet** [mi:t]	Let's *meet* after school and do our homework together.	(sich) treffen
	snack bar ['snæk bɑ:]		Imbissstube

Step B **At the boating lake**

	hour ['aʊə]	60 minutes = 1 hour	Stunde
	really ['rɪəlɪ]		wirklich
	to **cost** [kɒst]	The apples *cost* 60p.	kosten
4	**short** [ʃɔ:t]	long ←→ *short*	kurz

Step B **On the beach**

	crab [kræb]		Krebs
	to **live** [lɪv]	The Burtons *live* in Sherwood.	leben, wohnen
	rock [rɒk]		Fels
	water ['wɔ:tə]		Wasser
7	**room** [ru:m]		*hier:* Platz

Looking at the UK: At Skegness

	timetable ['taɪmteɪbl]		Fahrplan
	to **leave** [li:v]		*hier:* abfahren
	to **arrive** [ə'raɪv]	to leave ←→ *to arrive*	ankommen

Step C **The sandcastle**

	sandcastle ['sændkɑ:sl]		Sandburg
	promenade [ˌprɒmə'nɑ:d]		Promenade
	bucket ['bʌkɪt]		Eimer
	to **look** [lʊk]		aussehen
	small [smɔ:l]		klein
2	**bookshop** ['bʊkʃɒp]		Buchhandlung

Let's play with words

1 Word puzzle

Du kennst bereits viele englische Wörter, die im Deutschen gleich sind, wie z. B. COMPUTER. Kannst du alle Wörter aus dem Puzzle zusammensetzen?

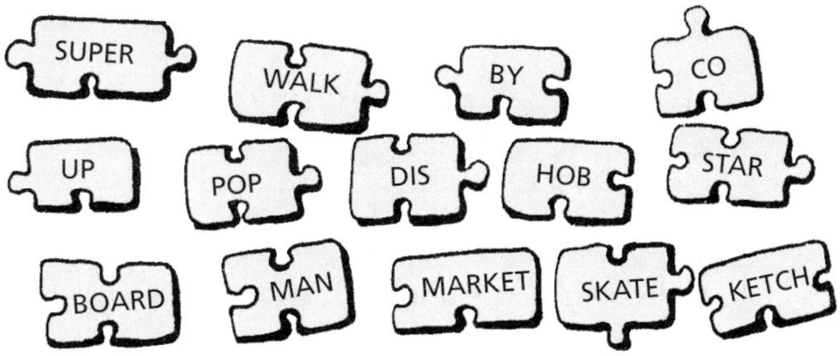

2 Word snakes

Welche Wörter findest du in den Schlangen? Schreibt man sie groß oder klein?

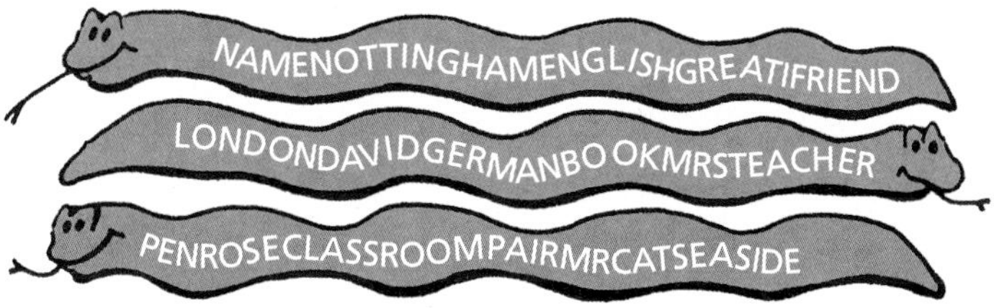

3 At the pond

Kannst du aus dem Teich die Wörter herausfischen, die zusammengehören? Bring sie auch in eine sinnvolle Reihenfolge. Welcher Fisch bleibt im Teich?

4 Word game

Denk an ein Wort. Wie viele andere Wörter kannst du finden, die etwas mit diesem Wort zu tun haben?

In dieser Spielwiese kannst du noch einmal mit den Wörtern spielen, die du in diesem Buch gelernt hast. Vielleicht kannst du auch selber solche Spiele mit anderen Wörtern zusammenstellen?

Step C **At a souvenir shop**

souvenir [ˌsuːvəˈnɪə]	Souvenir, Andenken, Mitbringsel
postcard [ˈpəʊstkɑːd]	Postkarte
to **say hello** [ˈseɪ həˈləʊ]	grüßen

Step D **Maxi's day at the seaside**

pet [pet]	Haustier
sandwich [ˈsænwɪdʒ]	belegtes Brot
to **understand** [ʌndəˈstænd]	verstehen
glad [glæd]	froh
to **sleep** [sliːp]	schlafen
duck [dʌk]	Ente
to **bark** [bɑːk]	bellen
rubbish [ˈrʌbɪʃ]	Abfall, Müll
to **show** [ʃəʊ]	zeigen
to **get lost** [get ˈlɒst]	verloren gehen, sich verirren

⟨Revision 3⟩

Cleethorpes [ˈkliːθɔːps]	*englischer Seebadeort*
Debbie [ˈdebi]	*weibl. Vorname*

Unit 10 On a Yorkshire farm

Eine Spielmöglichkeit ist die Vokabelkette, die du allein oder mit Freunden spielen kannst.
Einer nennt ein Wort. Der nächste muss ein zweites Wort finden, das mit dem letzten Buchstaben des ersten Wortes anfängt.
Schau dir Monnys Vokabelkette an.

Yorkshire [ˈjɔːkʃə]	*Grafschaft in England*
farm [fɑːm]	Bauernhof

Step A **Springfield farm**

Springfield [ˈsprɪŋfiːld]	*Name eines Bauernhofs*

Vocabulary

to **stay** [steɪ]		(zu Besuch) wohnen
Richards ['rɪtʃədz]		*Familienname*
guest house ['gest haʊs]	You can stay at a *guest house* at the seaside for a holiday.	Pension, Gästehaus
guest [gest]	 one *sheep*  two *sheep*	Gast
Jack [dʒæk]		*männl. Vorname*
sheep *(sg + pl)* [ʃi:p]		Schaf, Schafe
Sam [sæm]		*männl. Vorname*
sheepdog ['ʃi:pdɒg]		Hirtenhund
lamb [læm]	A *lamb* is a little sheep.	Lamm
lambing time ['læmɪŋ taɪm]		Zeit, in der Lämmer geboren werden
Lenny ['lenɪ]		*männl. Vorname*
animal ['ænɪməl]	Sheep, cats and dogs are *animals*.	Tier
cow [kaʊ]	We get milk from *cows*.	Kuh
pig [pɪg]	We get ham from *pigs*.	Schwein
hen [hen]	We get eggs from *hens*.	Henne
Grandpa ['grænpɑ:]		Opa
to **feed** [fi:d]	 Simon, Maxi and Mini are hungry. Can you *feed* them, please?	füttern
to **collect** [kə'lekt]		(ein)sammeln
to **lay** [leɪ]	Hens *lay* eggs.	legen

Step B **Jack's special friend**

enough [ɪ'nʌf]	 Do we need sugar? No, we've got *enough*. 	genug
to **drink** [drɪŋk]	You can *drink* tea, milk or lemonade.	trinken
all [ɔ:l]		ganz
3 **post office** ['pəʊst ˌɒfɪs]		Post, Postamt
Northallerton [nɔ:'θælətən]		*Ort in Yorkshire*
to **drive** [draɪv]	Can you *drive* a car? – No, I'm only 15.	fahren
⟨5⟩ had [hæd]		hatte
some [sʌm]		einige
chick [tʃɪk]		Küken
everywhere ['evrɪweə]		überall

Step B **The tractor**

tractor ['træktə]		Traktor, Trecker
who [hu:]		wen/wem

Step C **The seasons**

ⓐ **season** ['si:zn]		Jahreszeit
spring [sprɪŋ]		Frühling
holidays ['hɒlədɪz]	The summer *holidays* are in July and August.	Ferien

	summer ['sʌmə]		Sommer
	autumn ['ɔ:təm]		Herbst
	winter ['wɪntə]		Winter
	snow [snəʊ]	*Snow* makes everything white in winter.	Schnee
	night [naɪt]	day ⟷ *night*	Nacht
ⓑ	**milkshake** ['mɪlkʃeɪk]		Milchmixgetränk
	how many [haʊ 'menɪ]	*How many* seasons are there? – Four.	wie viele

Step D **Problems on the farm**

	Mary ['meərɪ]		*weibl. Vorname*
	to **be in trouble** [bɪ‿ɪn 'trʌbl]	I'm late. I'm *in trouble* again.	Schwierigkeiten haben
	trouble ['trʌbl]		Schwierigkeiten
	tired ['taɪəd]	 I'm *tired*. I want to go to bed.	müde
	shed [ʃed]		Stall, Schuppen
	to **wait** [weɪt]	I'm not ready! Please *wait*.	warten
	Alan ['ælən]		*männl. Vorname*
	Smith [smɪθ]		*Familienname*
	to **examine** [ɪg'zæmɪn]		untersuchen
	inside [ɪn'saɪd]	outside ⟷ *inside*	drinnen
	dead [ded]		tot
	to **save** [seɪv]	Firemen often *save* people from fires.	retten
	to **stay** [steɪ]		bleiben
	to **feel** [fi:l]	 I *feel* cold. – Well, don't stay outside too long. 	fühlen, sich fühlen
	to **die** [daɪ]		sterben
	to **trick** [trɪk]		austricksen
1	**trick** [trɪk]		Trick, Kunstgriff
	skin [skɪn]		Haut
6	**Walker** ['wɔ:kə]		*Familienname*
7	to **bring** [brɪŋ]	 Please *bring* bread and milk from the shop.	mitbringen
	free [fri:]		kostenlos

Alphabetical word list

In dieser alphabetischen Liste ist das gesamte Vokabular von *Red Line New 1* enthalten. Namen werden in einer gesonderten Liste nach dem Vokabular aufgeführt.

Der Wortschatz aus Übungen und Texten, die in Spitzklammern 〈 〉 stehen, ist wahlfrei.

Die Zahlen verweisen auf das erstmalige Vorkommen der Wörter, z. B.
afternoon [ˌɑːftəˈnuːn] Nachmittag **LS,** 14 = Let's start, Seite 14
again [əˈgen] **2,** 33 = Unit 2, Seite 33

A

a [ə] ein/eine **LS,** 9
to talk **about** [ˈtɔːk‿əˌbaʊt] reden über, sprechen über **2,** 32
What about ...? [wɒt‿əˈbaʊt] Was ist mit ...? **3,** 38
accident [ˈæksɪdənt] Unfall **8,** 86
to **act** [ækt] spielen, nachspielen **2,** 32
activity [ækˈtɪvɪtɪ] Tätigkeit **4,** 49
after [ˈɑːftə] nach **7,** 77
afternoon [ˌɑːftəˈnuːn] Nachmittag **LS,** 14
Good afternoon. [gʊd ˌɑːftəˈnuːn] Guten Tag. (*Anrede am Nachmittag*) **LS,** 16
in the afternoon [ɪn ðiː‿ɑːftəˈnuːn] nachmittags, am Nachmittag **LS,** 14
this afternoon [ðɪs‿ɑːftəˈnuːn] heute Nachmittag **3,** 40
again [əˈgen] wieder, noch einmal **2,** 33
airport [ˈeəpɔːt] Flughafen **3,** 37
all [ɔːl] ganz **10,** 108
all over [ˈɔːl‿ˌəʊvə] überall auf **7,** 83
all [ɔːl] alle/alles **3,** 43
alphabet [ˈælfəbət] Alphabet **4,** 47
always [ˈɔːlweɪz] immer **7,** 79
ambulance [ˈæmbjʊləns] Krankenwagen **8,** 91
an [ən] ein/eine **1,** 23
and [ænd] und **LS,** 8
angry [ˈæŋgrɪ] böse, verärgert **4,** 53
animal [ˈænɪməl] Tier **10,** 107
anorak [ˈænəræk] Anorak **6,** 70
another [əˈnʌðə] noch einen/eine/eins **5,** 63
answer [ˈɑːnsə] Antwort **LS,** 12
to **answer** [ˈɑːnsə] (be)antworten **6,** 70
Anything else? [ˈenɪθɪŋ ˈels] Sonst noch etwas? **7,** 82
apple [ˈæpl] Apfel **1,** 23
April [ˈeɪprəl] April **5,** 57
are [ɑː] bist/seid/sind **LS,** 11
arm [ɑːm] Arm **7,** 81
to **arrive** [əˈraɪv] ankommen **9,** 99
to **ask** [ɑːsk] fragen **1,** 21
to ask for [ˈɑːsk fɔː] bitten um **3,** 37
assembly [əˈsemblɪ] Versammlung **7,** 80
assistant [əˈsɪstənt] Helfer/in, Assistent/in **2,** 28
at [æt], [ət] an **LS,** 9
at home [ət ˈhəʊm] zu Hause **1,** 18
at ... o'clock [ət ... əˈklɒk] um ... Uhr **5,** 59
at the bottom of [ət ðə ˈbɒtəm‿əv] unten, am unteren Ende **6,** 69
at the top of [ət ðə ˈtɒp‿əv] ganz oben **2,** 33
August [ˈɔːgəst] August **5,** 57
aunt [ɑːnt] Tante **3,** 37
Aunty [ˈɑːntɪ] *Anrede für eine Tante* **3,** 39
autumn [ˈɔːtəm] Herbst **10,** 111

B

back [bæk] zurück **6,** 73
back door [ˈbæk ˈdɔː] Hintertür **8,** 92
bad [bæd] schlimm, schlecht **1,** 21
badminton [ˈbædmɪntən] Federballspiel **4,** 51
bag [bæg] Tasche **LS,** 10
ball [bɔːl] Ball **LS,** 10
balloon [bəˈluːn] Luftballon **5,** 58
banana [bəˈnɑːnə] Banane **7,** 82
bank [bæŋk] Bank **2,** 28
bank clerk [ˈbæŋk‿klɑːk] Bankangestellte/r **2,** 28
bar [bɑː] Tafel **7,** 82
to **bark** [bɑːk] bellen **9,** 102
bath [bɑːθ] Bad, Badewanne **5,** 62
to have a bath [hæv‿ə ˈbɑːθ] baden **5,** 62
bathroom [ˈbɑːθrʊm] Badezimmer **5,** 62
to **be** [bɪ] sein **2,** 33
Be careful! [bɪ ˈkeəfʊl] Pass auf!, Vorsicht! **2,** 33
to be good at [bɪ ˈgʊd‿ət] gut sein in ... **4,** 53
to be lucky [bɪ ˈlʌkɪ] Glück haben **3,** 38
to be on [bɪ‿ˈɒn] eingeschaltet sein **4,** 49
beach [biːtʃ] Strand **9,** 95
because [bɪˈkɒz] weil **6,** 69
bed [bed] Bett **1,** 23
bedroom [ˈbedrʊm] Schlafzimmer **5,** 62
beetle [ˈbiːtl] Käfer **7,** 81
behind [bɪˈhaɪnd] hinter **6,** 71
best [best] beste/bester/bestes **6,** 69
better [ˈbetə] besser **8,** 89
I hope you're better soon. [aɪ ˈhəʊp jʊə ˌbetə ˈsuːn] Ich hoffe, es geht dir bald besser. **8,** 89
big [bɪg] groß **1,** 21
bike [baɪk] Fahrrad **1,** 25
biro [ˈbaɪrəʊ] Kugelschreiber **LS,** 10
birthday [ˈbɜːθdeɪ] Geburtstag **5,** 56
biscuit [ˈbɪskɪt] Keks **1,** 18
a **bit** [əˈbɪt] etwas, ein bisschen **8,** 89
black [blæk] schwarz **2,** 28
blue [bluː] blau **2,** 28
boat [bəʊt] Boot **9,** 95
boating lake [ˈbəʊtɪŋ leɪk] Bootsteich **9,** 95
body [ˈbɒdɪ] Körper **7,** 81
book [bʊk] Buch **LS,** 10
boring [ˈbɔːrɪŋ] langweilig **4,** 47
bottle [ˈbɒtl] Flasche **7,** 82
box [bɒks] Schachtel, Kiste, Dose **LS,** 10
lunch box [ˈlʌntʃ bɒks] *Dose für belegte Brote zum Mittagessen* **LS,** 10
boy [bɔɪ] Junge **LS,** 12
bread [bred] Brot **3,** 42
breakfast [ˈbrekfəst] Frühstück **5,** 62
to **bring** [brɪŋ] bringen **LS,** 16; mitbringen **10,** 114

British [ˈbrɪtɪʃ] britisch **3,** 37
broken [ˈbrəʊkən] kaputt, zerbrochen **1,** 23
brother [ˈbrʌðə] Bruder **1,** 18
brown [braʊn] braun **2,** 28
bubble bath [ˈbʌbl ˌbɑːθ] Schaumbad **7,** 83
bucket [ˈbʌkɪt] Eimer **9,** 100
burglar [ˈbɜːglə] Einbrecher/in **8,** 93
bus [bʌs] Bus **6,** 69
bus stop [ˈbʌs stɒp] Bushaltestelle **6,** 69
busy [ˈbɪzɪ] beschäftigt **5,** 58
but [bʌt] aber **1,** 18
butter [ˈbʌtə] Butter **3,** 42
to **buy** [baɪ] kaufen **7,** 76
by [baɪ] mit **3,** 41
Bye. [baɪ] Tschüs! (*kurze gesprochene Form von* Goodbye.) **8,** 87

C

cake [keɪk] Kuchen, Torte **5,** 56
calendar [ˈkælɪndə] Kalender **6,** 69
to **call** [kɔːl] rufen, anrufen **8,** 91
⟨camcorder⟩ [ˈkæmkɔːdə] Videokamera **R2,** 66
camera [ˈkæmərə] Fotoapparat, Kamera **3,** 43
can [kæn] können **3,** 38
cannot [ˈkænɒt], [kɑːnt] nicht können **3,** 43
can't [kɑːnt] nicht können **3,** 38
candle [ˈkændl] Kerze **5,** 63
car [kɑː] Auto **1,** 18
card [kɑːd] Karte **8,** 90
Be **careful!** [bɪ ˈkeəfʊl] Pass auf!, Vorsicht! **2,** 33
case [keɪs] Etui, Hülle **LS,** 10
pencil case [ˈpensl keɪs] Federmäppchen **LS,** 10
castle [ˈkɑːsl] Burg **6,** 68
cat [kæt] Katze **2,** 28
CD [siː ˈdiː] CD **1,** 20
CD player [siː ˈdiː pleɪə] CD-Spieler **1,** 20
centre [ˈsentə] Mitte, Zentrum **6,** 68
chair [tʃeə] Stuhl **LS,** 13
⟨to check⟩ [tʃek] überprüfen, kontrollieren **LS,** 16
cheese [tʃiːz] Käse **3,** 42
⟨chick⟩ [tʃɪk] Küken **10,** 109
child [tʃaɪld], **children** *(pl)* [ˈtʃɪldrən] Kind, Kinder **2,** 28
chips *(pl)* [tʃɪps] Pommes frites **7,** 76
chocolate [ˈtʃɒklət] Schokolade **LS,** 15
church [tʃɜːtʃ] Kirche **6,** 68
cinema [ˈsɪnɪmə] Kino **6,** 69
city [ˈsɪtɪ] (Groß-)Stadt **6,** 68
⟨to clap⟩ [klæp] klatschen **1,** 19
class [klɑːs] Klasse (*in einer deutschen Schule*) **LS,** 9
classroom [ˈklɑːsrʊm] Klassenzimmer **LS,** 16
clerk [klɑːk] Büroangestellte/r **2,** 28
bank clerk [ˈbæŋk‿klɑːk] Bankangestellte/r **2,** 28
clever [ˈklevə] intelligent, klug **1,** 18
to **climb up** [ˌklaɪm ˈʌp] hochklettern, erklettern **8,** 93
to **close** [kləʊz] schließen, zumachen **8,** 92
clothes *(pl)* [ˈkləʊðz] Kleider **6,** 70
cold [kəʊld] kalt **4,** 52
to **collect** [kəˈlekt] abholen **7,** 78; (ein)sammeln **10,** 107
colour [ˈkʌlə] Farbe **2,** 28
to **come** [kʌm] kommen **4,** 49
Come on! [kəm‿ˈɒn] Komm schon!, Kommt schon! **2,** 33
to come home [kʌm ˈhəʊm] nach Hause kommen **7,** 77
⟨to come in⟩ [kʌm‿ˈɪn] hereinkommen **1,** 26
comic [ˈkɒmɪk] Comic **LS,** 10
competition [kɒmpəˈtɪʃn] Wettbewerb, Preisausschreiben **7,** 76
computer [kəmˈpjuːtə] Computer **1,** 20
cornflakes *(pl)* [ˈkɔːnfleɪks] Cornflakes **7,** 78
to **correct** [kəˈrekt] korrigieren, verbessern **LS,** 16
to **cost** [kɒst] kosten **9,** 97
to **count** [kaʊnt] zählen **4,** 47
cousin [ˈkʌzn] Cousin/e **3,** 37
cow [kaʊ] Kuh **10,** 107
crab [kræb] Krebs **9,** 98
Crash! [kræʃ] Rums! **4,** 53
crayon [ˈkreɪən] Buntstift **2,** 28
crazy [ˈkreɪzɪ] verrückt **LS,** 10
cricket [ˈkrɪkɪt] *englischer Rasensport* **4,** 51
crisps *(pl)* [krɪsps] Kartoffelchips **7,** 76
⟨'cross⟩ [krɒs] über **4,** 52
cupboard [ˈkʌbəd] Schrank **8,** 89

D

Dad [dæd] Vati, Papa **1,** 19
to **dance** [dɑːns] tanzen **5,** 56
date [deɪt] Datum **5,** 59
day [deɪ] Tag **5,** 56
in ... days [ɪn ... deɪz] in ... Tagen **5,** 56
dead [ded] tot **10,** 112
dear [dɪə] liebe/lieber/liebes **5,** 57
oh **dear** [əʊ ˈdɪə] Oh je! **7,** 79
December [dɪˈsembə] Dezember **5,** 57
desk [desk] Schreibtisch, Pult **LS,** 13
dialogue [ˈdaiəlɒg] Dialog, Gespräch **2,** 32
dice *(sg + pl)* [daɪs] Würfel **2,** 30
to **die** [daɪ] sterben **10,** 112
different [ˈdɪfrənt] unterschiedlich, anders **3,** 45
dirty [ˈdɜːtɪ] schmutzig, dreckig **7,** 81
to **do** [duː] tun, machen **3,** 38
to do the washing-up [ˈdʊ ðə ˌwɒʃɪŋˈʌp] spülen, abwaschen **7,** 79
doctor [ˈdɒktə] Arzt/Ärztin **8,** 91
dog [dɒg] Hund **LS,** 8
dog biscuit [ˈdɒg ˌbɪskɪt] Hundekuchen **1,** 19
dog-free zone [ˈdɒgfriː ˈzəʊn] hundefreie Zone **9,** 96
door [dɔː] Tür **7,** 79; (Garagen-)Tor **4,** 53
back door [ˈbæk ˈdɔː] Hintertür **8,** 92
front door [ˈfrʌnt ˈdɔː] Haustür **8,** 92
double [ˈdʌbl] zweimal, Doppel- **1,** 24
double decker [ˈdʌbl ˈdekə] Doppeldecker **6,** 69
down [daʊn] herunter, hinunter **6,** 71
to sit down [sɪt ˈdaʊn] sich hinsetzen **LS,** 16
downstairs [ˌdaʊnˈsteəz] unten (im Gebäude) **5,** 62
drama group [ˈdrɑːmə gruːp] Theatergruppe **7,** 80
to **draw** [drɔː] zeichnen **2,** 28
to **drink** [drɪŋk] trinken **10,** 108
to **drive** [draɪv] fahren **10,** 109
driver [ˈdraɪvə] Fahrer/in **6,** 73
duck [dʌk] Ente **9,** 102

E

⟨ear⟩ [ɪə] Ohr **7,** 81
early [ˈɜːlɪ] früh **7,** 78
easy [ˈiːzɪ] einfach, leicht **LS,** 14
to **eat** [iːt] essen **6,** 72

egg [eg] Ei **1,** 23
else [els] sonst (noch) **7,** 82
end [end] Ende **6,** 69
ending [ˈendɪŋ] Ende, Schluss (*bei Geschichten*) **8,** 93
English [ˈɪŋglɪʃ] englisch, Englisch **LS,** 10
enough [ɪˈnʌf] genug **10,** 108
evening [ˈiːvnɪŋ] Abend **4,** 48
in the evening [ɪnðiː‿ˈiːvnɪŋ] abends, am Abend **4,** 48
every [ˈevrɪ] jede/jeder/jedes **7,** 77
⟨everybody⟩ [ˈevrɪbɒdɪ] jede/jeder **9,** 95
everyone [ˈevrɪwʌn] jede/jeder, alle **5,** 58
everything [ˈevrɪθɪŋ] alles **2,** 33
⟨everywhere⟩ [ˈevrɪweə] überall **10,** 109
to **examine** [ɪgˈzæmɪn] untersuchen **10,** 112
example [ɪgˈzɑːmpl] Beispiel **1,** 18
exciting [ɪkˈsaɪtɪŋ] aufregend, spannend **4,** 49
Excuse me, please. [ɪkˈskjuːz mɪ pliːz] Entschuldigung., Entschuldigen Sie bitte. **6,** 71
exercise [ˈeksəsaɪz] Übung, Aufgabe **4,** 54
exercise book [ˈeksəsaɪz ˌbʊk] Heft **7,** 81
extra [ˈekstrə] zusätzlich **7,** 83
eye [aɪ] Auge **7,** 81

F

to **fall over** [fɔːl‿ˈəʊvə] hinfallen **7,** 83
family [ˈfæməlɪ] Familie **2,** 28
farm [fɑːm] Bauernhof **10,** 107
father [ˈfɑːðə] Vater **1,** 19
favourite [ˈfeɪvərɪt] Lieblings- **6,** 69
February [ˈfebrʊərɪ] Februar **5,** 57
to **feed** [fiːd] füttern **10,** 107
to **feel** [fiːl] fühlen, sich fühlen **10,** 112
feeler [ˈfiːlə] Fühler **7,** 81
⟨feet⟩ *(pl)* [fiːt] Füße **1,** 19
ferry [ˈferɪ] Fähre **3,** 41
to **find** [faɪnd] finden **LS,** 15
to find out [faɪnd ˈaʊt] herausfinden **4,** 49
I'm **fine.** [aɪm ˈfaɪn] Mir geht's gut. **5,** 57
to **finish** [ˈfɪnɪʃ] beenden, aufhören **7,** 77
fire brigade [ˈfaɪə brɪˌgeɪd] Feuerwehr **8,** 91
fireman [ˈfaɪəmən] Feuerwehrmann **8,** 91
firm [fɜːm] Firma **8,** 92
first [fɜːst] erste/erster/erstes **5,** 57
fish [fɪʃ] Fisch **8,** 92
fish finger [fɪʃ ˈfɪŋgə] Fischstäbchen **8,** 92
flat [flæt] Wohnung **1,** 22
flat [flæt] flach, platt **2,** 30
flat tyre [ˌflæt ˈtaɪə] platter Reifen, Platten **2,** 30
floor [flɔː] Boden **4,** 53
flowerpot [ˈlaʊəpɒt] Blumentopf **4,** 53
folder [ˈfəʊldə] Mappe, Hefter **LS,** 10
football [ˈfʊtbɔːl] Fußball **1,** 20
for [fɔː], [fə] für **1,** 18
to ask for [ˈɑːsk fɔː] bitten um **3,** 37
form [fɔːm] Form **3,** 39
free [friː] kostenlos **10,** 114
free [friː] frei **4,** 47
Friday [ˈfraɪdeɪ] Freitag **6,** 69
friend [frend] Freund/in **LS,** 9
frog [frɒg] Frosch **1,** 25
from [frɒm] aus, von **LS,** 8
from … to [frəm … tə] von … nach **3,** 41
front door [ˈfrʌnt ˈdɔː] Haustür **8,** 92
in **front of** [ɪn ˈfrʌnt əv] vor **6,** 68
fun [fʌn] Spaß **8,** 94
funny [ˈfʌnɪ] lustig, komisch **LS,** 16

G

game [geɪm] Spiel **LS,** 13
garage [ˈgærɑːdʒ] Garage **2,** 30
garden [ˈgɑːdən] Garten **1,** 21
⟨gay⟩ [geɪ] fröhlich **9,** 95
German [ˈdʒɜːmən] deutsch, Deutsch, Deutsche/r **LS,** 12
to **get** [get] bekommen **4,** 50; holen **2,** 33
Get out! [get ˈaʊt] Hinaus mit dir!, Hinaus mit euch! **7,** 81
Get well soon! [ˈget wel ˈsuːn] Gute Besserung! **8,** 90
to get lost [get ˈlɒst] verloren gehen, sich verirren **9,** 102
to get ready [get ˈredɪ] (sich) vorbereiten **5,** 58
to get stuck [get ˈstʌk] stecken bleiben **8,** 93
to get the bus [ˌget ðə ˈbʌs] den Bus nehmen **6,** 69
to get there [ˈget ðeə] hinkommen **3,** 41
to get up [get‿ˈʌp] aufstehen **7,** 77
girl [gɜːl] Mädchen **LS,** 11
to **give** [gɪv] geben **3,** 40
give my love to … [ˌgɪv maɪ ˈlʌv tə] grüß/grüßt … recht herzlich **8,** 92
to give … a lift [lɪft] … im Auto mitnehmen **6,** 73
glad [glæd] froh **9,** 102
to **go** [gəʊ] gehen, fahren **2,** 30
to go for a walk [ˌgəʊ fər‿ə ˈwɔːk] spazieren gehen **4,** 52
to go home [gəʊ ˈhəʊm] nach Hause gehen **8,** 88
to go on [gəʊ‿ˈɒn] weitermachen **LS,** 10
to go swimming [gəʊ ˈswɪmɪŋ] schwimmen gehen **9,** 95
to go to bed [gəʊ tə ˈbed] ins Bett gehen, schlafen gehen **7,** 77
to go to the shops [gəʊ tə ðə ˈʃɒps] einkaufen gehen **3,** 40
to go together [gəʊ təˈgeðə] zusammenpassen **7,** 82
goal [gəʊl] Tor (*beim Sport*) **4,** 53
good [gʊd] gut **LS,** 12
Good afternoon. [gʊd ɑːftəˈnuːn] Guten Tag. (*Anrede am Nachmittag*) **LS,** 16
Good morning. [gʊd ˈmɔːnɪŋ] Guten Morgen. **LS,** 12
It's good to see you. [ɪts ˌgʊd tə ˈsiː jʊ] Schön dich/euch zu sehen. **8,** 89
to be good at [bɪ ˈgʊd‿ət] gut sein in … **4,** 53
Goodbye. [gʊdˈbaɪ] Auf Wiedersehen., Tschüs. **LS,** 10
has **got** [hæz gɒt] hat **1,** 20
hasn't got [ˈhæznt gɒt] hat nicht/kein **1,** 20
have got [ˈhæv gɒt] haben, besitzen **1,** 21
Grandma [ˈgrænmɑː] Oma **6,** 72
Grandpa [ˈgrænpɑː] Opa **10,** 107
great [greɪt] toll, großartig **2,** 29
Greek [griːk] griechisch, Griechisch **3,** 37
green [griːn] grün **2,** 28
group [gruːp] Gruppe **LS,** 9
tutor group [ˈtjuːtə ˌgruːp] Klasse (*in einer englischen Schule*) **LS,** 9
guest [gest] Gast **10,** 107
guest house [ˈgest haʊs] Pension, Gästehaus **10,** 107
guitar [gɪˈtɑː] Gitarre **5,** 56

H

⟨had⟩ [hæd] hatte **10,** 109
half [hɑːf] halb; Hälfte **5,** 60
hall [hɔːl] Diele, Flur **5,** 62
ham [hæm] gekochter Schinken **3,** 42
hand [hænd] Hand **7,** 81

happy ['hæpɪ] fröhlich, glücklich **5**, 63
Happy birthday! [ˌhæpɪ 'bɜ:θdeɪ] Herzlichen Glückwunsch zum Geburtstag! **5**, 63
has got ... [hæz gɒt] hat ... **1**, 20
hasn't got ... ['hæznt gɒt] hat nicht/kein ... **1**, 20
⟨hat⟩ [hæt] Hut **9**, 95
to **have** [hæv] haben **3**, 42
have got ['hæv gɒt] haben, besitzen **1**, 21
haven't got ... ['hævnt gɒt] nicht haben **1**, 21
to have a bath [hæv‿ə 'bɑ:θ] baden **5**, 62
⟨to have on⟩ [hæv‿'ɒn] anhaben, tragen **9**, 95
he [hi:] er **LS**, 9
Is he ... ? ['ɪz 'hi:] Ist er ... ? **LS**, 9
head [hed] Kopf **7**, 81
headteacher [ˌhed'ti:tʃə] Schuldirektor/in **7**, 83
healthy living ['helθɪ 'lɪvɪŋ] gesunde Lebensweise **7**, 76
Hello. [hə'ləʊ] Hallo., Guten Tag. **LS**, 7
to say hello ['seɪ hə'ləʊ] grüßen **9**, 101
Help! [help] Hilfe! **8**, 91
to **help** [help] helfen **3**, 37
hen [hen] Henne **10**, 107
her [hɜ:] ihr/ihre **LS**, 12; ihr/sie **3**, 40
here [hɪə] hier **LS**, 10
Here you are. ['hɪə jʊ‿ˌɑ:] Hier, bitte schön. **2**, 28
here's (= here is) [hɪəz] hier ist **LS**, 10
Hey! [heɪ] He! **LS**, 13
Hi! [haɪ] Hallo! **1**, 25
hill [hɪl] Hügel **6**, 71
⟨on the hillside⟩ [ˌɒn ðə 'hɪlsaɪd] am Hang **2**, 35
him [hɪm] ihm/ihn **3**, 40
⟨hip, hip, hurray⟩ [hɪp hɪp hʊ'reɪ] hipp, hipp, hurra! **9**, 95
his [hɪz] sein/seine **LS**, 12
Hmm. Hm., Tja. **LS**, 15
hockey ['hɒkɪ] Rasenhockey **7**, 80
hole [həʊl] Loch **1**, 21
⟨holiday⟩ ['hɒlədɪ] Urlaub(stag) **9**, 95
holidays ['hɒlədɪz] Ferien **10**, 111
home [həʊm] Heim, Zuhause **1**, 22
at home [ət 'həʊm] zu Hause **1**, 18
to come home [kʌm 'həʊm] nach Hause kommen **7**, 77
to go home [gəʊ 'həʊm] nach Hause gehen **8**, 88
homework ['həʊmwɜ:k] Hausaufgaben **LS**, 16
to **hope** [həʊp] hoffen **8**, 89
hospital ['hɒspɪtl] Krankenhaus **8**, 89
hot [hɒt] heiß **6**, 72
hour ['aʊə] Stunde **9**, 97
house [haʊs] Haus **1**, 22
housework ['haʊswɜ:k] Hausarbeit **7**, 79
hovercraft ['hɒvəkrɑ:ft] Luftkissenboot **3**, 41
how [haʊ] wie **LS**, 11
How are you? [haʊ‿'ɑ: ju:] Wie geht es dir/euch/Ihnen? **5**, 57
how many [haʊ 'menɪ] wie viele **10**, 111
How much? [haʊ 'mʌtʃ] Wie viel? **7**, 76
hungry ['hʌŋgrɪ] hungrig **1**, 19
to **hurt** [hɜ:t] weh tun, schmerzen **8**, 89

I

I [aɪ] ich **LS**, 7
Am I ... ? ['æm‿aɪ] Bin ich ... ? **LS**, 10
I'm (= I am) [aɪm] ich bin **LS**, 7
I've got ['aɪv gɒt] Ich habe **1**, 21
ice cream [ˌaɪs 'kri:m] Eiskrem **8**, 92
idea [aɪ'dɪə] Idee **1**, 21
in [ɪn] in **LS**, 7
in ... days [ɪn ... deɪz] in ... Tagen **5**, 56
in front of [ɪn 'frʌnt əv] vor **6**, 68
in the afternoon [ɪn ði:‿ɑ:ftə'nu:n] nachmittags, am Nachmittag **LS**, 14
in the evening [ɪnði:‿'i:vnɪŋ] abends, am Abend **4**, 48
in the morning [ɪn ðə 'mɔ:nɪŋ] morgens, am Vormittag **LS**, 14
inside [ɪn'saɪd] drinnen **10**, 112
into ['ɪntʊ] in, hinein **6**, 69
invitation [ˌɪnvɪ'teɪʃn] Einladung **5**, 56
to **invite** [ɪn'vaɪt] einladen **5**, 56
irregular [ɪ'regjʊlə] unregelmäßig **7**, 78
is [ɪz] ist **LS**, 8
it [ɪt] es/er/sie **LS**, 13; ihn/sie/es; ihm/ihr **4**, 50
it's (= it is) [ɪts] es ist, er ist, sie ist **LS**, 13
Italian [ɪt'æljən] italienisch, Italienisch, Italiener/in **3**, 37
its [ɪts] sein, seine/ihr, ihre **2**, 29

J

January ['dʒænjʊərɪ] Januar **5**, 57
jeans *(sg + pl)* [dʒi:nz] Jeans **6**, 70
job [dʒɒb] Beruf, Arbeit **4**, 49
July [dʒʊ:'laɪ] Juli **5**, 57
June [dʒʊ:n] Juni **5**, 57
just [dʒʌst] eben, gerade, nur **4**, 49
⟨just the same⟩ [ˌdʒʌst ðə 'seɪm] genau gleich **2**, 35

K

to **kick** [kɪk] treten, mit dem Fuß stoßen **4**, 53
kitchen ['kɪtʃɪn] Küche **1**, 19
kite [kaɪt] Drachen **4**, 47
⟨knee⟩ [ni:] Knie **7**, 81
knife [naɪf], **knives** *(pl)* [naɪvz] Messer *(Sg/Pl)* **2**, 29
to **know** [nəʊ] wissen, kennen **8**, 86

L

ladder ['lædə] Leiter **8**, 92
lake [leɪk] (der) See, Teich **9**, 95
lamb [læm] Lamm **10**, 107
lambing time ['læmɪŋ taɪm] Zeit, in der Lämmer geboren werden **10**, 107
last [lɑ:st] letzter/letzte/letztes **4**, 47
late [leɪt] spät, zu spät **LS**, 10
to work late ['wɜ:k leɪt] länger arbeiten **4**, 49
to **laugh** [lɑ:f] lachen **4**, 53
to **lay** [leɪ] legen **10**, 107
lb (= **pound**) [paʊnd] *Abkürzung für* pound (*Gewicht*) **7**, 83
to **learn** [lɜ:n] lernen **LS**, 14
to **leave** [li:v] abfahren **9**, 99
left [left] (nach) links **6**, 71
on the left/right [ɒn ðə 'left], [ɒn ðə 'raɪt] links/rechts, auf der linken/rechten Seite **6**, 71
leg [leg] Bein **3**, 43
lemonade [lemə'neɪd] Limonade **7**, 82
to **lend** [lend] leihen, verleihen **7**, 76
lesson [lesn] Unterrichtsstunde **LS**, 16
Let's [lets] Lasst uns **LS**, 14
letter ['letə] Brief **5**, 57

letter ['letə] Buchstabe **4**, 47
to **lie** [laɪ] liegen **5**, 58
to give ... a **lift** [lɪft] ... im Auto mitnehmen **6**, 73
to **like** [laɪk] mögen, gern haben **8**, 86
like [laɪk] (so) wie **3**, 44
What's ... like? [wɒts ... laɪk] Wie ist ... ? **4**, 52
list [lɪst] Liste **5**, 58
to **listen** ['lɪsn] zuhören **LS**, 10
listening practice ['lɪsnɪŋ ˌpræktɪs] Hörverstehensübung **LS**, 15
little [lɪtl] klein **2**, 32
to **live** [lɪv] leben, wohnen **9**, 98
living-room ['lɪvɪŋrʊm] Wohnzimmer **2**, 33
locked [lɒkt] abgeschlossen **8**, 92
long [lɒŋ] lang **6**, 73
to **look** [lʊk] sehen, anschauen **LS**, 9; aussehen **9**, 100
Looking at the UK [ˌlʊkɪŋ‿ət ðə ju: 'keɪ] Ein Blick auf das Vereinigte Königreich! **1**, 22
to look at ['lʊk‿ət] anschauen **LS**, 9
a **lot of** [ə'lɒt əv] viel/viele, eine Menge **6**, 68
love [lʌv] alles Liebe *(als Briefschluss)* **5**, 57
lucky ['lʌkɪ] glücklich, Glücks- **7**, 83
to be lucky [bɪ 'lʌkɪ] Glück haben **3**, 38
You're lucky. [jɔ: 'lʌkɪ] Du hast Glück. **3**, 38
lunch [lʌntʃ] Mittagessen **LS**, 10
lunch box ['lʌntʃ bɒks] *Dose für belegte Brote zum Mittagessen* **LS**, 10

M

⟨made out of⟩ [ˌmeɪd 'aʊt‿əv] gemacht aus, hergestellt aus **2**, 35
magazine [ˌmægə'zi:n] Zeitschrift **8**, 86
to **make** [meɪk] machen **LS**, 9
man [mæn], **men** *(pl)* [men] Mann, Männer **2**, 28
how **many** [haʊ 'menɪ] wie viele **10**, 111
map [mæp] Landkarte **3**, 41
March [mɑ:tʃ] März **5**, 57
market ['mɑ:kɪt] Markt **6**, 68
mascot ['mæskət] Maskottchen **7**, 84
May [meɪ] Mai **5**, 57
maybe ['meɪbi:] vielleicht **3**, 40
me [mi:] mir/mich **3**, 40
mechanic [mɪ'kænɪk] Mechaniker/in **8**, 86
to **meet** [mi:t] (sich) treffen **9**, 96
mess [mes] Unordnung **7**, 79
milk [mɪlk] Milch **3**, 42
milkshake ['mɪlkʃeɪk] Milchmixgetränk **10**, 111
Never **mind.** ['nevə ˌmaɪnd] Mach dir nichts daraus., Macht euch nichts daraus. **9**, 95
minute ['mɪnɪt] Minute **4**, 49
In a minute. [ɪn‿ə 'mɪnɪt] Augenblick noch!, Warte/t mal einen Moment. **4**, 49
Monday ['mʌndeɪ] Montag **6**, 69
money ['mʌnɪ] Geld **7**, 76
month [mʌnθ] Monat **5**, 57
more [mɔ:] mehr, weitere **1**, 25
morning ['mɔ:nɪŋ] Morgen **LS**, 12
Good morning. [gʊd 'mɔ:nɪŋ] Guten Morgen. **LS**, 12
in the morning [ɪn ðə 'mɔ:nɪŋ] morgens, am Vormittag **LS**, 14
mother ['mʌðə] Mutter **1**, 19
mouth [maʊθ] Mund **7**, 81
Mr ['mɪstə] Herr *(Anrede für Männer)* **LS**, 12
Mrs ['mɪsɪz] Frau *(Anrede für verheiratete Frauen)* **LS**, 12
Mum [mʌm] Mama, Mutti **1**, 21
music ['mju:zɪk] Musik **4**, 51
pop music ['pɒp 'mju:zɪk] Popmusik **4**, 51
must [mʌst] müssen **3**, 40
my [maɪ] mein/meine **LS**, 8

N

name [neɪm] Name **LS**, 8
My name is ... ['maɪ neɪm‿ɪz] Ich heiße ... **LS**, 8
near [nɪə] in der Nähe von **6**, 68
⟨near⟩ [ni:ə] nahe **4**, 52
to **need** [ni:d] brauchen, benötigen **8**, 86
neighbour ['neɪbə] Nachbar/in **2**, 31
never ['nevə] nie **7**, 79
Never mind. ['nevə ˌmaɪnd] Mach dir nichts daraus., Macht euch nichts daraus. **9**, 95
new [nju:] neu **LS**, 8
next [nekst] nächste/nächster/nächstes **5**, 57
nice [naɪs] nett, schön **LS**, 9
night [naɪt] Nacht **10**, 111
no [nəʊ] kein/keine **4**, 53
no [nəʊ] nein **LS**, 10
nobody ['nəʊbədɪ] niemand, keiner **4**, 48
noise [nɒɪz] Lärm, Krach, Geräusch **2**, 33
⟨nose⟩ [nəʊz] Nase **7**, 81
nosy ['nəʊzɪ] neugierig **2**, 31
not [nɒt] nicht **LS**, 11
not ... yet [nɒt ... jet] noch nicht **1**, 25
nothing ['nʌθɪŋ] nichts **2**, 33
November [nəʊ'vembə] November **5**, 57
now [naʊ] jetzt, nun **LS**, 16
number ['nʌmbə] Nummer, Zahl **1**, 24
nurse [nɜ:s] Krankenschwester/Krankenpfleger **8**, 89
nursery school ['nɜ:sərɪ ˌsku:l] Kindergarten **7**, 78

O

o [əʊ] null *(bei Telefonnummern)* **1**, 24
at ... **o'clock** [ət ... ə'klɒk] um ... Uhr **5**, 59
October [ɒk'təʊbə] Oktober **5**, 57
of [ɒv], [əv] von **3**, 42
of course [əv‿'kɔ:s] natürlich, selbstverständlich **4**, 47
office ['ɔfɪs] Büro, Amt **6**, 72
police **officer** [pə'li:s‿ɒfɪsə] Polizist/in **8**, 91
often ['ɒfn] oft **7**, 79
oh [əʊ] oh **LS**, 8
Oh dear! [əʊ 'dɪə] Oh je! **7**, 79
OK [əʊ'keɪ] OK; in Ordnung **LS**, 12
old [əʊld] alt **LS**, 11
on [ɒn] auf **LS**, 13
⟨on the hillside⟩ [ˌɒn ðə 'hɪlsaɪd] am Hang **2**, 35
on (the radio) [ɒn] im (Rundfunk) **4**, 49
on the seventh of [ɒn ðə 'sevnθ‿əv] am siebten **5**, 59
on the telephone [ɒn ðə 'telɪfəʊn] am Telefon **3**, 40
to be on [bɪ‿'ɒn] eingeschaltet sein **4**, 48
on the left/right [ɒn ðə 'left], [ɒn ðə 'raɪt] links/rechts, auf der linken/rechten Seite **6**, 71
one [wʌn] ein/eine/eins **1**, 18
only ['əʊnlɪ] nur, erst **3**, 43
Oops! [u:ps] Hoppla! **1**, 21
to **open** ['əʊpən] öffnen, aufmachen **8**, 92
open ['əʊpən] offen, geöffnet **8**, 92
opposite ['ɒpəzɪt] Gegenteil **4**, 55
or [ɔ:] oder **LS**, 14
word **order** ['wɜ:d ˌɔ:də] Satzstellung **7**, 79

other ['ʌðə] andere, weitere **2,** 31
our ['aʊə] unser/unsere **1,** 19
out [aʊt] draußen, heraus **4,** 50
⟨made out of⟩ [ˌmeɪd 'aʊt‿əv] gemacht aus, hergestellt aus **2,** 35
outside [ˌaʊt'saɪd] draußen **2,** 33
over ['əʊvə] über **5,** 56
over there [əʊvə 'ðeə] da drüben, dort **1,** 23

P

packet ['pækɪt] Päckchen **7,** 76
page [peɪdʒ] Seite **LS,** 9
pair [peə] Paar **LS,** 14
parents *(pl)* ['peərənts] Eltern **2,** 29
park [pɑːk] Park **1,** 25
partner ['pɑːtnə] Partner/in **1,** 21
party ['pɑːtɪ] Party, Feier **5,** 56
to **pass** [pɑːs] reichen, weitergeben **3,** 42
past [pɑːst] nach (*bei Uhrzeiten*) **5,** 60
pen [pen] Füller **LS,** 10
pence (= **p**) *(pl)* [pens] Pfennige (*britisches Geld*) **7,** 76
pencil ['pensl] Bleistift **LS,** 10
pencil case ['pensl keɪs] Federmäppchen **LS,** 10
people *(pl)* ['piːpl] Leute **3,** 37
person ['pɜːsn] Person **6,** 72
pet [pet] Haustier **9,** 102
to **phone** [fəʊn] anrufen **3,** 40
photo ['fəʊtəʊ] Foto **3,** 41
to take a photo of [teɪk‿ə'fəʊtəʊ‿əv] ein Foto machen von **3,** 43
picture ['pɪktʃə] Bild **LS,** 14
pig [pɪg] Schwein **10,** 107
⟨pink⟩ [pɪŋk] rosa **2,** 35
pint [paɪnt] *etwa 0,5l* **7,** 82
plan [plæn] Plan **5,** 62
plane [pleɪn] Flugzeug **3,** 41
to **play** [pleɪ] spielen **LS,** 13
playground ['pleɪgraʊnd] Schulhof, Spielplatz **LS,** 15
please [pliːz] bitte **LS,** 9
pocket ['pɒkɪt] Tasche (*bei Kleidung*) **8,** 86
pocket money ['pɒkɪt ˌmʌnɪ] Taschengeld **8,** 86
police [pə'liːs] Polizei **8,** 91
police officer [pə'liːs‿ˌɒfɪsə] Polizist/in **8,** 91
pond [pɒnd] Teich **1,** 21
poor [pɔː] arm **1,** 25
pop music ['pɒp 'mjuːzɪk] Popmusik **4,** 51
popular ['pɒpjʊlə] beliebt **8,** 88
post office ['pəʊst ˌɒfɪs] Post, Postamt **10,** 109
postcard ['pəʊstkɑːd] Postkarte **9,** 101
poster ['pəʊstə] Poster, Plakat **LS,** 9
potato, potatoes *(pl)* [pə'teɪtəʊ] Kartoffel, Kartoffeln **6,** 72
pound (= **lb**) [paʊnd] Pfund *(Gewicht)* **7,** 82
pound (= **£**) [paʊnd] Pfund *(britisches Geld)* **7,** 76
Word **power** ['wɜːd ˌpaʊə] Die Kraft der Wörter **1,** 23
practice ['præktɪs] Übung, Training **LS,** 10
listening practice ['lɪsnɪŋ ˌpræktɪs] Hörverstehens-übung **LS,** 15
sound practice ['saʊnd ˌpræktɪs] Aussprache-übung **LS,** 10
present ['prezənt] Geschenk **3,** 39
prize [praɪz] Preis, Gewinn **7,** 76
problem ['prɒbləm] Problem **5,** 56
promenade [ˌprɒmə'nɑːd] Promenade **9,** 100
pullover ['pʊlˌəʊvə] Pullover **6,** 70
pump [pʌmp] Luftpumpe **2,** 30
pupil ['pjuːpl] Schüler/in **7,** 80
to **put** [pʊt] setzen, stellen, legen **2,** 33
to put in ['pʊt‿ɪn] einsetzen, hineintun **1,** 27

Q

quarter ['kwɔːtə] Viertel **5,** 60
question ['kwestʃən] Frage **LS,** 15
quiet ['kwaɪət] still, ruhig **LS,** 16
quiz [kwɪz] Quiz, Ratespiel **3,** 38

R

radio ['reɪdɪəʊ] Radio **1,** 20
to **rain** [reɪn] regnen **4,** 52
to **read** [riːd] lesen **4,** 47
ready ['redɪ] fertig, bereit **1,** 25
to get ready [get 'redɪ] (sich) vorbereiten **5,** 58
really ['rɪəlɪ] wirklich **9,** 97
red [red] rot **2,** 28
reduced in size [rɪˌdjuːst‿ɪn 'saɪz] verkleinert **7,** 76
to **remember** [rɪ'membə] behalten, sich merken, sich erinnern **5,** 57
to **repair** [rɪ'peə] reparieren **4,** 47
request [rɪ'kwest] Bitte, Wunsch **8,** 90
restaurant ['restərɒnt] Restaurant **6,** 68
⟨revision⟩ [rɪ'vɪʒn] Wiederholung **R1,** 46
rhyme [raɪm] Reim **4,** 47
right [raɪt] (nach) rechts **6,** 71
on the left/right [ɒn ðə 'left], [ɒn ðə 'raɪt] links/rechts, auf der linken/rechten Seite **6,** 71
right [raɪt] richtig **LS,** 12
right away ['raɪt‿ə'weɪ] sofort **3,** 43
ring [rɪŋ] Ring **2,** 33
road (= **Rd.**) [rəʊd] Straße **1,** 22
rock [rɒk] Fels **9,** 98
role play ['rəʊl pleɪ] Rollenspiel **1,** 24
room [ruːm] Raum, Zimmer **1,** 20; Platz **9,** 98
round [raʊnd] um ... herum **4,** 50
rubbish ['rʌbɪʃ] Abfall, Müll **9,** 102

S

⟨to sail⟩ [seɪl] segeln **4,** 52
salad ['sæləd] gemischter Salat **3,** 42
same [seɪm] gleich **4,** 51
⟨all the same⟩ [ˌɔːl ðə 'seɪm] alle gleich **2,** 35
⟨just the same⟩ [ˌdʒʌst ðə 'seɪm] genau gleich **2,** 35
sandcastle ['sændkɑːsl] Sandburg **9,** 100
sandwich ['sænwɪdʒ] belegtes Brot **9,** 102
Saturday ['sætədeɪ] Samstag, Sonnabend **4,** 53
sausage ['sɒsɪdʒ] Würstchen, Wurst **7,** 76
to **save** [seɪv] sparen **8,** 86
to **save** [seɪv] retten **10,** 112
to **say** [seɪ] sagen **LS,** 10
to say hello ['seɪ hə'ləʊ] grüßen **9,** 101
scene [siːn] Szene **R2,** 66
school [skuːl] Schule **LS,** 8
sea [siː] Meer **3,** 41
at the **seaside** ['siːsaɪd] an der See **9,** 95
season ['siːzn] Jahreszeit **10,** 111
seat [siːt] Sitz, Sitzplatz **9,** 95
to **see** [siː] sehen **2,** 33
to **sell** [sel] verkaufen **8,** 86
sentence ['sentəns] Satz **LS,** 14

September [sep'tembə] September **5,** 57
she [ʃi:] sie **LS,** 9
she isn't (= she is not) [ʃi:‿'ɪznt] sie ist nicht **LS,** 15
she's (= she is) [ʃi:z] sie ist **LS,** 9
shed [ʃed] Stall, Schuppen **10,** 112
sheep *(sg + pl)* [ʃi:p] Schaf, Schafe **10,** 107
sheepdog ['ʃi:pdɒg] Hirtenhund **10,** 107
shelf [ʃelf], shelves *(pl)* [ʃelvz] Regal, Regale **2,** 29
shirt [ʃɜ:t] Hemd(bluse) **6,** 70
shoe [ʃu:] Schuh **4,** 47
shop [ʃɒp] Geschäft, Laden **2,** 31
shop assistant ['ʃɒp‿ə,sɪstənt] Verkäufer/in **8,** 86
to go to the shops [gəʊ tə ðə 'ʃɒps] einkaufen gehen **3,** 40
shopping [ʃɒpɪŋ] Einkaufs-, Einkaufen **5,** 58
shopping centre ['ʃɒpɪŋ ,sentə] Einkaufszentrum **6,** 68
shopping list ['ʃɒpɪŋ lɪst] Einkaufsliste **5,** 58
short [ʃɔ:t] kurz **9,** 97
⟨shoulder⟩ ['ʃəʊldə] Schulter **7,** 81
to **show** [ʃəʊ] zeigen **9,** 102
silly ['sɪlɪ] dumm, albern **2,** 33
to **sing** [sɪŋ] singen **5,** 56
sister ['sɪstə] Schwester **1,** 21
to **sit** [sɪt] sitzen **4,** 52
Sit down. [sɪt 'daʊn] Setz dich., Setzt euch. **LS,** 16
to sit down [sɪt 'daʊn] sich hinsetzen **LS,** 16
size [saɪz] Größe **7,** 76
skateboard ['skeɪtbɔ:d] Skateboard **1,** 20
skin [skɪn] Haut **10,** 113
to **sleep** [sli:p] schlafen **9,** 102
small [smɔ:l] klein **9,** 100
snack bar ['snæk bɑ:] Imbissstube **9,** 96
snake [sneɪk] Schlange **LS,** 13
snow [snəʊ] Schnee **10,** 111
so [səʊ] also **3,** 39
soap [səʊp] Seife **7,** 83
⟨some⟩ [sʌm] einige **10,** 109
sometimes ['sʌmtaɪmz] manchmal **7,** 79
song [sɒŋ] Lied **8,** 87
soon [su:n] bald **8,** 89
Sorry! ['sɒrɪ] Entschuldigung!, Tut mir Leid. **LS,** 11
sound practice ['saʊnd ,præktɪs] Ausspracheübung **LS,** 10
souvenir [,su:və'nɪə] Souvenir, Andenken, Mitbringsel **9,** 101
spade [speɪd] Spaten **4,** 50
Spanish ['spænɪʃ] spanisch, Spanisch **3,** 37
to **speak** [spi:k] sprechen **3,** 38
special ['speʃl] besondere/r/s; Spezialität des Hauses **6,** 72
to **spell** [spel] buchstabieren **4,** 47
spoon [spu:n] Löffel **2,** 29
spring [sprɪŋ] Frühling **10,** 111
square ['skweə] Platz **6,** 68
⟨to stamp⟩ [stæmp] stampfen **1,** 19
⟨Stamp your feet.⟩ [,stæmp jɔ: 'fi:t] Stampf/t mit deinen/euren Füßen. **1,** 19
to **stand** [stænd] stehen **6,** 73
to **start** [stɑ:t] anfangen, beginnen **3,** 37
Let's start. [,lets 'stɑ:t] Lasst uns anfangen. **LS,** 7
station ['steɪʃn] Bahnhof **9,** 96
statue ['stætʃu:] Statue, Denkmal **6,** 68
to **stay** [steɪ] (zu Besuch) wohnen **10,** 107; bleiben **10,** 112
step [step] Schritt, Stufe **1,** 18
stone [stəʊn] Stein **4,** 50
to **stop** [stɒp] anhalten **6,** 73
⟨stormy⟩ ['stɔ:mɪ] stürmisch **4,** 52
story ['stɔ:rɪ] Geschichte, Erzählung **3,** 43
straight on [streɪt‿'ɒn] geradeaus **6,** 71
street [stri:t] Straße **6,** 68
sugar ['ʃʊgə] Zucker **3,** 42
summer ['sʌmə] Sommer **10,** 111
⟨sun⟩ [sʌn] Sonne **9,** 95
Sunday ['sʌndeɪ] Sonntag **6,** 69
sunny ['sʌnɪ] sonnig **4,** 52
superdogs *(pl)* ['su:pədɒgz] Superhunde **1,** 18
supermarket ['su:pə,mɑ:kɪt] Supermarkt **7,** 82
sure [ʃɔ:] sicher **LS,** 15
I'm not sure. [aɪm nɒt 'ʃɔ:] Ich bin mir nicht sicher. **LS,** 15
surprise [sə'praɪz] Überraschung **5,** 56
sweatshirt ['swetʃɜ:t] Sweatshirt **4,** 51
sweet [swi:t] Bonbon **8,** 86
to go **swimming** [gəʊ 'swɪmɪŋ] schwimmen gehen **9,** 95

T

T-shirt ['ti:ʃɜ:t] T-Shirt **4,** 51
table ['teɪbl] Tisch **1,** 25
to **take** [teɪk] nehmen **7,** 83; bringen **8,** 91
to take a photo of [teɪk‿ə'fəʊtəʊ‿əv] ein Foto machen von **3,** 43
to take home [teɪk 'həʊm] nach Hause bringen **7,** 79
to **talk about** ['tɔ:k‿ə,baʊt] reden über, sprechen über **2,** 32
tea [ti:] Mahlzeit am frühen Abend **3,** 42; Tee **3,** 42
teacher ['ti:tʃə] Lehrer/in **LS,** 10
team [ti:m] Mannschaft **4,** 53
telephone ['telɪfəʊn] Telefon **1,** 24
on the telephone [ɒn ðə 'telɪfəʊn] am Telefon **3,** 40
to **tell** [tel] erzählen **3,** 38; sagen, mitteilen **6,** 71
to tell the time ['tel ðə 'taɪm] die Uhrzeit angeben **5,** 60
tennis ['tenɪs] Tennis **4,** 51
terrible ['terəbl] schrecklich, furchtbar **3,** 40
text [tekst] Text **8,** 93
Thank you. ['θæŋk‿ju] Danke schön **LS,** 10
Thanks! [θæks] Danke! **1,** 19
that's (= that is) [ðæts] das ist **LS,** 8
the [ðə] der/die/das **LS,** 12; **the** [ði:] der/die/das **LS,** 14
their [ðeə] ihr/ihre *(Pl)* **1,** 19
them [ðem] sie/ihnen **4,** 50
then [ðen] dann **4,** 47
there [ðeə] da, dort **1,** 23
over there [əʊvə 'ðeə] da drüben, dort **1,** 23
there are [ðeər‿'ɑ:] es gibt, es sind **3,** 37
there is [ðeər‿'ɪz] es gibt, es ist **3,** 37
these [ði:z] diese hier **2,** 32
they [ðeɪ] sie *(Pl)* **LS,** 12
they aren't (= they are not) [ðeɪ‿'ɑ:nt] sie sind nicht **LS,** 15
they're (= they are) [ðeə] sie sind **LS,** 12
thing [θɪŋ] Ding, Sache **1,** 26
to **think** [θɪŋk] denken, glauben **4,** 47
to think of ['θɪnk‿əv] ausdenken **4,** 49
this [ðɪs] dies/dieser/diese/dieses **1,** 22
this afternoon [ðɪs‿ɑ:ftə'nu:n] heute Nachmittag **3,** 40
those [ðəʊz] die da drüben **2,** 32
through [θru:] durch **3,** 41
to **throw** [θrəʊ] werfen **2,** 30

Thursday ['θɜ:zdeɪ] Donnerstag **6**, 69
ticket ['tɪkɪt] Fahrkarte **9**, 95
⟨ticky tacky⟩ ['tɪkɪ 'tækɪ] billiges Material **2**, 35
tidy ['taɪdɪ] ordentlich, aufgeräumt **7**, 79
to **tidy up** ['taɪdɪ‿ʌp] aufräumen **7**, 79
time [taɪm] Zeit **4**, 47
It's time for … [ɪts‿'taɪm fə] Es ist Zeit für … **4**, 47
to tell the time ['tel ðə 'taɪm] die Uhrzeit angeben **5**, 60
What **time is it?** [ˌwɒt 'taɪm‿ɪz‿ɪt] Wie spät ist es?, Wie viel Uhr ist es? **5**, 60
timetable ['taɪmteɪbl] Fahrplan **9**, 99
tired ['taɪəd] müde **10**, 112
to [tʊ] zu **3**, 40; vor **5**, 60
from … to [frəm … tə] von … nach **3**, 41
today [tə'deɪ] heute **2**, 29
⟨toe⟩ [təʊ] Zeh **7**, 81
together [tə'geðə] zusammen **1**, 24
toilet ['tɔɪlɪt] Toilette **5**, 62
tomato, tomatoes *(pl)* [tə'mɑ:təʊ] Tomate, Tomaten **6**, 72
tomorrow [tə'mɒrəʊ] morgen **5**, 61
too [tu:] auch **LS**, 9; allzu, zu **6**, 69
town [taʊn] Stadt **6**, 68
tractor ['træktə] Traktor, Trecker **10**, 110
train [treɪn] Zug **3**, 41
tree [tri:] Baum **1**, 21
trick [trɪk] Trick, Kunstgriff **10**, 113
to **trick** [trɪk] austricksen **10**, 112
to **trip** ['trɪp] stolpern **7**, 83
trouble ['trʌbl] Schwierigkeiten **10**, 112
to be in trouble [bɪ‿ɪn 'trʌbl] Schwierigkeiten haben **10**, 112
trousers *(sg + pl)* ['traʊzəz] Hose, Hosen **6**, 70
to **try on** [traɪ‿'ɒn] anprobieren **6**, 70
Tuesday ['tju:zdeɪ] Dienstag **6**, 69
tunnel ['tʌnl] Tunnel **3**, 41
Turkish ['tɜ:kɪʃ] türkisch, Türkisch **3**, 37
Your **turn.** ['jɔ: tɜ:n] Du bist an der Reihe. **LS**, 8
to **turn** [tɜ:n] abbiegen **6**, 71
tutor ['tju:tə] Klassenlehrer/in, Betreuungslehrer/in **LS**, 9
tutor group ['tju:tə ˌgru:p] Klasse *(in einer englischen Schule)* **LS**, 9
TV [ˌti:'vi:] Fernsehen **4**, 47
twin [twɪn] Zwilling **6**, 72
twin town ['twɪn 'taʊn] Partnerstadt **6**, 72
Twinning Office ['twɪnɪŋ ˌɒfɪs] Städtepartnerschaftsbüro **6**, 72
tyre ['taɪə] Reifen **2**, 30

U

uncle ['ʌŋkl] Onkel **3**, 37
under ['ʌndə] unter **LS**, 13
to **understand** [ʌndə'stænd] verstehen **9**, 102
uniform ['ju:nɪfɔ:m] Uniform **3**, 40
unit ['ju:nɪt] Lektion, Kapitel **1**, 18
untidy [ʌn'taɪdɪ] unordentlich **2**, 29
upstairs [ˌʌp'steəz] oben (im Gebäude) **5**, 62
us [ʌs] uns **4**, 50
to **use** [ju:z] benutzen **8**, 90
usually ['ju:ʒʊəlɪ] gewöhnlich, normalerweise **8**, 92

V

verb [vɜ:b] Verb **7**, 84
very ['verɪ] sehr **2**, 29
vet [vet] Tierarzt/Tierärztin **2**, 28
vet's assistant ['vets‿ə'sɪstənt] Tierarzthelfer/in **2**, 28
video ['vɪdɪəʊ] Video **5**, 63

W

to **wait** [weɪt] warten **10**, 112
to wait for ['weɪt fɔ:] warten auf **8**, 92
walk [wɔ:k] Spaziergang **4**, 52
to go for a walk [ˌgəʊ fər‿ə 'wɔ:k] spazieren gehen **4**, 52
to **walk** [wɔ:k] (zu Fuß) gehen **6**, 69
to **want** [wɒnt] (haben) wollen **8**, 86
warm [wɔ:m] warm **4**, 52
to **wash up** [wɒʃ‿'ʌp] abwaschen, (Geschirr) spülen **4**, 49
washing-up [ˌwɒʃɪŋ'ʌp] Abwasch **7**, 79
to **watch** [wɒtʃ] (zu)schauen, gucken **4**, 47
water ['wɔ:tə] Wasser **9**, 98
⟨waters⟩ ['wɔ:təz] Gewässer **4**, 52
way [weɪ] Weg **6**, 71
⟨all the way⟩ [ˌɔ:l ðə 'weɪ] den ganzen Weg **1**, 19
we [wi:] wir **LS**, 12
we're (= we are) [wɪə] wir sind **LS**, 12
to **wear** [weə] tragen, anhaben **6**, 70
weather ['weðə] Wetter **4**, 52
Wednesday ['wenzdeɪ] Mittwoch **6**, 69
week [wi:k] Woche **6**, 69
Welcome to … ['welkəm tʊ] Willkommen in … **3**, 37
well [wel] gut, nun, na ja **4**, 47
Get well soon! ['get wel 'su:n] Gute Besserung! **8**, 90
Well done! [wel 'dʌn] Gut gemacht!, Bravo! **7**, 79
wet [wet] nass **4**, 52
what [wɒt] was **LS**, 8
What's … like? [wɒts … laɪk] Wie ist … ? **4**, 52
What a … ['wɒt‿ə] Was für ein/e … **2**, 29
when [wen] wann **5**, 59
where [weə] wo **LS**, 13
where's (= where is) [weəz] wo ist **LS**, 13
white [waɪt] weiß **7**, 76
who [hu:] wer **3**, 38; wen/wem **10**, 110
why [waɪ] warum **6**, 69
window ['wɪndəʊ] Fenster **8**, 92
windy ['wɪndɪ] windig **4**, 52
winner ['wɪnə] Gewinner/in **7**, 81
winter ['wɪntə] Winter **10**, 111
with [wɪð] bei, mit **1**, 18
without [wɪð'aʊt] ohne **5**, 57
woman ['wʊmən], **women** *(pl)* ['wɪmɪn] Frau, Frauen **2**, 28
word [wɜ:d] Wort **LS**, 14
word order ['wɜ:d ˌɔ:də] Satzstellung **7**, 79
Word power ['wɜ:d ˌpaʊə] Die Kraft der Wörter **1**, 23
to **work** [wɜ:k] arbeiten **1**, 21
worried ['wʌrɪd] besorgt, beunruhigt **6**, 73
to **write** [raɪt] schreiben **LS**, 14
wrong [rɒŋ] falsch **LS**, 16

Y

year [jɪə] Jahr, Jahrgang **LS,** 14
yellow ['jeləʊ] gelb **2,** 28
yes [jes] ja **LS,** 8
not … **yet** [nɒt … jet] noch nicht **1,** 25
you [ju:] du, Sie **LS,** 10; ihr/Sie **LS,** 12; dich/euch/Sie; dir/euch/Ihnen **4,** 50
Are you … ? [ɑ: ju:] Bist du … ?/Sind Sie …? **LS,** 11
you're (= you are) [jʊə] du bist/Sie sind **LS,** 11
you're (= you are) [jʊə] ihr seid/Sie sind **LS,** 12
your [jɔ:] dein/deine, Ihr/Ihre **LS,** 8; euer/eure; Ihr/Ihre **LS,** 12

Boys' names

Alan ['ælən]
Colin ['kɒlɪn]
David ['deɪvɪd]
Eddy ['edɪ]
Jack [dʒæk]
Lenny ['lenɪ]
Mark [mɑ:k]
Michael ['maɪkəl]
Peter ['pi:tə]
Robert ['rɒbət]
Sam [sæm]
Simon ['saɪmən]
Tim [tɪm]

Girls' names

Anna ['ænə]
Annabel ['ænəbel]
Audrey [ɔ:drɪ]
Becky ['bekɪ]
Debbie ['debi]
Helen ['helɪn]
Janet ['dʒænɪt]
Jenny ['dʒenɪ]
Kim [kɪm]
Margaret ['mɑ:grɪt]
Mary ['meərɪ]
Pat [pæt]
Sarah ['seərə]
Suvina [sə'vi:nə]
Victoria [vɪk'tɔ:rɪə]

Surnames

Adib [ə'dɪb]
Barker ['bɑ:kə]
Benson ['bensn]
Burton ['bɜ:tn]
Cooper ['ku:pə]
Croft [krɒft]
Dane [deɪn]
Dixon ['dɪksn]
Hilton ['hɪltən]
Hunt ['hʌnt]
Miller ['mɪlə]
Nosy ['nəʊzɪ]
Penrose ['penrəʊz]
Richards ['rɪtʃədz]
Smith [smɪθ]
Walker ['wɔ:kə]
Wall [wɔ:l]
White [waɪt]
Wood [wʊd]

Geographical names

Africa ['æfrɪkə]
⟨Albania⟩ [æl'beɪnjə]
Angel Row ['eɪndʒəl 'rəʊ]
Arndale Road ['ɑ:ndeɪl 'rəʊd]
Arnot Hill Park [ˌɑ:nət hɪl 'pɑ:k]
⟨Austria⟩ ['ɒstrɪə]
Beastmarket Hill ['bi:stmɑ:kɪt 'hɪl]
Beeston ['bi:stən]
Belgium ['beldʒəm]
⟨Belorussia⟩ [ˌbeləʊ'rʌʃə]
Berlin [bɜ:'lɪn]
Bestwood ['bestwʊd]
⟨Bosnia Herzegovina⟩ ['bɒznɪə ˌheətsəgəʊ'vi:nə]
⟨Bulgaria⟩ [bʌl'geərɪə]
Castle Gate ['kɑ:sl 'geɪt]
Channel Tunnel ['tʃænl 'tʌnl]
Cleethorpes ['kli:θɔ:ps]
⟨Croatia⟩ [krəʊ'eɪʃə]
⟨Czech Republic⟩ [ˌtʃek rɪ'pʌblɪk]
⟨Denmark⟩ ['denmɑ:k]
Edward's Lane ['edwədz ˌleɪn]
England ['ɪŋglənd]
⟨Estonia⟩ [es'təʊnjə]
⟨Europe⟩ ['jʊərəp]
Exchange Walk [ɪks'tʃeɪndʒ 'wɔ:k]
⟨Finland⟩ ['fɪnlənd]
France [frɑ:ns]
Friar Lane ['fraɪə 'leɪn]
Germany ['dʒɜ:mənɪ]
⟨Greece⟩ [gri:s]
Heathrow [ˌhi:θ'rəʊ]
the **High Street** ['haɪ stri:t]
⟨Hungary⟩ ['hʌŋgərɪ]
⟨Iceland⟩ ['aɪslənd]
⟨Ireland⟩ ['aɪələnd]
⟨Italy⟩ ['ɪtəlɪ]
Larwood Grove ['lɑ:wʊd 'grəʊv]
⟨Latvia⟩ ['lætvɪə]
⟨Lithuania⟩ [ˌlɪθju:'eɪnjə]
London ['lʌndən]
⟨Luxembourg⟩ ['lʌksəmbɜ:g]
Maid Marian Way [ˌmeɪd 'mærɪən 'weɪ]
⟨Malta⟩ ['mɔ:ltə]
Mansfield Road ['mænsfi:ld 'rəʊd]
⟨Moldavia⟩ [mɒl'deɪvjə]
⟨Montenegro⟩ [ˌmɒntɪ'ni:grəʊ]
Mount Street ['maʊnt ˌstri:t]
The **Netherlands** [ðə 'neðələndz]
North Sea [nɔ:θ 'si:]
Northallerton [nɔ:'θælətən]
⟨Norway⟩ ['nɔ:weɪ]
Nottingham ['nɒtɪŋəm]
Old Market Square [əʊld 'mɑ:kɪt 'skweə]
Parliament Street ['pɑ:ləmənt ˌstri:t]
Poland ['pəʊlənd]
⟨Portugal⟩ ['pɔ:tʃʊgl]
⟨Romania⟩ [ru:'meɪnjə]
⟨Russia⟩ ['rʌʃə]
⟨Serbia⟩ ['sɜ:bjə]

Sherwood [ˈʃɜːwʊd]
Skegness [skegˈnes]
⟨Slovakia⟩ [sləʊˈvækjə]
⟨Slovenia⟩ [sləʊˈviːnjə]
South Parade [ˈsaʊθ pəˈreɪd]
⟨Spain⟩ [speɪn]
⟨Sweden⟩ [ˈswiːdn]
⟨Switzerland⟩ [ˈswɪtsələnd]
⟨Turkey⟩ [ˈtɜːkɪ]
The **UK (= The United Kingdom)** [juː ˈkeɪ], [juːˈnaɪtɪd ˈkɪŋdəm]
⟨Ukraine⟩ [juːˈkreɪn]
Yorkshire [ˈjɔːkʃə]

Other names

Greenwood [ˈgriːnwʊd]
Haywood School [ˈheɪwʊd ˈskuːl]
Maxi [ˈmæksɪ]
7MD [ˌsevn emˈdiː]
Mini [ˈmɪnɪ]
Monny [ˈmɒnɪ]
Robin Hood [ˈrɒbɪn ˈhʊd]
Sneaky Snake [ˈsniːkɪ ˌsneɪk]
Springfield [ˈsprɪŋfiːld]
St. Peter's Church [snt ˌpiːtəz ˈtʃɜːtʃ]
Tabby [ˈtæbɪ]

⟨In the classroom⟩

What you can say to your friends or to the teacher

Before and after the lesson

• Good morning, Mr/Mrs … .	Guten Morgen, Herr/Frau … .
Good-bye. Bye.	Auf Wiedersehen. Tschüs.
Thanks. Thank you (very much).	Danke. Vielen Dank.
• I'm sorry I'm late.	Tut mir Leid, dass ich mich verspätet habe.
I'm not feeling well.	Ich fühle mich nicht gut.
Can I open the window?	Kann ich das Fenster aufmachen?
• What's that in English/German?	Was heißt das auf Englisch/Deutsch?
What does … mean?	Was bedeutet …?
• Can I have your crayon/ruler/…?	Kann ich deinen Buntstift/dein Lineal/ … haben?
How do you do this exercise?	Wie macht man/geht diese Übung?
Can you help me, please?	Können Sie/Kannst du mir bitte helfen?
I'm not sure.	Ich bin nicht sicher.
Sorry I don't know.	Tut mir Leid, das weiß ich nicht.
Is this right?	Ist das richtig?
I don't think this is right/wrong.	Ich glaube nicht, dass dies richtig/falsch ist.
Can you repeat the sentence, please?	Können Sie/Kannst du bitte den Satz wiederholen?
Pardon?	Wie bitte?
Can you write it on the board?	Können Sie es an die Tafel schreiben?
• Let's act the story/play a game.	Wir möchten die Geschichte/ein Spiel spielen.
Can we sing a song?	Können wir ein Lied singen?
• What's for homework?	Was haben wir als Hausaufgabe auf?

… and what the teacher says to you

• Open your books at page … .	Öffnet eure Bücher auf Seite … .
Read the text on page … .	Lies den Text auf Seite … .
• Please get me some chalk.	Bitte hol mir Kreide.
Would you collect the exercise books/ worksheets/workbooks, please?	Würdest du bitte die Übungshefte/Arbeitsblätter/ Arbeitsbücher einsammeln?
Do this exercise for homework.	Macht diese Übung als Hausaufgabe.
Who would like to write on a transparency?	Wer möchte auf Folie schreiben?
• Good. Very good. That's good.	Gut! Sehr gut! Das ist gut.
You can do better. Try again.	Das kannst du besser. Versuch es noch einmal.
That's it. Well done.	So ist es richtig. Gut gemacht.
• Be quiet.	Sei/Seid ruhig.
Sit down, please.	Setz dich/Setzt euch, bitte.
Please speak up.	Sprich/Sprecht lauter, bitte.

Bildquellen:

Bavaria, München: p. 91 (6)
Camera Press, London: p. 91 (1, Stewart Mark)
J. Allan Cash Ltd., London: p. 41 (3); p. 91 (2)
dpa, Frankfurt/Main: p. 41 (4, Ian Turner)
East Lindsey District Council, Louth: p. 99 (2, 3)
Dieter Gebhardt, Graphic- und Foto-Design BFF, Asperg: p. 9; p. 10; p. 22 (6); p. 28; p. 34; p. 59; p. 62 (7); p. 70; p. 76; p. 80; p. 101
Heathrow Airport Ltd., Public Affairs: p. 41 (1)
Images, Bavaria: p. 91 (7)
Joachim Krüger, Korntal (Karten): p. 22 (2, 3); p. 41 (5); p. 99 (1); Innenumschlag hinten
Wolfgang Metzger, Mühlacker: Innenumschlag vorne
Mauritius, Stuttgart: p. 9 (Superstock); p. 41 (6, Rosenfeld)
Picturepoint, London: p. 91 (5)
Regional Railways North East: p. 99 (5)
Rex Features, London: p. 41 (2); p. 51 (2, Agence France)
Rolf W. Roth, Idar-Oberstein: p. 22 (5, Schild); p. 91 (3, 4)
Trevor Scotcher, Cambridge: p. 51 (1, 5)
Melanie Smith, Peabody's Communications Group, Nottingham: p. 22 (1, 5); p. 51 (3, 4); p. 60, p. 62 (1–6); p. 68 (1–4); p. 80 (1–5)
John Sumpter, jms Photography, Nottingham: p. 14; p. 22 (4); p. 42
Norman Thelwell, "Belt up", Methuen, London: p. 94
Klett-Archiv, Stuttgart: p. 91 (8, Christa Weck)

Textquellen:

At the door: p. 26, © Text: Alan Posener, Berlin, Melodie: Petra Scheil, Berlin
Little boxes: p. 35, © Text und Melodie: Malvina Reynolds; Essex Musikvertrieb GmbH, Köln
Sailing: p. 52, © Text und Melodie: Gavin Sutherland; Polygram Songs Musikverlag GmbH, Hamburg
Happy birthday: p. 63, © Text: Patti Smith-Hill, Melodie: Mildred J. Hill; Musikverlag Intersong GmbH, Hamburg
The sun has got his hat on: p. 95, © Text und Melodie: Ralph Butler, Noel Gay, Phylip Seeley; 1932 Reproduced by permission of West's Limited 138–40 Charing Cross Road, London WC2H OLD

Bye!!

ICELAND
NORWAY
SWEDEN
FINLAND
RUSSIA
ESTONIA
LATVIA
LITHUANIA
RUSSIA
BELARUS
DENMARK
THE UNITED
KINGDOM
IRELAND
Nottingham
London
THE NETHER-
LANDS
E U R O P E
POLAND
GERMANY
BELGIUM
LUXEMBOURG
CZECH
REPUBLIC
THE UKRAINE
SLOVAKIA
MOLDAVIA
FRANCE
SWITZER-
LAND
AUSTRIA
HUNGARY
ROMANIA
SLOVENIA
CROATIA
BOSNIA–
HERZEGOVINA
SERBIA
BULGARIA
PORTUGAL
SPAIN
ITALY
MONTENEGRO
ALBANIA
GREECE
TURKEY
MALTA
0
500
1 000 km
A F R I C A